ORLANDO

like a

By Rick Namey

Previously published as *Fodor's Disney Like a Pro*
Fodor's Travel Publications, Inc.
New York • Toronto • London • Sydney • Auckland
www.fodors.com/

Orlando Like a Pro
EDITOR: Karen Cure
Editorial Contributors: Rita Aero, Janet Atkins, Susan Blake, Howard and Donald Bradfute, Janet Tucker Butler, Audra Epstein, Ken Jones, Charles Namey, Ricky Namey, Terrie Namey, Tiffany Namey, Jennifer Paull, Donald Schutz
Editorial Production: Linda K. Schmidt
Maps: David Lindroth, Inc., cartographer; Robert Blake, *map editor*
Production/Manufacturing: Robert B. Shields
Cover Photograph: Kevin Kolczynski

Copyright
Copyright © 1998 by Fodor's Travel Publications, Inc.
Fodor's is a registered trademark of Fodor's Travel Publications, Inc.
All rights reserved under International and Pan-American Copyright Conventions. Published in the United States by Fodor's Travel Publications, Inc., a subsidiary of Random House, Inc., New York, and simultaneously in Canada by Random House of Canada Limited, Toronto. Distributed by Random House, Inc., New York. No portions of this book may be reproduced in any form without written permission from the publisher.
Second Edition
ISBN 0-679-00222-7
Cover Photograph © Universal Studios Florida. All rights reserved.
Walt Disney World® is a registered trademark of The Walt Disney Company; Universal Studios Florida™ is a registered trademark of a MCA/Rank Organization Joint Venture.

Special Sales
Fodor's Travel Publications are available at special discounts for bulk purchases for sales promotions or premiums. Special editions, including personalized covers, excerpts of existing guides, and corporate imprints, can be created in large quantities for special needs. For more information, contact your local bookseller or write to Special Markets, Fodor's Travel Publications, 201 East 50th Street, New York, NY 10022. Inquiries from Canada should be directed to your local Canadian bookseller or sent to Random House of Canada, Ltd., Marketing Department, 2775 Matheson Boulevard East, Mississauga, Ontario L4W 4P7. Inquiries from the United Kingdom should be sent to Fodor's Travel Publications, 20 Vauxhall Bridge Road, London SW1V 2SA, England.

Important Advice
You can use this book in the confidence that all prices and opening times are based on information supplied to us at press time; Fodor's cannot accept responsibility for any errors. Time inevitably brings changes, so always confirm information when it matters.

Acknowledgments
Robert Stricker, Rita Aero, Tom Schroder, Kevin Kolcynski, Glenn Haddad, Elias Fadool, Greg Galloway, Paul Meena, Lonnie Conte, Kalin Thomas Samuel, Blaise Mercadante, Charles Namey, Pamela Tuscany Warren, John Sleasman, Bob Kaplus, Carol Biallas, Jim Canfield, David Milov, Jennifer Theilhelm, Jack Young, and Kim Dawson.

Dedication
An extra special thank you to our family's favorite rock stars, the incredibly talented group "Sister Hazel," especially lead singer Ken Block, his wife, Tracy, and manager Andy Levine, and to the House of Blues' Stephanie Jones, for making a little boy feel very special at a very important time.

PRINTED IN THE UNITED STATES OF AMERICA
10 9 8 7 6 5 4 3 2 1

contents

Dear Reader .... *vii*

1. **Grab the Mouse by the Tail!** *1*
   Figure the Hourly Cost of Your Vacation *2*
   Go Where You Want to Go, Do What You
   Want to Do! *8*
   How to Save Money on Lodgings *10*
   Save Big on Tickets (or Get Them Free) *12*
   Save Money on Shopping and Incidentals! *20*
   Don't Waste Time Getting Around *21*
   Beat the Lines! *22*
   Have a Great Time! *28*

2. **Admission Prices
   and Where to Find Out More** *33*

3. **Universal Studios Florida** *36*
   Islands of Adventure: A Preview *55*

4. Sea World **59**

5. Busch Gardens.. **68**

6. The Magic Kingdom **81**

7. Epcot Center **107**

8. Disney–MGM Studios Theme Park.................... **131**

9. Disney's Animal Kingdom **145**

10. Downtown Disney.. **149**

    The West Side *151*
    Pleasure Island *157*
    The Marketplace at Downtown Disney *159*

11. Universal's CityWalk... **165**

12. More Eatertainment **171**

    My Short List *171*
    Character Meals *173*
    Theme Restaurants *174*
    Church Street Station and Downtown *175*
    Disney's BoardWalk *179*
    Dinner Theaters *180*
    Sushi and Seafood *184*
    Off the Beaten Path *184*

13. Water Parks **186**

    Orlando and Kissimmee Water Parks *188*
    Disney Water Parks *189*

14. The Wider World of Sports *192*
Disney's Wide World of Sports *192*
Golf *195*

15. Grand Old Florida Attractions and Other Diversions *197*
Grand Old Florida Attractions *199*
Inside Walt Disney World *203*
International Drive and Orlando *205*
Around Kissimmee *208*

16. The Space Coast *211*
What to See *212*
On the Way *216*

17. Beach, Beach, Beach *218*
Daytona Beach and North *218*
South of Daytona *223*

18. Shoppertoonities *226*

19. Sleeping Beauties *231*
My Short List *236*
Other Good Bets *243*

20. Cruising Like a Pro *255*

Index *261*

Coupons *265*

dear reader

Since childhood, I have believed that "when you wish upon a star, your dreams come true." When I was growing up in Baltimore, distant Disneyland was an impossible dream. So I simply wished the Magic Kingdom to come to me. My wish required the Russians to launch Sputnik, thereby necessitating the transfer of most of America's rocket engineers (including my father) to an unknown town in the middle of Florida. Then, in the mid-1960s, I asked my waterskiing buddy Craig Linton, whose dad was in real estate, "Hey Craig, why don't you get your dad to sell 30,000 acres of orange grove to Walt Disney to build a theme park so we could all go to it?" After graduating from college as a TV major, I didn't want to leave Orlando, and while most of my graduating class went off to seek fame and fortune in New York and Los Angeles. I had no choice but to wish Universal Studios to me.

The rest is history.

Obviously, the person who originally wished the Disney and Universal parks all the way from California to Orlando is the person most qualified to show you around. You will also get three genuine natives at no additional charge: my wife, Terrie; 13-year-old Tiffany; and 10-year-old Ricky, who has not missed a single season at the theme parks in his entire life.

This is, and always has been, a family effort. Our goal is to help you and your family benefit from the knowledge that has taken us many years to acquire. We've tried our best to be accurate and complete (omitting only attractions we don't like and a lot of changeable details you can easily get elsewhere). Our wish is that our work makes your dreams come true.

–Rick Namey
Orlando, Florida

chapter 1
GRAB THE MOUSE BY THE TAIL!

The average room rate in Central Florida is around $50. A soda in a Disney theme park costs around $2. If each person in a family of four has a soft drink with lunch and dinner and takes three cold drink breaks—a reasonable proposition under the Florida sun—the group's daily cost for sodas will be $40. This comes close to the price of nightly lodging for many visiting families. And a full week of sodas costs the same as one discounted round-trip airplane ticket to Orlando from many major cities. Walt Disney World's press kit says that the Magic Kingdom serves more than 46 million Coca-Colas each year—and that's only Coca-Colas, and not any other beverages. That sounds to me like an enormous number of sodas. Yet in all the years I've been going to the theme parks, never once have I heard anyone say that the highlight of his or her vacation was the fabulous cola in the parks.

I'm not saying that you should go without cold drinks on hot days. I'm not trying to pick on the cola guys. But as you read this book you will learn that I hate to be taken advantage of.

I wrote this book to help you avoid little things that rob you of your vacation dollars. I wrote this book to teach you things that only a person who's been here since they opened the place would know, to help you save money—and to show you how to save time. Because, ultimately, when you're on vacation, time is also money.

FIGURE THE HOURLY COST OF YOUR VACATION

Let me explain. To understand the real cost of your visit to each Central Florida attraction, you also have to prorate what you spent to get to the area and stay there. The corollary is that the real cost of riding, say, Space Mountain is not just the cost of getting into the Magic Kingdom. Riding Space Mountain also involves your transportation, lodging, meals, and multiday admission tickets during your entire trip. And you can prorate this figure to give you an idea of how much each waking hour you spend in Orlando actually costs. The hourly figure, together with my exclusive Worth-It Ratings, which I give for nearly every attraction in this book, provide a great answer to the question that arises each time you start a new activity or step into a long line: "Is my experience going to be worth my time and my money?" My one- to five-star Worth-It Ratings reflect my opinion of whether the experience you'll have there is worth the money it will cost you to get it.

GRAB THE MOUSE BY THE TAIL!

(You may notice that the ratings are generally high. That's because we've just left out attractions that aren't worth it—to spare you wasting time and money acquiring information about them.)

Here's how I figure the hourly cost.

Transportation: Start here. Figure the family's airfare, airport transportation at both ends, parking, and/or car rental. If you drive to Orlando, allow for fuel, lodging, and meals en route, and around 25 cents per mile for wear and tear on your car. Add the cost of transportation around Orlando, including bus fares or tour fees.

Food: Give yourself a daily budget that reflects meals you expect to have. In Orlando, a meal in a moderately priced restaurant might cost $20 to $30, excluding drinks, service, and tax; $30 to $40 in an expensive restaurant; and over $40 in a very expensive restaurant. In the theme parks, restaurants with table service are usually moderately priced. Fast food costs the same here as everywhere. To be perfectly accurate about your vacation costs, subtract your normal food budget for the period from your estimated vacation expenditure (after all, you'd have to eat anyway).

Lodging: Add the cost of your hotel. Be sure to include tax and allow for phone and incidentals.

Tickets and Souvenirs: You know about the tickets. The souvenirs are inevitable, too. To keep these costs down, give each family member an allowance over which they cannot go.

To get your estimated total vacation cost, add all these figures. Multiply the number of days you plan to be in Orlando by 12 (about how many hours most people tolerate in a theme park at a time). Then divide your total cost by total hours.

Let's look at how this works for the hypothetical Martin family, New Yorkers staying eight days: Marvin, Mavis, 13-year-old Elizabeth, and 9-year-old Michael.

FIGURE THE HOURLY COST OF YOUR VACATION

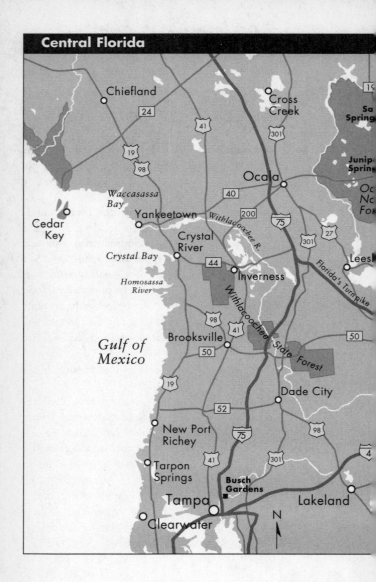

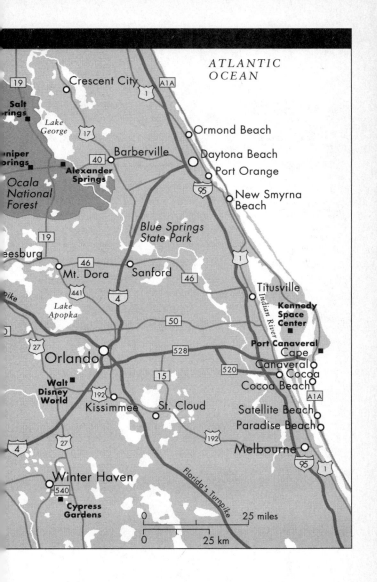

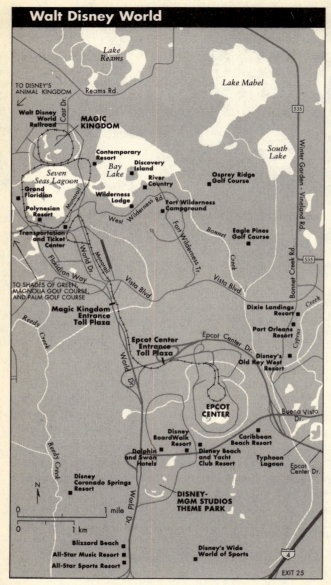

The round-trip Newark–Orlando flight costs $230 per person, $920 for the family. In New Jersey, they spend $30 per person for airport transportation each way. In Orlando, they rent a mid-size car for a flat $150. Add $10 a day for gas for a total of $80.

They plan to eat mostly at inexpensive family restaurants, and they've allowed $960 for food, $560 more than they spend at home.

Lodging costs $52 a night. They budget $50 for movies and other incidentals at their hotel.

At Walt Disney World, they plan to visit the Magic Kingdom and Epcot. So they're buying two single-day, single-park Disney passes at $42.14 per day for each family member over 12 and $33.92 for Michael. They get the seven-day Orlando FlexTicket to Universal Studios Florida, Sea World, and Wet 'n Wild for $100.65 each ($82.63 for Michael). With one day left, they're heading for the Kennedy Space Center for $10 a head ($7 for Michael). At each park, each person gets $10 in spending money; the family's total shopping allowance is $320.

Here's a recap of their budget:

Airfare and airport transport	$980
Rental car and gas	$230
Vacation food	$560
Hotel	$414
Magic Kingdom and Epcot passes	$321
Universal Studios Florida, Sea World, Wet 'n Wild passes	$385
Kennedy Space Center	$37
Shopping	$320
Total	$3,247

At 12 hours per day, the Martins have a total of 96 waking hours during their eight-day vacation. Dividing the $3,247 by 96 yields the hourly cost of the Martins' vacation: $33.82.

FIGURE THE HOURLY COST OF YOUR VACATION

Substitute your own figures. Then, when it looks like you're going to have to wait an hour to ride Dumbo, you won't just ask yourself if you want to take the time to ride. You'll also, inevitably, ask yourself whether you feel that a ride on Dumbo is *really* worth $33.82.

GO WHERE YOU WANT TO GO, DO WHAT YOU WANT TO DO!

Central Florida has no fewer than 13 theme parks. There are also seven water parks, over a dozen dinner shows, and several ticketed nightclub attractions. One of the reasons I wanted to write this book is that I've seen over and over that many people miss some of the best of them. When I was at Visitor Information Television and later at Visitor Information Radio, people constantly told us that the Kennedy Space Center was one of the top three places they wanted to visit. Yet surveys of what visitors actually saw always put the Kennedy Space Center below that. What happened? Why did so many people who wanted to go to the Space Center travel all the way to Central Florida, then miss it? Most of the locals I know agree with me that Universal Studios Florida is the best attraction in town. Although millions of people see it every year, millions still miss it. Why?

Part of the answer is probably the simple fact that after most families take in the Walt Disney World theme parks, they have neither time nor money left over. That's why I recommend an alternative strategy for your Central Florida vacation.

DO IT BACKWARDS Most people visit Disney first, and Disney does a really great job of taking advantage of that fact to keep them there—spending their money before they have a chance to spend it anywhere else. So by all means, figure out what you want to do in Orlando. And do it all. But if it includes destinations outside WDW, save the Mouse for last so that *you* see what *you* want.

I encourage you to begin your vacation at the park I consider the best in the world: Universal Studios Florida (around here we always call it "Universal" for short).

Universal is now positioning itself in direct competition to Walt Disney World. With the new CityWalk shopping and nightlife attraction and a second full-fledged theme park, Islands of Adventure, soon to open—not to mention a resort with four new hotels and two golf courses—Universal is fast becoming a complete vacation destination.

MINIMIZE YOUR MOUSE We all know that Walt Disney World is the magnet that brings most people to Central Florida. However, some things at the parks are extremely expensive. And although some of them here (and at other theme parks) are not duplicated anywhere else in the world, many things are available elsewhere—and at a lower cost.

Outside Walt Disney World, for instance, you can buy enough stuff with pictures of Mickey, Donald, Goofy, and the other Disney characters to last you a lifetime. Ditto for food, supplies, and other necessities. And the prices for all this are significantly lower elsewhere.

Plus, Central Florida has a full complement of the national chains that save you money at home: Wal-Mart, KMart, Target, and others. There are also several chains of local discount outlets created to serve the attractions area. When you need film, videotape, or sunscreen, don't buy it in the theme parks—Disney or otherwise. Visit a discount specialist. The Wal-Marts in the Disney area, among the world's

GO WHERE YOU WANT TO GO, DO WHAT YOU WANT TO DO!

largest, with food, pharmacy items, and liquor, are almost destination attractions!

GO WHEN YOU WANT TO GO Other guides make a lot of noise about the benefits of traveling off-season, when crowds are smaller and lines shorter. There are three problems with this theory.

First, it may not be possible to travel then. If your kids are in school, staying as long as you need to in order to see what you want means either missing school—or traveling when everyone else does.

Second, although lines may be shorter off-season, they may not move as quickly. Theme parks have the ability to open or close lines and add or subtract ride vehicles. This is not some conspiracy to cheat off-season guests. It's a way for parks to lower costs when there are fewer guests around.

Third, park hours are shorter off-season, so for any given length of vacation, the parks are available to you for fewer hours overall. Moreover, there may be fewer parades and shows. So, although you're paying less, you're also getting less.

My advice? Go when you want to go. The basic experience varies little from season to season. Don't be afraid of peak times, because the parks are geared up to provide a peak experience. And don't stay away from off-peak times, either. Room and travel rates are lower, compensating for what you may be missing.

HOW TO SAVE MONEY ON LODGINGS

GET THE LOWEST RATE If you're looking for a low rate on a room, you could go from hotel to hotel or stop at a pay phone and check around. But you still wouldn't know where the lowest rates are.

That's where room brokers come in. Try the **Central Florida Tourist Information Center** (tel. 800/396–1883), **Central Reservations Service** (tel. 800/873–4683), or **Tamar Inns** (tel. 800/999–6327).

There is a standing rule in the hotel business that says, "An unsold room night is gone forever." Therefore, anything that a hotel can get out of a room is better than nothing. Room brokers purchase blocks of room nights from hotels; typically, they either commit to a high number of room nights in advance, or they pick up leftover rooms on a daily basis. Either way, they get incredibly low rates and pass the savings on to you. So a family of four can pay as little as $23 a night with no extra-person charges in a decent chain property. Or up to six can stay in a two-bedroom suite with a kitchen for an incredible $49 a night at a major chain hotel in the attractions area.

AVOID PHONE-RATE RIPOFFS During my years in the tourist industry, many hotels have told me that phone charges are their number-one source of extra revenue. For instance, there was the very nice hotel on U.S. 192, a major thoroughfare, where I used to book business associates at an unbelievably low $32 a night. The catch was that the phone charges were outrageous. For business people who had to make a lot of calls, that $32 quickly became $100. When planning your trip to Orlando, be sure to consider your need for a telephone when you book your lodging. Remember that you'll probably be calling locally a lot, to make reservations and get information. Even local charges add up. And just because the hotel uses AT&T, Sprint, or MCI doesn't mean you're protected: Prices on calls for access to them can be horrendous. So can making credit-card calls from your room.

In advance, find out rates for local and long-distance calls (including those you make with your calling card or via Sprint, AT&T, or MCI). Then negotiate a better deal. And get it in writing.

SAVE BIG ON TICKETS (OR GET THEM FREE)

It's a lot easier than you imagine to save a few bucks.

NEVER PAY FULL PRICE Don't buy theme-park tickets at the gate. That may be the worst possible place to buy them. Not only will you pay more—you'll have to wait in line to do it. You'll find little booths with signs inviting you to ask about free or discount attraction tickets at convenience and souvenir stores, in parking lots, and in hotel lobbies as far north as Pedro's South of the Border, a hotel and attraction complex near Dillon, South Carolina. These booths are known in the trade as OPCs, short for Off-Premises Contractors, and they sell tickets at between 10% and 20% off the walk-in price. For a family of four, the savings is about $20 a day—$100 for a five-day vacation! Plus, you'll also save time standing in line.

(By the way, children under 3 are usually admitted to theme parks free—though I wouldn't be surprised to see that change. I can still recall a time when the parks allowed children to stay "children" until the age of 12. Now the theme parks define "children" as people nine and under. I feel uncomfortable with that designation. I don't know about you, but I don't think of 10-year-olds as adults.)

NEGOTIATE WITH YOUR HOTEL FOR FREEBIES A travel agent may not get you the best deal on a hotel room, at least one in Orlando. For that, you have to deal with the hotel directly—preferably from home rather than while you're standing at the front desk, credit card in hand, with the kids just over your shoulder impatiently asking questions.

At chain hotels, which tend to have smaller staffs—Days Inns, Holiday Inns, and the like—ask for the manager, who is usually easily accessible. Say when you're coming and how long you plan to stay, and mention that you are comparing a number of properties to get the best deal. I usually say something like, "Sharpen your pencil, now. I'm going to be calling a lot of properties and comparing what they offer. If you want my business, I need your very best deal, now. Otherwise, if I get a better one down the street, you probably won't hear from me again." Actually, if they're at all competitive, they will probably hear from me again regardless, because—and this is my favorite part—I always call them back to tell them my best deal and let them bid against it. Believe me, if you don't use a wholesale broker, you have to shop the hotels this way. Even if you call a couple of places, if you just take the rate they give you, you'll overpay.

When you negotiate, it helps to understand a little about the local hotel business. One of the yardsticks by which hotel owners measure their managers and staffs is by the hotel's "average room rate," an average of what's taken in for all the hotel's room nights per night, per season, and per year. You probably already know that air fares vary widely; you can sit next to someone who paid half as much or even twice as much. That's also true of room rates. Because the management is so conscious of its average room rate, there is a rate beneath which they will not go. But the fact that your negotiations have brought you to this rate does not mean that the manager has nothing left to offer.

Most hotels have a stash of attraction tickets. Hotel employees often get them as personal gifts from the various theme parks, who hope to persuade staffers to recommend a visit. The more people they send, the more free tickets they get. Other tickets may have been purchased from the theme parks, often at a discount, to resell to guests at a profit. If a manager really needs the room night, he or she may part with a few tickets.

Although you will seldom find these so-called comps at $22-a-night motels along U.S. 192, there are exceptions—particularly if you promise to stay a week or longer. In general, the closer the attraction, the more likely a hotel is to have comps to give away. For free Disney tickets, your best chance is at hotels on property in the Walt Disney World Village area and off property in the Lake Buena Vista area. For Universal, best odds are at motels on the north end of International Drive, another tourist main drag; for Sea World, next door to the park on the south end of I-Drive (as International Drive is known around town). And so on.

Go for comps for water park and dinner shows first. They're easier to get, though the normal prices are similar to theme parks'. Basically, if you're going to pay for some of your tickets and get some free, it doesn't matter which are which.

Remember that the hotels get discounts, even on passes they buy. You should, too. So if you can't get comps (maybe because you got such a good deal on your room), try to buy tickets outright at a discount. Just say that you know that the hotel is selling tickets at a markup and that you want to buy tickets at the wholesale price as a condition of choosing that hotel.

GRAB THE MOUSE BY THE TAIL!

If shuttle service to attractions is not included in your room rate, ask for a freebie when you negotiate over your room. Many hotels offer shuttles to attractions, and usually some passengers have paid and some haven't. Don't be one of the losers. Mears, the area's largest shuttle operator (tel. 407/423–5566), charges between $12 and $14 or more, per person for one round trip between any given hotel and any given theme park. For a family of four, that would be as much as $56. A family's total outlay for lodging and transportation, when staying in a $40 room in a hotel without free shuttle service, would be comparable to the $96 they might pay for a room in a hotel that includes transportation. In other words, that $40 room is not the bargain they think. If you're not renting a car, a $74 room at the All-Star Resort, which is in Walt Disney World and includes all Disney transportation, actually leaves you with more money at the end of the day than a $30-a-night room on U.S. 192 that doesn't include any transportation.

Just because you're driving your own car doesn't mean the shuttle has no value to you. The hotel doesn't know that you have your own transportation. Transportation is worth something. When you're negotiating for your best rate, make sure that the hotel knows that you know this. Tell the manager that you've spoken with Mears and that you know what the value of the transportation and are factoring that into the equation when comparing various room rates. All other things being equal, a room that doesn't include transportation should not sell for the same rate as one that does.

Always keep in mind that Orlando has more hotel rooms than any other single locality on the entire planet. Though rates are extremely low and supply is very high, local developers keep building more. Except for a few peak weeks of the year, there is tremendous competition for your business. The

SAVE BIG ON TICKETS (OR GET THEM FREE)

hotels need you a lot more than you need them. You have the power—use it! If a hotel, including any of those on my list, acts like they don't want your business, move on! There are plenty more who do.

TOUR A TIME SHARE AND SAVE! When you buy a time share, as so-called interval-ownership resorts are informally known, you buy partial ownership of a town house or apartment, which you are then allowed to use for a given length of time during the year, usually one week. Whereas full ownership of this apartment would normally go for, say, $50,000 to $100,000, each time-share purchaser, buying a 1/52 interest, may pay only $8,000 to $20,000. Consequently, the developer extracts a total of between $400,000 and $1,000,000 from the unit. Because there is so much profit to be made, time-share promoters are willing to offer valuable incentives to induce you to tour their properties.

Time-share resorts offer some of Orlando's best accommodations, with excellent facilities. So you may well *want* to tour a time share. But if you're really serious about saving money, there's another good reason to do so. Some big operators pay cash—sometimes $50 to $75 to people who agree to take a 90-minute tour. Most others offer free attraction tickets. There are enough different properties offering free attraction tickets that if you'll simply let the developers feed you breakfast and entertain you every morning, you could conceivably spend every day of your vacation at a theme park for free. (And because you get breakfast as well as the free tickets, you'll come out ahead, even given the hourly cost of your vacation I figured above.)

To find out about these, keep your eyes open for OPCs, described above, who contract with time-share resorts to deliver people who are willing to take the tours. If you ask about the free tickets (as opposed to discounted tickets), the OPC operator will tell you about time-share tours.

Know the Rules: A time-share tour can be a relatively painless way to get free tickets, providing you know the rules. Always remember that time-share promoters are required by law to abide by any offer they make. If the terms read "No purchase necessary," then you are under no obligation to buy anything.

Many developers give the OPCs budgets with which to buy tickets to give away as premiums—enough to give you tickets to a Disney park, Universal, or another major attraction. But because anything they don't spend is profit, they try to get away with giving you the least expensive premium possible. Insist on tickets to a major park. And walk away if you don't get them. If you settle for a vague promise like, "I'll see what I can do," chances are you'll end up with tickets to Ralph's Roach Ranch and Ball of String Museum.

The invitation to tour the property, which the OPC gives you when you agree to take the tour, spells out the rules of the game. Always get the premium offer in writing. If the OPC offers you two free tickets to Universal, the invitation should say "two free tickets to Universal Studios Florida." The invitation also details the qualifications you must meet. Generally, you must be married and traveling with your spouse, have at least $40,000 annual household income, live outside Florida, and be "creditworthy."

Always Take the Morning Tour: This usually gets you free breakfast. It interferes least with your day. Remember that by law, the operator has to abide by his offer. If the offer mentions a 90-minute presentation, then 90 minutes are all you are obligated to give. When 90 minutes are up, you are free to go, and they must provide transportation.

Don't Leave Without Your Premium: When the tour ends, the salesperson completes and verifies your certificate. You

SAVE BIG ON TICKETS (OR GET THEM FREE)

then turn it in at the time share's redemption office and get your premium—in this case, your theme park tickets.

You may actually want to buy a time share. If that's the case, take my advice: Look for a property that has the facilities you want and good security—that's only sensible. Go for a larger property. Smaller ones don't offer the extras, and it's the extras that will affect how easy your property is to exchange. Most larger time shares belong to an international network of properties and you can probably exchange your week for a week at another resort in the group. The more you have, the more you have to trade. And the quality of the network's other properties has significant impact on your property's resale value.

If you are considering a previously owned time share, which costs less than a new one, make sure that it comes with the exchange privilege; sometimes it's not transferable, so the resale is not the bargain it seems.

USE THE ORLANDO FLEXTICKET Remember, this guide is meant to help you find the best values. Single day, single park tickets to most major attractions are just over $40 each, including tax. I recommend the Orlando FlexTicket, which offers substantial savings over the single-day single-park price of admissions to Universal, Sea World, and Wet 'n Wild. In fact, at only $100.65 for seven days, including tax, the cost per day is only $14.38, about a third of the cost of single-day single-park tickets.

DON'T PAY TO PARK HOP! Disney's multiday passes do not offer significant savings over single-day admissions. Instead, Disney heavily promotes the "Park Hopping" feature (which allows you to visit more than one park on any given day) and suggests that there is an added value with this privilege, available only on multiday passes.

I disagree. In my experience, the Park Hopper feature has practically no value. That's because getting into a theme park takes time (and remember, time is very closely related to money). Getting into a theme park requires parking your car, waiting for a tram, riding it to the entrance, waiting in line there, and then walking from the entrance some distance past the shops and eateries to the attractions. Leaving is the same process in reverse. Traveling between parks means taking a tram, bus, boat, or shuttle, and more waiting. Only the Magic Kingdom and Epcot are really convenient to each other. (But not all that convenient. A couple of years ago, in the off season, I left the Disney–MGM Studios at 4:30 PM headed for Disney's Old Key West Resort, where my companion intended to freshen up before a 6:30 dinner in Pleasure Island. Although we moved as quickly as we could and spent only 15 minutes at the hotel, we were an hour late for dinner.)

I simply can't recommend that you waste perfectly good ride-and-attraction time on the leaving-and-arriving routine. So I advise you against park-hopping. And I certainly don't recommend that you pay extra to do it.

(And the one-day, three-park Waterpark Hopper pass just baffles me. I can think of few vacation activities that appeal less to me than traveling between Disney water parks in a wet bathing suit—let alone doing it twice in a day!)

STICK WITH ONE-DAY, ONE-PARK TICKETS AT DISNEY I base this recommendation on years of experience. Disney makes a big deal out of the fact that multiday passes, which cost somewhat less per day than one-day, one-park tickets,

SAVE BIG ON TICKETS (OR GET THEM FREE)

are good forever. They are. However, by state law (which says a lot about Florida politics), theme park passes can't be transferred or sold. So if you live far from Orlando and never get back, the extra days may turn out to be worthless to you—and you wouldn't even be able to give them away to your friends. (The Four-Day Value Pass, without park-hopping, costs $142.04 including tax, or $35.51 a day, just $6.63 a day less than the $42.14 with-tax cost of a single-day theme park ticket. If your plans change and you use the pass for only three days, the prorated per-day cost is $47.35, over $5 a day more than the cost of single tickets.) Buying one-day, one-park tickets buys you flexibility.

As I said, it will also leave you free to take advantage of Central Florida tourism's best-ever deal, the $95 Orlando FlexTicket ($100.65 including tax), which buys unlimited admissions to Universal, Sea World, *and* Wet 'n Wild for seven days—and which works out to an absolutely unheard-of $14.38 a day. This is a spectacular value, so inexpensive that even if you use the pass for only three days, your cost per day is still only $33.55, way less than the $42.14 with-tax tab for a single-day ticket to Universal.

SAVE MONEY ON SHOPPING AND INCIDENTALS!

BYO DRINKS If you really want to save money, one excellent place to cut back is on sodas. It absolutely galls me to pay $2 for a cola when a juice box that's easy to tote in my backpack or stash in a locker costs between a quarter and fifty cents. (I'll tell you more about the great lockers below.) And, as I said, I have yet to run into a family who told me how great the soft drinks were in the theme parks.

BYO FOOD The more you feed yourself, the more you can save. Theme-park fast food for four costs between $20 and $30 per meal; packing sandwiches can trim $40 to $50 a day off your budget. And no one ever seems to mind when we brown-bag it.

USE SHOPPING PASSES If there's something you must have that's available only inside one of the Disney theme parks, don't pay another admission: You can get a complimentary, limited-time shopping pass, a really nice feature made for us locals. Go to Guest Relations, ask for a shopping pass, tell them what you want to buy, and pay for a one-day admission. If you convince them you don't have the time to go elsewhere, they'll give you about an hour. Return to Guest Relations within the specified time, show your purchases, and claim a refund.

DON'T WASTE TIME GETTING AROUND

LEAVE THE DRIVING TO SOMEONE ELSE Surprisingly, you can get just about anywhere, even the Space Center, more easily and cheaply on a shuttle. Buses to WDW, whether run by Disney or not, get you closer to the parks' entrance turnstiles and get you in and out of the park area with a lot less hassle. The same is true at other parks. You'll really appreciate the convenience at the end of the day, when the last thing you feel like doing is waiting in another line just to get to your car.

ALWAYS KNOW WHERE YOU ARE GOING Get good directions (and a good map) at your hotel or the airport, and use them. Bad directions can waste your time or, worse, get you in trouble. The popular Church Street Station, for example, borders a part of town where you really don't want to be lost—trust me.

Central Florida directions can be very confusing. Interstate 4, which is marked east and west (because it's an east–west highway, running between Daytona and Tampa), actually runs north and south through Orlando. When you're thinking about I-4, just remember that east is actually north, and west is really south.

Don't make the mistake that many visitors do of confusing I-4 with the area's other "I," I-Drive, the nickname for International Drive. The main attractions strip in the Magic Kingdom area, U.S. 192, also goes by many names. In this book we use its impossibly long formal name, the Irlo Bronson Memorial Highway. It's also called Space Coast Parkway; in downtown Kissimmee, it's Vine Street. U.S. 441 is also known as Orange Blossom Trail. There's not much here unless you're into XXX, except for the huge Florida Mall, which is worth your while only if your hometown malls are few and basic. Don't go without dependable transportation, good directions, and plenty of gas.

BEAT THE LINES!

I once saw a comedian on the Tonight show who began his stand-up act with the lines, "I just got back from Orlando. I'd like to do my impression of a day at Disney World." Then, he walked up and down the stage in small square patterns, simulating the mazelike path of a line at a theme park. The audience howled, then applauded. Everyone recognized a shared and despised experience.

Believe it or not, the parks are full of shortcuts, short lines, off-peak times at attractions and restaurants, and many other opportunities to save time. Think like a football player and look for the openings. Keep your eyes peeled and keep reprioritizing your schedule. Yes, it's a good idea to have a plan. But keep yourself open to the timesaving opportunities that are always popping up. The minutes you save will add up to extra rides at the end of the day.

I'm not promising freedom from lines. Unfortunately, they're part of the deal. I *can* promise that if you follow my advice, the lines you do wait in will be shorter and fewer.

PARK SMART As I've said before, just arriving at the theme parks offers several opportunities to wait in line; leaving, you do the whole thing in reverse, minus the wait at the ticket windows. However, although arriving guests usually straggle in throughout the day, most visitors leave at closing time. That's when you find the worst lines at the monorails and parking-lot trams (at the Disney parks)—and everyone's tired. That's why I devised my system of parking at the Disney hotels.

For the Magic Kingdom: With my system here, I skip the lines to park, I skip the wait for the tram to the main gate, and I skip the lines waiting for Magic Kingdom transportation. It's even better at the end of the day.

As I approach the toll booth at the main entrance, I get into the lane furthest to the right. I pay the parking fee and continue to keep to the right. When I see signs pointing to the hotels, I go either to the Polynesian Village Resort or the Contemporary Resort Hotel.

From the Poly (that's what the insiders call it), I turn in at the first entrance, stay to the right, and go to the last lot. This puts me next to the walkway into the Magic Kingdom. Then, I just walk down the path to the Transportation and Ticket Center (a.k.a. the TTC). Sometimes, during peak seasons, in the entrance lane to the Polynesian's parking lot, an attendant asks to see my hotel ID. I answer that I'm having breakfast in the hotel. In over 20 years, at least 100 times, this system has failed only twice, on some of the busiest days on record. The attendant who turned me back told me that only registered guests could park at the hotel. He told me that in order to have breakfast there I should park in the main lot and take the bus to the Poly from the TTC. This left me in exactly the same position that I would have been in had I not tried.

At the Contemporary, I park as close to Space Mountain as possible since the walkway from the hotel to the Magic Kingdom is nearby. On the occasions that I was challenged and didn't get through, I went into the hotel and up to the Grand Canyon Concourse to catch the monorail, which stops right in the hotel. It's almost never crowded and takes me right into the park.

To Epcot and Disney–MGM Studios: Our new route for these is to park at Disney's BoardWalk (just follow the Epcot Resorts signs to Epcot Resorts Boulevard) and take the boats directly to the parks. We haven't had any trouble; Disney seems to want to encourage people to visit BoardWalk, which is a really neat place. Parking is free and so is the boat.

Universal, Sea World, Busch Gardens: All three are currently offering something they call Preferred Parking. For $5 above the regular $5 parking fee at Sea World and Busch Gardens, you park right near the front gate. At Universal, for an extra $7, you get valet parking. This is a big worth-it when you arrive, but it's even more so at the end of the day.

ARRIVE LATE AND LEAVE LATE Most people take an unrealistic view of how long they'll spend in a park. During peak seasons, when hours are extended, they may arrive at 9 AM and expect to leave at midnight. Some visitors even attempt this endurance contest with children. Few make it. As a result, park crowds thin considerably around dark.

That's why I always advise my friends, no matter which of our Orlando theme parks they're visiting, to sleep in (or to attend a free time-share breakfast and pick up free theme park tickets). Relaxed and rested, they'll arrive late. They'll start at the front of their chosen park, where lines have abated, and stay late enough to see the fireworks. Then they'll have the park practically to themselves, along with a few thousand parkwise visitors.

Related to this is my advice to:

BE CONTRARY Most people are creatures of habit, engaging in predictable behavior at predictable times. In theme parks, most visitors arrive between 9 and 10 AM. They eat lunch between 11 AM and 1:30 PM. They have dinner between 4 and 7 PM. Waits for all rides are shorter around lunch—and there are almost no lines for food between 2 and 3 PM.

While in the theme parks, my advice is the same: Be contrary. If you arrive early, head first for the back. Most people start at the front. If you arrive after the park has been open for at least an hour, start at the front.

And remember that you can save a couple of hours a day eating at off-peak times. My family usually has lunch at about 2 PM.

Decide which attractions you want to visit most and do them in REVERSE order. Most people have the same favorites. As the day goes on the most popular rides become less crowded. If you visit them in reverse order, you'll see

BEAT THE LINES!

more and spend less time standing in lines. Lines for some popular attractions almost never thin out, particularly when they're still relatively new. My suggestion is to line up when your tour through the park brings you to them. Then bite the bullet and wait.

The parades and fireworks at the theme parks are spectacular. But remember, you can't do everything and life is full of trade-offs. Lines are shortest during the parades and fireworks (and, during parades, particularly at the rides and shows nearest the parade route). Parades are usually late in the day, in the afternoon and at night. Decide what's more important—to see the parade or to catch that major ride.

KEEP LEFT AND DON'T FOLLOW THE CROWD I am constantly amazed by the behavior of people in a crowd. Most people follow the crowd, any crowd. Crowds usually flow to the right. Most people in a hurry pass on the left. If you make it a practice to stay left, you will usually be in the shortest and fastest lines. Also, many attractions run two lines. Because people follow each other and because the crowd moves right, there is often no line at all on the left. It's a Catch-22—no one is in the left line because no one is in the left line to follow. I've seen park attendants walk way out into a long line and remind people that there is another line open. Even on peak days, I have often entered rides with no lines at all, just by walking up the left lane—while hundreds waited patiently on the right.

I remember once in the Magic Kingdom when the line at Big Thunder Mountain stretched all the way down the hill. Looking up at the entrance, I noticed that the left lane was open. My family and I ran up to it, all the way to the entrance, and walked right onto the ride. We entered ahead of hundreds of people who had waited 45 minutes or more, simply because we knew enough not to follow the crowd.

In the Magic Kingdom's Haunted Mansion, the line suddenly moves into a big open area that is a sort of a free-for-all, just before visitors get into the little black ride vehicles. These are on the right. So the crowd always pushes in that direction. This always leaves a large open space along the left wall. We walk through this space—right to the head of the line. It works every time.

Remember, in any area where ropes mark off different queues, a line that's closed will always be indicated by a chain across the opening. If you see no chain, walk on in!

DON'T LINE UP WHEN THERE'S NO LINE Many rides and shows have lobby areas or other collection spots where people are asked to wait. The expectation is that they'll wait in a sort of orderly mob. However, most visitors form a line—out of habit—leaving large open spaces empty. As a fast-track opportunist, you can move right in.

Look for the door and stand near it. If you can't see where it is (because often these doors are disguised), ask the attendants: They'll tell you cheerfully where you'll be going next.

BE PARKWISE There are times that you find unusually short lines at even the most popular rides. Be parkwise: Don't bypass a short line to stick to a schedule, thinking that a particular ride always has short lines and you can come back to it later. Finding a short line is like finding money on the sidewalk. It won't be there for long.

PRAY FOR RAIN A typical summer day in Orlando starts out cloudy and gets progressively more so until mid- to late afternoon, when it rains for an hour or two. That days like this come frequently—sometimes daily—sounds like bad news. But it's not. These are ideal days to visit the theme parks. The cloudy weather scares many people away. Although some hardy souls brave the clouds, many more are flushed out by the rain. When the rain lets up, you may find the theme park practically to yourself.

So come prepared. Or buy a rain poncho with Mickey's picture on it (about $5) or a souvenir umbrella bearing the likeness of the Mickster, Woody Woodpecker, or Shamu. Since most lines are covered most of the time, find a long line you've been avoiding as soon as the rain starts. By the end of the ride, the shower may be over.

Also remember that Florida is the lightning capital of the world and an umbrella can be a lightning rod. Put it down before crossing wide-open spaces.

HAVE A GREAT TIME!

DRESS FOR THE WEATHER—AND FOR COMFORT Did you hear the one about the man who survived a fall from the Tower of Terror? He was wearing his light fall suit! Bad jokes notwithstanding, this is important. Always check the forecast before you leave for Orlando. Check again every day before you leave your hotel. And dress appropriately.

In winter, cold air masses from the north occasionally push southward, and temperatures drop. Thinking back on Christmases past, I can remember many in the 80s and many in the 30s or 40s. But once a cold front moves through, the weather instantly becomes tropical again. Many 40-degree days are followed by 80-degree days and vice versa. Sometimes cold nights follow warm days. Around Thanksgiving and between Christmas and New Year's, when the theme parks are open late, this is a consideration. Bring a jacket or even a change of clothes.

SHIP YOUR PURCHASES—DON'T CARRY THEM If you're staying at a theme-park hotel, one of your many perks as a guest is free delivery of theme-park purchases to your room. Request it when you pay. And note that whether or not you're staying on property, you can have purchases shipped home or to anywhere in the world directly from the park. You pay only for the shipping—the parks generally do not tack on an extra charge for this service.

USE THE LOCKERS All parks have them, and I can't stress enough how helpful they can be, especially when the weather obliges you to bring warm clothes. Putting your things in a convenient locked box inside the theme park can make your whole day better. Over the years, I have seen many thousands of miserable people, slogging around in the afternoon heat loaded down with gear and purchases.

Although no one can guarantee the safety of your stuff, I myself have never had a problem in over 20 years. Security in the parks is good, particularly around the lockers. And the lockers are a heck of a lot safer than the trunk of your car in the parking lot.

I use the locker for heavy, bulky things, like jackets, sweaters, and rain ponchos. You will want your cameras to record the day's events on film and video. But you will be miserable if you lug this equipment around all day. Use the locker (discreetly) to give yourself a break.

HAVE A GREAT TIME!

We also bring:

- A couple of towels to dry off with.
- Extra clothes, at least for your small fry. Getting splashed has always been part of the fun, and several parks now have fountains and other water features meant for playing in—younger children invariably end up soaked.
- A change of socks for every member of the family. You'll be amazed how much a pair of dry socks can do for you after a rain or a hot, sweaty day.
- Frozen box drinks.
- Sandwiches and snacks.
- Extra film and videotape.

RIDE THE FRONT CAR While hundreds or thousands of visitors wait in line for a seat in one of the Disney monorails, my family and I are being personally escorted to the front of the train by a uniformed attendant to ride with the driver. I have overheard first-time visitors to Walt Disney World whisper "Who are they?" or "They must be VIPs." There's a trick to this, and I can tell you what it is.

We ask.

That's it. That's all.

We just ask.

Disney's absolutely unadvertised policy is that anyone who asks can usually get a front seat. This is true on almost any ride—the monorail, Space Mountain, Big Thunder Mountain, Splash Mountain, Pirates of the Caribbean, even It's a Small World. You may have to wait until the next ride, or even the one after that, but if you want a front seat, they'll try to accommodate you. As for the monorail, the panorama you see through the Plexiglas bubble is spectacular. As often as we have done it (50 times or more), it's always a thrill.

USE SUNSCREEN This may seem obvious, but believe me, it's not. At the end of the day in the theme parks I see way too many sunburned noses. Remember that Florida sun will burn you even on overcast days and in winter. So put on your sun block—preferably one with a sun protection factor of 15 or higher—before you leave your motel, and bring extra. If you're going to a water park, be sure your sun block is waterproof and refresh it every few hours if you're in the water.

BRING MOSQUITO REPELLENT You may think of this when you go camping. But lots of people never even imagine they'll need it in theme parks. I speak from experience. If you're planning on visiting Discovery Island, Fort Wilderness, or a water park with a lot of nature like River Country, you'll need mosquito repellent. And you may even need it in the parks on summer evenings.

PREPARE TO GET WET In many parks (and not only the water parks), at least part of the fun is getting wet. As I said above, you may want to bring a round of dry clothes for the family. And, because seeing your kids get wet makes for great pictures, I always bring a zip-closing bag to put over my camera. (I use a gallon-size bag over my video camera.) Then I shoot right through the plastic—a poor man's sports camera! If you're worried, leave your camera at home and bring one of those waterproof one-time FunSaver cameras.

BEAT THE HEAT The Florida sun can wear you down. Next to staying inside where it's air-conditioned, the best way to beat

HAVE A GREAT TIME!

the heat is to get wet. Our family used to cool off by spritzing each other with a spray bottle filled with water; lately we've discovered a version with electric fan attached, known as a "Squeeze and Breeze" (around $18 in the parks and only $8 at Wal-Mart and KMart). We can also be seen sticking our heads under the stream of water in the drinking fountains. Now and then, I step into the rest room, soak my T-shirt in the sink, and put it back on. It works! I'm cool for hours. (The one drawback: Tiffany, my daughter, and Ricky, my son, don't think so.)

BE KIND TO YOUR KIDS All too frequently I overhear parents in the theme parks yelling at their children, even hitting them. Sometimes even the best children need a little discipline. That's not what I'm talking about. I'm talking about overbearing parents who are herding their children through the parks, determined to make them have a good time or else. Yes, there are ways to get through the parks faster, but don't overdo it! Don't try so hard to do so much that you miss the most important thing of all—a good time.

chapter 2

ADMISSION PRICES AND WHERE TO FIND OUT MORE

If you're visiting Universal Studios, Sea World, and Wet 'n Wild, don't forget about the multipark **Orlando FlexTicket** ($99.95, $82.95 for kids 3–9). A 10-day FlexTicket costs $129.95 ($107.95 children 3–9) and includes Busch Gardens.
These prices and those below do not include tax. Be sure to ask about special AAA and senior citizen rates.

BUSCH GARDENS Tickets cost $37.95 for one day, $10.95 per extra day. Save $6 when you combine a ticket to Sea World. A combined ticket to Busch Gardens and the adjacent Adventure Island water park is $45.19 ($38.77 children 3–9). Parking is $5 for cars ($10 for Preferred Parking; *see* Chapter 5), $6 for trucks or campers, $4 for motorcycles.
Hours Daily 9:30–6, longer during peak periods.
More Information: Busch Gardens, Box 9158, Tampa 33674, tel. 813/987–5082.

SEA WORLD One-day tickets cost $39.75 ($32 for children 3–9). Save $6 when you combine a ticket to Busch Gardens. Parking is $5 per car (Shamu's Preferred Parking $10), $7 per RV or camper.
Hours: Daily 9–7, as late as 10 during peak periods.
More Information: Sea World, 7007 Sea Harbor Dr., Orlando 32821, tel. 407/351–3600.

UNIVERSAL STUDIOS Tickets cost $39.75 for one day, $59.75 for two days ($32 and $49.75 respectively, for children 3–9), plus tax. Get them at the Orlando/Orange County Convention and Visitors Bureau office at 8723 International Dr. and you'll save a couple of dollars per ticket. Parking is $6 for cars, $10 for campers ($12 for valet parking).
Hours: Daily 9–7, as late as 10 during peak periods.
More Information: Universal Studios, 1000 Universal Studios Plaza, Orlando 32819–7610, tel. 407/363–8000.

WALT DISNEY WORLD Here, we're talking about the major parks (**Magic Kingdom, Epcot,** and **Disney–MGM Studios**), the water parks (**Typhoon Lagoon, Blizzard Beach,** and **River Country**), and **Discovery Island**. Single-day *tickets* admit you to just one of the major parks at a time, multiday *passes* to more than one. At press time, four-day passes are good for the major parks but not the water parks or Discovery Island; longer passes cover all parks, including the water parks, Pleasure Island, and Discovery Island. Prices, which change regularly, are as follows, with prices for kids 3–9 in parentheses: one-day ticket $39.75 ($32); Four-Day Value Pass $134 ($107); Four-Day Park Hopper $150 ($120); Five-Day All-in-One Hopper $205 ($164); River Country $15.95 ($12.50); Discovery Island $11.95 ($6.50); combined River Country/Discovery Island $20.95 ($15.50); Blizzard Beach

ADMISSION PRICES AND WHERE TO FIND OUT MORE

and Typhoon Lagoon $25.95 ($20.50); Pleasure Island $17.95 for all. Six- and seven-day passes are also available. *See* pages 18–20 for more on tickets and passes.

Tickets and passes can be ordered by mail (c/o Mail-Order Tickets, Walt Disney World, Box 10140, Lake Buena Vista, FL 32830; add $2 per order for postage and handling and allow two weeks for processing). Or they can be purchased at local Disney Stores, the theme parks, at on-site resorts (registered guests only), and at the WDW kiosk in Orlando International Airport. AAA offices nationwide sell discounted admissions.

To park in the theme parks you'll pay $5 ($6 for RVs and campers; free to Walt Disney World resort guests with ID and at Typhoon Lagoon, River Country, and Blizzard Beach). Save your receipt; if you visit another park on the same day, you won't have to pay twice to park.

Hours: Hours vary but are longest during peak periods, when the Magic Kingdom may stay open until midnight or later. Note that although the Magic Kingdom, Disney–MGM, and Epcot's Future World officially open at 9 (World Showcase opens at 11), visitors may enter at 8:30, even 8. If you stay at a Disney-owned hotel, you can enter earlier. Discovery Island, River Country, Typhoon Lagoon, and Blizzard Beach operate Daily 10–5 (during summer until 7 or occasionally 10).

Animal Kingdom: Revised prices that include Disney's Animal Kingdom were not available at press time. Call as your visit approaches to check on Animal Kingdom operating hours.

More Information: For **general matters,** contact Guest Relations or Guest Services in any Disney theme park or hotel (tel. 407/824–4321). For **accommodations and shows,** call WDW Central Reservations (tel. 407/W–DISNEY).

ADMISSION PRICES AND WHERE TO FIND OUT MORE

chapter 3
UNIVERSAL STUDIOS FLORIDA

From I–4, take Exit 30B. This puts you practically on top of the main entrance on Kirkman Road, which intersects with International Drive at its north end. You can follow signage (which takes you around to the back of the park). Or do as I do to avoid the extra drive: Turn right onto Major Boulevard, the street that runs alongside the Twin Towers and the Mystery Fun House and is directly opposite the park entrance; then make a legal U-turn, which points you straight at the entrance. (If you enter from I-Drive on Kirkman, the U-turn is unnecessary.)

★★★★★ +

Subtract 1 if you're traveling with children under 6.

The best theme park in the world—that's what you'll hear me say over and over about Universal Studios Florida. The rides are the most spectacular, the shows the most thrilling, the attention to detail unequaled anywhere. And now, with the opening of two new shows, Twister and Hercules and Xena: Wizards of the Screen, the best theme park in the world is even better. The park is now also part of Universal Florida, soon to be a three-park destination attraction. Universal's CityWalk, opening in 1998, is a dazzling new nightlife attraction. And Universal's unbelievable new Islands of Adventure theme park, scheduled to open in 1999 and previewed at the end of this chapter, promises to eclipse everything that has ever been done in theme-park history!

Remember, the Universal complex isn't the product of some second-rate outfit. Established in 1918, during the Silents Era, Universal is the studio that releases Steven Spielberg films, and its history during the the 1930s and 1940s is star-studded. True, lines can be painfully long and very hot, and the park has too much concrete and not enough green space and shade. But despite that, and as great as the Disney parks are, Universal Studios Florida is better than anything at Walt Disney World.

I use a process of elimination.

The Magic Kingdom is a wonderful park. It's based on Disneyland, which opened in 1956, the original. It's full of neat things to see and do. But it's still based on many concepts from the 1940s.

Epcot Center is too much about shopping and eating and not enough about rides and shows.

Disney–MGM Studios is the newest and the best of the Disney parks. Since it's movie-based, like Universal, comparisons between the two are easy. Both parks offer back lot tours that give you a behind-the-scenes look at how movies and TV shows are made. Both have first-class thrill rides and multimillion-dollar media productions.

In contrast to Disney's Star Tours, where your simulator is a small square room and the screen is even smaller than those in your average mall multiplex cinema, Back to the Future has you in an eight-passenger replica of a DeLorean sports car that literally hangs you out in space in front of a nine-story IMAX screen. Star Tours is great, and my whole family loves it. But Back to the Future is about a gazillion times more exciting.

In no other theme park do you find the attention to detail that you do at Universal Studios Florida. For instance, Universal's rides not only look real, they smell real, from the salt tang in the air at the northeastern wharf outside Jaws to the scent of bananas on King Kong's breath at Kongfrontation.

As you read this chapter, you will see why ride for ride, show for show, this is my family's favorite park. The rides and shows are similar in structure from park to park: There are simulators and thrill rides, special effects and stunt shows, interactive film shows and robotics (called Audio-Animatronics at Disney). However, in almost every case, Universal's version is bigger, more detailed, more powerfully presented, or just plain better. Universal has a lot to please the little ones with Barney and Baby Bop, Fievel's Playland, and my favorite kid's ride anywhere, The Funtastic World of Hanna-Barbera. Still, I have to give Disney the edge for cuteness and appeal to small children. But for kids old enough to appreciate the slimy goo at Nickelodeon and for the pure power of motion-picture magic, sound, light, and spectacle, my envelope says the winner is Universal Studios Florida.

WHAT'S NEW Be sure to catch Twister, complete with indoor tornado and water effects, when it opens in summer 1998. Hercules and Xena, based on the TV series, is also a must.

TIMING Because it is the best of all the parks, I recommend two days here. And do it *before* you visit any of the Disney parks.

EATERTAINMENT Okay, I've said that I don't recommend theme-park restaurants. But Universal Studios has a bunch of decent munching stops that you may want to try for the experience or the convenience. There's a **character breakfast,** complete with Woody Woodpecker. (Bonus: Depending on how quickly you finish, you can get an early jump on park activities.) I list my other picks below. Reservations usually aren't necessary but if you have your heart set on a specific place, book ahead (you can call up to 48 hours in advance). I give the numbers below, along with the descriptions.

SHOPPERTOONITIES Universal offers a number of unique shopping opportunities, starting at the front gate with **On Location** and **Studio Gifts**.

SHOWS AND TAPINGS A schedule of shows is posted on a sign board near the entrance. You get a printed schedule when you buy your ticket. If you lose yours, you can replace it at Guest Relations. But it's better to call ahead to find out what will be taping when and then schedule your day in the park accordingly. Also ask how long the taping will take: Because it's hard to slip out early and because even a half-hour show can easily take half a day or more to make, a taping can really cut into your theme-park time if you're not careful. If you do decide to go, remember: The early bird gets first shot at tickets. Depending on the show, you will have to grab a seat or a place in line early, and you will have to wait; bring refreshments to help pass the time and beat the heat. The number to call is 407/363–8000.

THE LAY OF THE LAND Universal Studios Florida is laid out like a Hollywood back lot, with areas that simulate Hollywood and Beverly Hills, New York City and Chicago, and the wharves of New England and San Francisco, plus an area called Expo Center. Finally, the Production Central section highlights the mechanics of show biz. These "lands" are arranged around a central lagoon.

THE FAST TRACK Most visitors bear right when they enter the park. Do what other people don't: Bear left when you

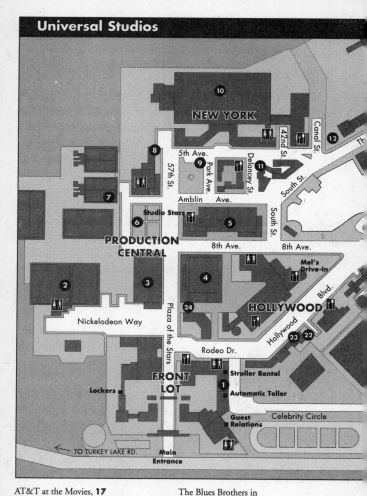

AT&T at the Movies, **17**
Alfred Hitchcock–the Art of Making Movies, **4**
Animal Actors Stage, **18**
Back to the Future...The Ride, **16**
Barney, **19**
Beetlejuice's Rock and Roll Graveyard Revue, **12**

The Blues Brothers in Chicago Bound, **11**
The Boneyard, **6**
E.T. Adventure, **21**
Earthquake: The Big One, **13**
Fievel's Playland, **20**
Funtastic World of Hanna-Barbera, **3**

40

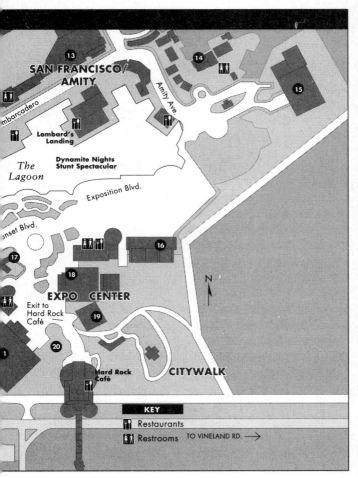

Gory, Gruesome & Grotesque
Horror Make-Up Show, **22**
Hercules and Xena: Wizards of the
Screen, **5**
Islands of Adventure Preview Center, **9**
Jaws, **14**
Kongfrontation, **10**
Lucy: A Tribute, **24**

Nickelodeon Studios Tour, **2**
Production Center Information, **1**
Studio 54, **7**
Terminator 2: 3-D, **23**
Twister, **8**
Wild, Wild, Wild West
Stunt Show, **15**

enter, and proceed clockwise around the park. Why fight the crowds? Do the shows (Wild West, Beetlejuice, Animal Actors, Barney) first. Rides are most crowded in the mornings, then thin out dramatically by afternoon. Be sure to take your time as you stroll: One of our favorite family pastimes is to try to recognize buildings and what movie we saw them in. If you overlook the little things, you'll miss a lot.

What to See

PRODUCTION CENTRAL

NICKELODEON STUDIOS TOUR According to recent A.C. Nielsen ratings, Nickelodeon is one of the highest rated cable networks—not just among kids, but among everybody. The line to tour the studios forms at the **Slime Geyser,** the giant fountain that blasts green goo high into the Florida sky. Glassed-in catwalks above the soundstages give you a unique view of real TV shows in progress. Kids get to see how their favorite substances, gak and slime, are made, and may even get a taste! **Game Lab,** at the very end of the Nick tour, is like a fake game show with people in your tour group chosen to participate based on enthusiasm. (The kids and I know the drill, and one or more of us almost always get in.) The games are quintessential Nick—very physical and messy, ending with one lucky (?) kid getting slimed.
Worth-It Rating ★★★★★ Minus 1 if you're traveling without kids.

FUNTASTIC WORLD OF HANNA-BARBERA This is the first ride you see in the park and the best ride for little kids any-

where. I wish Disney would do as well with Peter Pan. Bill and Joe (Hanna and Barbera) give you a quick look at computer animation. Then you enter a large simulator where you join Yogi Bear in a daring rescue of Elroy Jetson from the evil clutches of Dick Dastardly and his sniveling mutt, Muttley. The lines are often short.
Worth-It Rating ★★★★★

ALFRED HITCHCOCK—THE ART OF MAKING MOVIES I remember being scared to death in 1963, when Tippi Hedren was attacked in Alfred Hitchcock's *The Birds*. But that was long ago and for most of the X and Echo generations, this show may be dated. The effects are pretty neat, though: You may want to check your clothes for droppings.
Worth-It Rating ★★★

HERCULES AND XENA: WIZARDS OF THE SCREEN For 1998, both studios had a Hercules. Universal's attraction is based on the TV version with Kevin Sorbo as Hercules and Lucy Lawless as Xena. Even for old TV pros like me, the demonstrations of cutting-edge special effects and digital animation are impressive. The scenario is that the production is way behind, and you have to help the cast and crew, in an interactive participation event that takes you from filming to sound effects and voice-overs. Along the way, things get completely out of hand—that's the fun part!
The Fast Track: Act up and you could get a part. Have a camera ready, just in case.
Worth-It Rating ★★★★★

STAGE 54 An inside look at the props, costumes, and special effects that go into the latest Universal TV or film production. At this writing, it's *The Lost World of Jurassic Park, Be-*

hind the Screams, an exhibit of props and sets (including robotic dinosaurs) that's so large that it bursts out of its small building and takes over the street. No lines, no waiting and lots to see!
Tip: Have your camera ready—photo ops abound.
Worth-It Rating ★★★★★

THE BONE YARD Many visitors completely miss this not-necessarily-final resting place of props and gadgets from films gone by. That tarnished metal hulk once had the title role in *Jaws* and was as big a star as Richard Dreyfuss. Take a minute to stop and smell the rust.
Worth-It Rating ★★★★★

PRODUCTION CENTER, SOUNDSTAGE WALK-THROUGHS One of the things I love about Universal Studios Florida is that it is a real, working, major motion picture studio. Although the entrance to the movie studios is heavily guarded, doors to one side of the actual soundstages open right onto the park. There's always a chance that a movie star (like Sly or Arnold) or a director (like Spielberg) will walk out into the park. I just saw Henry Winkler. Plus, there's almost always a walk-through tour where you can see a real movie soundstage complete with the sets. Nowhere else in the world do you get such an authentic experience of the way movies are made. This is a must-see for any movie buff, regardless of what is on view when you arrive.
Worth-It Rating ★★★★★

EATERTAINMENT Studio Stars, a cafeteria between Hollywood and New York, gives you hot and cold options galore. Still, I miss those all-you-can-eat buffets that used to be here. To reserve, call 407/224–9530.

NEW YORK

ISLANDS OF ADVENTURE PREVIEW CENTER Depending on when you read this, you will either be looking at a preview of the most awesome theme park ever conceived, or going to it. (For my own preview, *see* Islands of Adventure, A Preview, *below.*)

TWISTER The stars of *Twister*, Helen Hunt and Bill Paxton, greet you in a short film that introduces the premise of the movie—two scientists chasing tornadoes across the country. This kicks off your journey into a fabulous soundstage demonstration. Set designers experiment with the equipment that creates the spectacular weather effects for *Twister* and the forthcoming *Twister II*. As so often happens in theme parks, things spin out of control until you find yourself in the middle of an indoor tornado. The effects are all around you—spectacular. Everyone always asks, will you see the flying cow? Yes, and expect to get wet!
Tip: The line is air-conditioned; this is a great place to cool off during the hottest parts of the day.
Worth-It Rating ★★★★★

KONGFRONTATION New York City's transit system brings you face to face with the movies' biggest mechanical menace—Ol' Banana Breath himself! It even smells like New York, sort of (only they left the gross parts out).
The Fast Track: Beware of lines here—there's a lot more inside than you might guess. The best time we've found to do this ride is late in the day.
Worth-It Rating ★★★★★

WHAT TO SEE

THE BLUES BROTHERS IN CHICAGO BOUND This show takes place in the street, in front of a reproduction of Jake and Elwood's walk-up from the movie. These guys are better than Aykroyd and Belushi! Check your program for times.
Worth-It Rating ★★★★★

BEETLEJUICE'S ROCK AND ROLL GRAVEYARD REVUE Rock and roll with the ungrateful dead in this loud, last-gasp blast from the passed. It takes place on an outdoor stage, with lots of bright and smoky pyrotechnics. Bring earplugs.
Worth-It Rating ★★★★

BITES Remember *The Godfather*? I have it memorized. Really, the whole movie. **Louie's Italian Restaurant,** a Little Italy–style establishment, wasn't in the movie, but it could've been. Great pizza, of course. **Finnegan's Bar and Grill,** an Irish pub where Universal staffers hang out after work, serves British beers along with live entertainment, happy hours, and hearty fare like shepherd's pie. Draw me a Guinness! To reserve at Finnegan's, call 407/363–8757.

BUYS Doc's, on Delancey Street, is where the Blues Brothers shop. And you can outfit yourself in khaki and a pith helmet at **Safari Outfitters,** next to Kongfrontation. Or have your photo taken with the giant simian. Nearby is **Second Hand Rose.** Only Universal Studios has this kind of bargain basement full of its discounted clothing and souvenirs.

SAN FRANCISCO/AMITYVILLE

EARTHQUAKE: THE BIG ONE Charlton Heston narrates a behind-the-scenes look at how the special effects for this classic film were made. Then you ride a subway into an 8.3 quake, complete with spectacular effects involving explosions and a lot of water. You might get wet.
The Fast Track: Act loud and crazy at the beginning and you could get picked to be an extra. Bring a camera.
Worth-It Rating ★★★★

JAWS You are greeted with the unmistakable smell of wharf, then board a tour boat for a routine cruise around Amityville's harbor when suddenly you are attacked by a terrifying shark. It took over four years for the Universal Studios engineers to get this thing to work (in tests, the mechanical sharks actually sank the boats). The delay was worth it.
The Fast Track: Before you line up, stop at a shop and get a plastic bag to hold anything you don't want to get wet.
Worth-It Rating ★★★★★

WILD, WILD, WILD WEST STUNT SHOW This is a nifty look at how those shoot-'em-ups and blow-'em-ups are made. These daring stunt men are "real" men and almost as good as the stunt women. At Halloween, this becomes Bill & Ted's Excellent Halloween Adventure and Stunt Show—a show so great that even Disney folks pay to visit their competition.
The Fast Track: It's loud. Bring ear plugs, especially for little tots.
Worth-It Rating ★★★★ +

WHAT TO SEE

BITES The steaks and seafood at **Lombard's Landing** are excellent, and it's a great place to watch the stunt show. To reserve, call 407/224-6400. Outside on the pier, a stand serves clam chowder in a bread bowl. Yum! **Richter's Burger Company** offers giant burgers and a fixin's bar, plus grilled chicken, hot dogs, huge shakes, mountains of fries, and the trademark—*cheesequake* dessert.

BUYS Check out the wood and leather items at lagoon's-edge **Bayfront Crafts. Quint's Nautical Treasures** sells *Jaws* merchandise. At **Salty's Sketches,** in Amityville, you can have a caricature drawn. Then there's **Shaiken's Souvenirs,** across from the Epicenter, where you can actually feel the ground shake while you're shopping for San Francisco and *Earthquake* stuff.

EXPO CENTER

BACK TO THE FUTURE: THE RIDE I rate Back to the Future the number-one theme-park ride in the world. One of the greatest thrills of my career was when I attended its star-studded opening, along with Michael J. Fox, Mary Steenburgen, and Tom Wilson, who plays the ride's villain, Biff. We rode nine times in a row! I also talked to Douglas Trumbull, the renowned Hollywood special-effects wizard who designed this amazing ride, using the same simulator technology developed for NASA to replicate space-flight conditions.

The adventure begins in line as you are greeted by a research assistant from Doc Brown's Institute for Future Living. Pay close attention to the TV monitors—they're not up there just to help you pass the time. The presentation will bring you up to speed on your mission to capture Biff, with impressive detail. Check the halls for memorabilia from previous visitors such as Albert Einstein and Leonardo da Vinci.

Your simulator is a model DeLorean, similar to the car in the film trilogy (the actual vehicle is out front). Once you're buckled up, a garage door opens to reveal the fact that you are suspended several stories up in front of one of the largest theater screens in the world, 90 feet high!

The Fast Track: The very best seat in the house is the center car on level five. Go ahead and ask the attendant for it. (You may even get it.) Occasionally, you can fast-track the left lane, but don't count on it.

Worth-It Rating ★★★★★ +

BARNEY Too quickly, kids grow up. Sadly, mine are beyond Barney. Yours may still want to meet the famous purple dinosaur, Baby Bop, and pals at this live outdoor sing-along, play-along show on a high-tech revolving stage. One highlight is an outdoor play area where kids make music by touching glowing, singing rocks. Check your schedule for show times.

The Fast Track: Get there early to sit up front—little kids are short and have trouble seeing over crowds.

Worth-It Rating ★★★★★ Subtract 4 if you're over 5.

ANIMAL ACTORS STAGE Meet Lassie, Mister Ed, and many other four-legged stars. You won't believe that animals can do what they do here until you see them do it here, and then you may still not believe. Like many of the Orlando theme-park experiences, this trained-animal show is the best of its kind.

Worth-It Rating ★★★★★

WHAT TO SEE

FIEVEL'S PLAYLAND Everyday household items are huge in Fievel Mouskewitz's land of the little. This world-class kids' playground has the obligatory ball pits and moon walks, but its centerpiece is a water slide that will soak riders of any age—wonderful on a hot day.

The Fast Track: Plan to be here when the mid-afternoon heat peaks, around 2 or 3 PM. Then you can cool off and relax in this wet, shady, fun spot.

Worth-It Rating ★★★★★

E.T. ADVENTURE The most popular ride in the park gives you another excellent look at how movies are made. The setting is a realistic re-creation of a Hollywood set, a forest full of topless concrete trees, filled with props from *E.T.* You ride the bike with E.T. and see how many scenes and special effects were done.

The Fast Track: Long lines—and nothing to be done about it; get there early.

Worth-It Rating ★★★★★ Add 1 if you have small children or don't like thrill rides.

AT&T AT THE MOVIES Fans of America's largest phone company will love this showcase of its role on film. What, you've never gone to a movie to see an AT&T phone?

Worth-It Rating ★★★ Subtract 2 if you think your phone bill is too high.

BITES The **International Food Bazaar** is just like the food court at the mall, only better, with Italian, Greek, and American (among others).

BUYS Just outside the world's greatest ride, you'll find **Back to the Future Gifts** and about a million different reproductions of the time-traveling DeLorean. You can also find your size in a Hill Valley High School class ring. Want to own the shower curtain from the most famous shower scene in history? Or take home a towel or ash tray from the Bates Motel? Stop by the **Bates Motel Gift Shop.** Then there's **E.T.'s Toy Closet and Photo Spot,** with hard and soft E.T. toys and a place to have your photo taken with the famous alien. **Fievel's Playland Kiosk** is your source for Fievel toys.

HOLLYWOOD

GORY, GRUESOME & GROTESQUE HORROR MAKE-UP SHOW This how-to demonstration on the making of Hollywood's grossest goo is only for the strong of stomach, liver, and intestines. In fact, you'll see all the above entrails and then some. Would it surprise you to know that many human body parts on film are actually bloody meat and animal organs?
The Fast Track: Don't go at lunchtime.
Worth-It Rating ★★★★ Subtract 3 if you are easily nauseated.

TERMINATOR 2: 3D When I was growing up in the 1950s, 3D film promoters predicted that exhibitors of the future would proffer their wares in special theaters showing only 3D movies. So far that has happened only at the theme parks. All these shows are worth seeing, but along with the number-one ride in the world, Back to the Future, Universal Studios Florida is also home to T2, which I consider the number-one theme-park show in the world and the most spectacular production anywhere. Directed by *Titanic* director James Cameron, it cost $65 million to make.

WHAT TO SEE

At the beginning, you enter the headquarters of a fictitious CyberDyne Systems (frighteningly similar to a not-so-fictitious West Coast company). You are shown a wonderfully satirical film depicting the amazing things that computers will soon be doing for you. Fans of the Terminator movies will already know what everyone else will soon understand: The machines are trying to take over the world. If Linda Hamilton can't stop them with the help of renegade Terminator robot Arnold Schwarzenegger, humanity is doomed. Along with a 3D movie featuring Arnold, Linda, and other stars from the films, there are giant robots, incredibly realistic 3D effects, fast-moving props, and live actors on motorcycles zooming in and out of the screen so that it's difficult to distinguish what's real and what's not. Audiences typically give this show a standing ovation. I went home and hugged my Apple computer.

The Fast Track: There are three opportunities to fast-track here. When you enter the building, the left lane may be open. Next, look for the place where the line changes to an assembly area; most people try to stay in line, so you can move ahead. Finally, in the holding lobby just before the theater, you can move directly to the area in front of the doors. Try not to sit in the front row. It's too close, and you don't see as much on the sides and in the back.

Worth-It Rating ★★★★★ +

LUCY: A TRIBUTE Anywhere else, this often-overlooked tribute to Lucille Ball would stand out. Now, thanks to *Nick at Nite,* a whole new generation loves Lucy.

Worth-It Rating ★★★★

PRODUCTION TOURS Productions are often in progress on Universal soundstages, so call ahead to request a schedule. You'll generally come in through the back lot entrance, then

ride the tram into the soundstage area and end up as a member of the audience for a national TV show like *WCW Wrestling* or *Country Music Showdown.* If you're lucky, you might just catch a movie being filmed. Big stars work here all the time (I've personally seen Steven Spielberg, Steve Martin, Roy Scheider, Michael J. Fox, and a few others).
Worth-It Rating ★★★★★

BITES **Schwab's Pharmacy** re-creates the soda fountain where 40s film star Lana Turner was discovered. You can discover overstuffed sandwiches and excellent old-fashioned fountain treats. Try the chocolate ice-cream soda. **Mel's Drive-In**, the scene of George Lucas's classic, *American Graffiti,* is just like you remember. In **Café La Bamba,** they speak Tex-Mex. Try the yucca (it's a vegetable) or the ribs (Ricky loves 'em).

BUYS In the **Brown Derby Hat Shop,** you'll find every kind of hat. **Bull's Gym & Sports Merchandise** is the place to get Universal sweats and active wear. **Cyber Image-T2 Merchandise** sells replicas of Arnold's zippered leather jacket and a special cut of the movie with some great scenes that were left out. The **Dark Room**, a film store, displays great black-and-white photos on the walls. The color film you can buy is strictly modern. So is the developing. Check out **It's a Wrap.** You can make yourself feel like Hollywood royalty, if you have enough money for its pricey 30s and 40s fashion. In **Movietime Portrait and Celebrity News,** you can step into vintage outfits and get your photo on the cover of *Variety* or some other rag. Need a klieg lamp for the den? A plastic Oscar or a clapboard scene slate for your home videos? Stop at **Silver Screen Collectibles,** next to Alfred Hitchcock. In the **Universal Cartoon Store,** next to E.T., you'll find character toys and everything imaginable that relates to Universal

WHAT TO SEE

cartoons. **Universal Studios Store,** the biggest store in the park, has items from all the other theme shops plus Nickelodeon merchandise. In **Williams of Hollywood Photo Studio,** you pose in period-style costumes. In the Bone Yard, between New York and Hollywood, you'll find the dinosaurs and **Jurassic Park Merchandise:** toys, hats, shirts, and other paraphernalia boldly emblazoned with the logo of the world's most famous fictitious theme park.

THE SHOW AT THE END OF THE DAY

DYNAMITE NIGHTS STUNTACULAR Remember those great speedboat chases on *Miami Vice*? They're performed nightly on the lagoon, right in the middle of the park, along with fireworks and lots of explosions. It is spectacular.
Worth-It Rating ★★★★ +

SPECIAL EVENTS

Universal has some of Orlando's best special and seasonal events. Halloween Horror Nights focuses on the horror genre with such classic characters as Frankenstein and Dracula, along with new material like Bill and Ted's Excellent Halloween Adventure and Stunt Show, which I consider the best live theme park show in town. Mardi Gras is also a major event. If your vacation plans coincide with either season, call 407/363–8000 to get the details so that you don't miss the fun.

Islands of Adventure:
A Preview

Universal is planning to corner the market on superlatives with this new attraction. Working with park creative consultant Steven Spielberg, Universal's Mark Woodbury and his design team have used cutting-edge technology to work with such disparate themes as Marvel superheroes, Dr. Seuss, and Jurassic Park to produce what promises to be a masterpiece.

THE LAY OF THE LAND Islands of Adventure will consist of several themed islands. The hub, **Port of Entry**, will be an eclectic mixture of the classic buildings of the ancient world.

MARVEL SUPER HERO ISLAND Spider Man Adventure, a multimedia adventure, will combine amazing 3D filmed special effects with an action ride on a moving vehicle. Sometimes you'll whiz past the 3D screens, sometimes they'll move with you; other effects may involve live action, robotics, and pyrotechnics. At night, the **Incredible Hulk Coaster** should glow green like its namesake. Plans call for the ride to start by duplicating the thrust of a U.S Air Force F-16 attack jet, going from zero to 40 mph in two seconds. An ensuing 100-foot-high inversion will have you experiencing honest-to-goodness weightlessness and six more upside-down rolls. And you'll plunge underground twice. **Dr. Doom's Fearfall** is Universal City's answer to Disney–MGM's Tower of Terror, but unlike TOT, which is indoors, this one will be in the open, so that you can see the ground coming straight at you in your terrifying free-fall.

TOON LAGOON At **Dudley Do-Right's Ripsaw Falls**, you'll help save Nell from the evil Snidely Whiplash in the only flume ride ever to take you underwater. At **Popeye and Bluto's Bilge Rat Barges**, a 16-feet-per-second white-water rafting adventure, other guests will fire water cannons at you; the ride is to end in a drive-through boat wash where there will be absolutely no chance you won't get soaked—that is, if you aren't already. **Popeye's Boat** is planned as a nifty twist on the giant playground concept, with another water cannon in addition to the ropes, ladders, and slides. In **Comic Strip Lane**, you'll stroll through the habitat of Beetle Bailey, Blondie, Cathy, Hagar the Horrible, and many more famous funny-paper characters, over 80 in all.

JURASSIC PARK The dinosaurs at **Jurassic Park River Adventure** should be the most realistic ever created. Among them will be a five-story T-Rex that will brush against your vehicle just before you meet up with a torrential storm and plunge down an 85-foot water slide, the fastest and steepest ever built. In **Triceratops Encounter**, you can pet a 24-foot-long, 10-foot-high interactive robotic dinosaur, complete with facial tics and muscle flinches. The interactive **Jurassic Park Visitor Center**, a faithful re-creation of the point of debarkation in the movie, will mix real exhibits of fossilized dinosaurs with robotics such as the hatching of baby raptor. **Pteranodon Flyers** will repackage the old familiar skyride—the vehicles are a prehistoric bird/reptile with a 10-foot wingspan. **Camp Jurassic** will update the Magic Kingdom's Tom Sawyer Island, with lava pits, caves, and a rain forest.

LOST CONTINENT Another spectacular multimedia event, like Terminator 2: 3D, **Escape from the Lost City** will put you in the middle of a battle between Zeus, who is armed with 25-foot fire balls, and Poseidon, backed by a mere 350,000 gallons of water. Billed as the only ride of its kind in the world, **Dueling Dragons** will be the park's signature roller coaster. Plans are for a single lift to take two coasters up 125 feet, then drop them down on two different tracks, where they will avoid a head-on collision by a mere 12 inches, one of three near-misses. In all, you'll be upside down five times. The **Eighth Voyage of Sinbad** should be one of the most ambitious stunt shows ever produced, involving explosions in the water and what promise to be amazing pyrotechnics, including a stunt person, on fire, who falls 22 feet.

SEUSS LANDING It's about time somebody designed something truly cutting-edge for little ones. In **Cat in the Hat: Ride Inside**, six-passenger couches will whirl through 18 amazing multidimensional adventures, with 130 effects including a wallpaper-peeling tunnel and multiple appearances by that silly goldfish who tries to keep things under control. Remember **One Fish, Two Fish, Red Fish, Blue Fish**? If you listen to the rhyme carefully, you may be able to steer your two-passenger fish 15 feet up and down through the air, and pass the 18-foot squirt posts well enough to stay dry. Don't plan on it, though. And don't forget the **Caro-Seuss-El.** Thanks to an effect known formally as Guest-Activated Interactive Animation, you will be able to control the action on this merry-go-round and clamber up on Seuss's most beloved characters: the cowfish from *McElligot's Pool*, the elephant birds from *Horton Hears a Who*, the aqua mop-tops and twin camels from *One Fish, Two Fish*, the dog-a-lopes and mulligatawnies from *If I Ran the Zoo*, and the birthday katroo from *Happy Birthday to You*. **Sylvester McMonkey McBean's Very Unusual Driving Machines** will have you traveling 15 feet above Seuss Landing through six different scenes from the story. You'll control your vehicle's speed and set off wacky sound and visual effects by bumping the car ahead. **If I Ran the Zoo,** similar to Fievel's Playland at Universal Studios Florida, will have lots of water effects and 19 different play stations.

chapter 4
SEA WORLD

Take I–4. Use Exit 27A, Sea World, eastbound; Exit 28, Route 528/the Beeline Expressway, westbound. The park can also be easily reached directly from the south end of International Drive and from the I-Drive exit on the westbound Beeline.

It's the best of its kind anywhere.

Sea World is a wonderful educational experience, and kids learn without being lectured. Knowledgeable staffers are on hand at every attraction to share their knowledge and answer questions. On our last visit a guide gave us a personal hour-long presentation on everything we'd ever wanted to know about polar bears. I am constantly amazed at the level of perception shown by even the smallest children here.

Moreover, attractions such as Sea World and Busch Gardens—both owned and operated by Anheuser-Busch—provide funding and expertise to protect many endangered animals. Every year Sea World staff respond to hundreds of calls for help, including many from state and federal authorities in need of an aquatic rescue.

WHAT'S NEW? My wife, Terrie, and I swam with the dolphins! Awesome! The **Dolphin Interactive Program** (DIP for short) is admittedly pricey, but it's a totally unique, once-in-a-lifetime experience you will never forget—well worth the money. **Journey to Atlantis,** a unique and breathtaking water coaster ride, features two giant drops.

TIMING Stay as long as you can—from opening to closing during the off season and around 12 hours when Sea World stays open late. (You *could* stay 15 hours, but that's too long for anyone to spend in a theme park, even Sea World.) Because of how shows are timed, it's nearly impossible to see them all. If you do, you'll have no time left for exhibits. So set your priorities based on what interests *you*—there are no bad shows at Sea World.

THE LAY OF THE LAND Sea World attractions, exhibits, and shows are arranged around a small lagoon.

THE FAST TRACK Except at the Wild Arctic, Sea World has few lines. Most people go to the right when they get here. My family goes the other direction, and I advise you to do the same. Here are some other tips:

- If you begin early, start in the back of the park and work forward. If you arrive late, start at the front. You'll get the best seats and views at shows.
- Near the entrance, pick up a computer printout with the day's shows; based on when you arrive, this recommends what to see. Plan your day around them.
- The bridge across the lake at Sea World's center is long and open. Because Florida lightning can be dangerous, people sometimes stampede when a storm threatens.

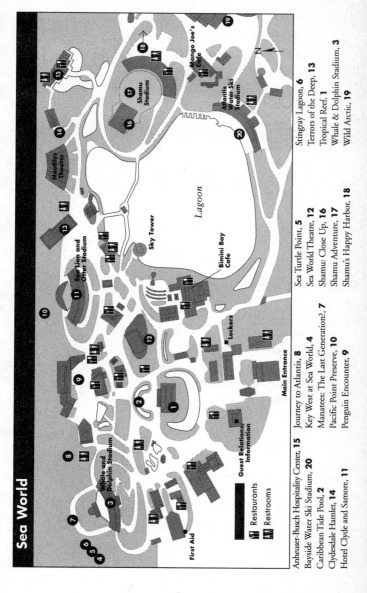

Watch out—and if it looks like rain, stay off the bridge.
- Consider a behind-the-scenes tour. The **Polar Expedition** takes you to meet polar bears, penguins, and beluga whales; the **Shark Tour** lets you feed and touch the ocean's most feared creatures; and the **Bird's Eye View** teaches you about the many species that live at Sea World and allows you to feed many of them. Cost is $5 per adult, $4 per child 3 and up. Reservations are neither required nor available, but it's best to sign up as early as you can; stop at the service desk, on your left immediately after you enter the park.

WHAT TO SEA

TROPICAL REEF A cool refuge on a hot day, this giant aquarium would be a stand-alone attraction anywhere but Orlando. Little signs identify thousands of species, most from the Caribbean.
Worth-It Rating ★★★

SEA WORLD THEATER "Pets on Stage" is a live action, performing animal show similar to Animal Actors at Universal.
Too new to rate.

DOLPHIN NURSERY Newborn baby Flippers and their moms splash around in this nursery. My kids love it.
Worth-It Rating ★★★★

CARIBBEAN TIDE POOL Grab a surface scope (like a dive mask that you hold against the surface of the water to look

through). You can see sea urchins, starfish, and anemones, and even handle them. A Sea World staffer hovers nearby and helps the kids ask the right questions. Cool pool!
Worth-It Rating ★★★★ Add 1 if you have kids.

WHALE AND DOLPHIN SHOW Trained humans run around the enormous Whale and Dolphin Stadium and fetch fish for the highly intelligent sea mammals performing the breathtaking leaps of a graceful, intricate water ballet. Hundreds of whale hours have gone into teaching these two-legged land mammals to perform their tricks.
The Fast Track: One lucky child is picked to be in the show. Get there extra early and beg, and it might be yours.
Worth-It Rating ★★★★★

DOLPHIN INTERACTIVE PROGRAM For this two-hour education-and-participation program, you actually get into the water with the trainer and the dolphins, and get to pet, feed, and hug your very own dolphin pal. Easily worth the extra cost ($148 for participants 13 and up, $53 for observers), it's available at 7 and 10:30 daily.
The Fast Track: In peak season, this books up months in advance. If you want to DIP, find out what's available and schedule your vacation around it.
Worth-It Rating ★★★★★ +

MANATEES, THE LAST GENERATION? Thanks to legislation championed by the folks here and by Florida's own Jimmy Buffett, these gentle sea cows are making a comeback. In this nifty environment, you can view them above the water and beneath it, peacefully coexisting with some jumbo gators.
Worth-It Rating ★★★★★

WHAT TO SEA

KEY WEST AT SEA WORLD In this charming re-creation of Ernest Hemingway's Key West, you can have stingrays eating right out of your hand; learn the differences between porpoises and our home-grown Atlantic bottle-nosed dolphins; and, at designated times, buy smelts and toss them into the pool—smelly but fun.
Worth-It Rating ★★★★★

HOTEL CLYDE AND SEAMORE This show in the Sea Lion and Otter Stadium stars the Laurel and Hardy of the water, Clyde Otter and Seamore Sea Lion.
The Fast Track: There are lots of obstructions. You'll miss some of the best gags if you're too close to the stage or too far to either side. Go for the middle, halfway back.
Worth-It Rating ★★★★★

PACIFIC POINT PRESERVE This man-made tidal pool is complete with the rocky Pacific coast and rolling waves. Here, you'll learn the differences between sea lions and seals, and get the chance to throw 'em a fish! (The fish is on you.)
Worth-It Rating ★★★★ Add 1 if the cost of fish is not a factor.

PENGUIN ENCOUNTER Pop quiz! How do you tell a penguin from a puffin? Hint: There are no penguins at the North Pole. Both are here, in icy splendor. They're fast, they're funny, and they're all dressed up in black tie and tails.
Worth-It Rating ★★★★★

JOURNEY TO ATLANTIS This is the first of a new generation of rides called water coasters. Not flumes, these are more like a giant roller coaster except that you get wet. This one has two 60-foot drops. Special effects en route tell the tale of your mission: to warn the inhabitants of Atlantis about a terrible storm that threatens to submerge the entire continent. *Too new to rate.*

TERRORS OF THE DEEP Don't miss this one! Live sharks circle right in front of you in an enormous tank. But wait, there's more! Step onto a moving sidewalk and you are slowly propelled through an enormous Plexiglas tube right through the middle of the shark tank!
Worth-It Rating ★★★★★

CLYDESDALE HAMLET Home of the world-famous Budweiser Clydesdales, the pride of Anheuser-Busch.
Worth-It Rating ★★★

SHAMU ADVENTURE If you guessed that the Shamu Stadium is home of Shamu, you're right. Themes change, so the show may well be called something else by the time you visit, but so what? You see the big guy on a big screen and in person with baby Shamu, too! Shamu is huge, jumps a lot, and lands with a thud (just like a few professional basketball players who get paid $20 million a year). At night, the show is "Shamu's Night Magic." Personally, I like Shamu best under the lights.
Worth-It Rating ★★★★★

SHAMU CLOSE-UP Here's your chance to see Shamu's family up close and personal in the world's largest fish bowl (okay, mammal bowl).
Worth-It Rating ★★★★★

SHAMU'S HAPPY HARBOR Imagine one of those McDonald's play places that's five stories high! This awesome playground is complete with giant pirate ship and water cannons.

WHAT TO SEA

Grown-ups can go, too—when accompanied by a child. And there's no waiting. Get wet, cool off—we do!
Worth-It Rating ★★★★★

WILD ARCTIC First, you take a simulator trip through the Arctic. Then you go through the world's largest walk-in freezer to view polar bears and other Arctic animals. The finale? A high-tech educational area to answer all your questions.
Worth-It Rating ★★★★★

BAYSIDE WATER SKI STADIUM The current show is "Baywatch at Sea World Water Adventure." Ricky, my son, calls it "Babe Watch"! It's a wild and funny stunt exhibition with lots of buffed bodies in spandex. After dark? There must be a law that says that every theme park must have a fireworks show. "Red, White, and Blue Fireworks Spectacular," in the water-ski stadium after dark, is currently the town's biggest.
Worth-It Rating ★★★★★

ANHEUSER-BUSCH HOSPITALITY CENTER Free beer! (Or you could stop here for sandwiches and snacks.) Check out the flamingos out front.
Worth-It Rating ★★★★★

EATERTAINMENT

The big deal is the **Luau**, a Polynesian dinner show (*see* Chapter 12). At the **Spinnaker Sidewalk Cafe,** we get clam chowder in a bread bowl, a family favorite. At the **Polar Parlor,** also near the entrance, the specialty is the giant waffle cone. The **Cypress Bakery**, near the front gate, serves up fresh-baked goodies—arrive early and do breakfast. **Bimini Bay Cafe,** next to the Luau, serves mostly sandwiches and burgers but also has a good island-style chowder. **Buccaneer Smokehouse,** in front of the Sea World Theater, and **Dockside Smokehouse,** next to Terrors of the Deep, are barbecue specialists. **Mama Stella's Italian Kitchen,** across from Penguin Encounter, serves pizza and pasta. At **Chicken 'n' Biscuit,** between the Sea World Theater and the Sea Lion and Otter Stadium, I love the double-chocolate cherry cake. Sandwiches are the fare at **Waterfront Sandwich Grill,** next to the Sea Lion and Otter Stadium, and the **Deli,** in the Anheuser-Busch Hospitality Center. At **Mango Joe's Cafe,** the sizzling fajitas are a great deal, and the seafood salad is wonderful.

SHOPPERTOONITIES

For aquatic mementos, Sea World is the place. **Shamu's Emporium, Shamu Souvenirs, Crosswalk, Outrigger, Sand Castle Toys 'n' Treats, Coconut Bay Trader,** and **Stadium Gifts** all stock a bit of everything, many items bearing pictures of Shamu. Check **Discovery Cove** for educational toys; **Ocean Treasures, Pearl Factory,** and **Wild Arctic** for sea stuff. At **Cruz Kay Harbor,** you'll find that Hawaiian print whatever you've been wanting (not necessarily needing). **Flamingo Point** has hats and T-shirts. Bunches of people buy Anheuser-Busch logo souvenirs at the **Label Stable, Gulf Breeze Trader,** and **Gangway Gift Shop.** We love the frogs. Personalized souvenirs? **Kaman's Photo, Key Hole Photo,** and **Amazing Pictures** do novelty photos. You can have your face sketched at **Kaman's Artist** or painted at **Enjoy Your Face. The Ringcutter, Pearl Factory, Your Name in Gold,** and **Brewster Glassmith** make jewelry.

chapter 5
BUSCH GARDENS

Take I–4 west to Tampa, then I–75 north to Busch Boulevard or follow the signs. The park is about an hour and a half from Orlando.

Add 1 if you love animals or roller coasters.

*It's a great park and a great deal,
especially if you use the Orlando FlexTicket.
One of my family's favorite parks.*

In this 335-acre park from the brewers of the King of Beers, the theme is a trip across Africa, and each area is based on a different country; the park's ubiquitous German motifs are reminders of the Germans' colonization of the continent (and the German heritage of Busch beer). The roller coaster and thrill ride selection is second to none—Busch Gardens is known for its world-ranked, hang-you-upside-down roller coasters. They're the modern kind, with tubular steel tracks, different from the sometimes larger rides with tracks built on wooden scaffolding; the thrills come not from climbs and falls but from speeding through tight turns and hanging upside down.

But the rides are only part of the show. Surrounding the part of the park devoted to rides, shows, and exhibits is a huge botanical garden and zoological park, one of the world's first to abandon cages in favor of habitats. We've brought both Tiffany and Ricky frequently since infancy, and I believe this park has sparked an intense interest in animals that will remain with them for the rest of their lives. So take your time and be aware of your surroundings as you move from place to place.

WHICH ANIMAL KINGDOM? Even with the similar but bigger and newer Disney's Animal Kingdom in the attractions lineup, the original of the genre may still be your choice. Due to the distance from Orlando, Busch Gardens will probably be a lot less crowded. And, because it can be so difficult to slog through Walt Disney World traffic, the difference in drive time may be a toss-up.

WHAT'S NEW? Edge of Africa, an exhibit of African animals, includes lions and several varieties of primates, displayed behind glass windows in the style that worked so well in the Myombe Reserve Gorilla Exhibit. People are protected from the animals but close enough to get a good look at them; just as importantly, the animals are protected from people.

EATERTAINMENT The food here is among the best at any theme park, prices are reasonable, and the beer, which is stored, served, and chilled as only a master brewer can, is as good as it gets. In some cases, it's also free!

SHOPPERTOONITIES Some of the park's best values are in the leather and brass shops of the Moroccan Bazaar. Busch Gardens is also a great place to get safari- and tropical-style clothing as well as Anheuser-Busch logo gear.

THE LAY OF THE LAND Basically, the rides and attractions are in the center and the animal areas are around the perimeter. Moving clockwise from the main entrance at Morocco, areas

Akbar's Adventure Tours, **21**

Anheuser-Busch Hospitality Center, **4**

Animal Nursery Tour, **15**

Bird Show Theater, **3**

Clydesdale Hamlet, **20**

Congo River Rapids, **9**

Curiosity Caverns, **16**

Dolphin Theater, **12**

King Tut's Tomb, **23**

Kumba, **11**

Land of the Dragons, **5**

Midway and Arcade, **13**

Monorail, **18**

Montu, **24**

Moroccan Palace Theater, **2**

Myombe Reserve, **17**

Python, **8**

Sand Dig, **22**

Scorpion, **14**

Skyrider, **19**

Stanley Falls Log Flume Ride, **7**

Sultan's Tent, **1**

Tanganyika Tidal Wave, **6**

Ubanga-Banga, **10**

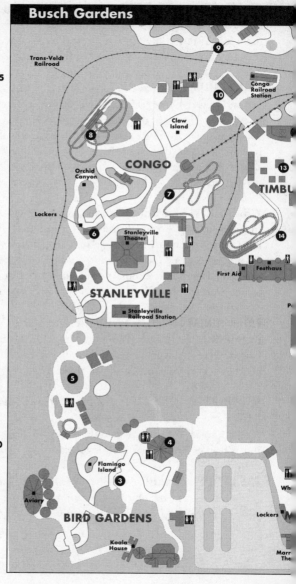

70

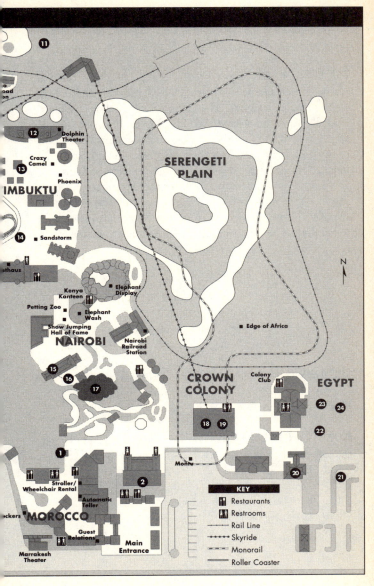

include Bird Gardens, Stanleyville, Congo, Timbuktu, Nairobi, and the Crown Colony. I discuss my favorite attractions below; check the map for other fun stops.

THE FAST TRACK Be prepared to walk a lot. Like the real Africa, Busch Gardens is vast. Dress lightly in clothes you won't mind getting wet. The Congo River Rapids and Stanley Falls leave you soaked; put valuables in resealable plastic bags. More than any other park, Busch Gardens lends itself to my go-left strategy. You enter through Morocco and flow naturally to the right. But if you bear hard left into Morocco, you'll find a small walkway past the Hospitality House through the Bird Gardens. If you enter this way—the way that most people leave—you'll meet minimal crowds early in the day. You'll wind up in Egypt, where crowds will be much sparser than they would have been earlier.

MOROCCO

Don't miss the alligators, the musical performances, and the close-order drills by the Mystic Sheiks Marching Band.

SULTAN'S TENT You'll know you've arrived when you see the scantily clad belly and snake dancers.
Worth-It Rating ★★★★★

MOROCCAN PALACE THEATER Back home, you could pay the full-ticket price to see a world-class ice show like "Hollywood on Ice," presented here. It's a spectacularly costumed and choreographed tribute to the movies—climaxed, of course, by a Busby Berkeley number.
Worth-It Rating ★★★★

BITES The **Zagora Café** and the adjacent **Boujad Bakery** serve huge pastries and wonderful coffees. Next door, an ice-cream shop dishes up giant waffle cones.

BUYS In the **Moroccan Bazaar,** leather and brass is hand-crafted before your eyes (and customized, if you like). Prices are great, especially on leather. On more than one occasion, I have traveled to Busch Gardens just to shop for it.

THE BIRD GARDENS

In the mid-60s, when I first started coming here, these beautifully landscaped gardens were the main attraction, along with the brewery tour, which is now just a memory, and the bird show.

BIRD SHOW THEATER After all these years, the hourly exotic bird show has changed little. Trainers interact with several species of parrots and other tropical birds and explain where each bird comes from and its markings, characteristics, and habits. The birds do a number of charming fetch-its.
Worth-It Rating ★★★★

ANHEUSER-BUSCH HOSPITALITY CENTER Free beer here! Plus pizza, sandwiches, snacks, live entertainment, and an excellent view of the park.

LAND OF THE DRAGONS

One of the best children's play areas anywhere, this land is a world of giant children's tree houses, where kids can climb, explore, and slide.

DRAGON FLUME RIDE A delightful, kid-sized version of the park's trademark flume rides. Small children who are old enough to walk but still under 56 inches can ride a dragon upstream and over the falls.
Worth-It Rating ★★★★★

STANLEYVILLE

Don't miss the beautiful gardens of the Orchid Canyon; there's a spectacular view from the Tanganyika Tidal Wave.

TRANS-VELDT RAILROAD On the narrow-gauge choo-choo that chugs its way around the park, you get the most extensive view of the African Veldt, if not necessarily the best. The train also gets you around the park.
Worth-It Rating ★★★★★

TANGANYIKA TIDAL WAVE The truth is that I liked Stanley Falls fine until I tried this bigger, better variation. The much larger ride vehicle at this splash-a-rama holds 24 (or more, with small children). Don't be fooled by the long, leisurely cruise—it ends with a 55-foot plunge, the equivalent of a fall from a six-story building. You WILL get soaked.
Worth-It Rating ★★★★★

STANLEY FALLS For many years this was the definitive flume ride, with two to four passengers shooting the falls together in a floating log. Okay, it creaks a little, it's kind of slow, and the big drop is not as thrilling as the one on its newer cousin next door. But it does have character.
Worth-It Rating ★★★★

BITES Some of the park's best food is here. At the **Smokehouse** you'll find barbecued chicken and ribs. At the **Bazaar Café** the specialty is a generous barbecue sandwich.

CONGO

When you travel deep into the Congo, don't miss the view of Claw Island, home of Busch Gardens' majestic white tigers. There's also a Trans-Veldt Railroad station here.

PYTHON Busch Gardens' original steel coaster loops you over twice, but it ends so quickly!
Worth-It Rating ★★★★

UBANGA-BANGA Regular amusement-park bumper cars, plain and simple.
Worth-It Rating ★★★

CONGO RIVER RAPIDS Accompanied by music that takes you straight to the world of Indiana Jones, Florida's best

water ride has you floating down white-water rapids in a 10-passenger raft made from a monster truck tire. You may recall the Greek myth of Tantalus, whose punishment was to spend eternity with an unquenchable thirst, inches from water he could never reach. That's how you'll feel in the interminable line to ride. To keep cool, I soak my T-shirt. I know I'll be soaked when I get off, anyway.
Worth-It Rating ★★★★★

KUMBA Two double-upside-down loops and 13 upside-down turnovers make this coaster truly impressive. It's also one of the longest and most exciting rides in the country.
Worth-It Rating ★★★★★

BITES The **Vivi Storehouse Restaurant**, between the Monstrous Mamba and Ubanga-Banga, sells fast food. An ice-cream stand at the base of the Python serves cold treats.

TIMBUKTU

We call it Timbuk-3 (as in, a little farther than Timbuk-2), because by the time we get this far, we're ready for the park's best eatertainment stop. In addition to the amusements below, there are some good toddler rides.

DOLPHIN THEATER Anheuser-Busch also owns Sea World, so they put on a good dolphin show here. It's amazing how they train these mammals to swim! They also jump, fetch, sing, dance, kiss the trainer, and eat a lot of raw fish.
Worth-It Rating ★★★★

MIDWAY AND ARCADE This may be the only midway you'll ever visit where you feel that someone actually wants you to win something. You pay extra, but you win: We've won at least half a dozen life-size stuffed animals here.
Worth-It Rating ★★★★★

SCORPION If roller coasters are your thing, this single-loop thing is your coaster. You zip through all 360 degrees of the loop, hanging 100% upside down all the way.
Worth-It Rating ★★★★★

BITES In **The Festhaus**, a replica of a German beer hall the size of an aircraft hangar, you lunch next to total strangers at long wooden tables. German dancers, singers, and oompah bands entertain. Portions are generous, prices are reasonable, and the beer is the best.

NAIROBI

On a hot day, you'll envy the Asian elephants as they bathe in Nairobi's cool waterfall. A petting zoo allows kids of the human kind to meet the animals they're named for—friendly, playful young goats—along with other gentle farm animals. There's another Trans-Veldt Railroad station, too.

ANIMAL NURSERY TOUR There's always a new population of adorable babies here. We have seen eagles and other rare birds, some of the park's endangered wild and African deer, and plain old baby critters just opening their eyes.
Worth-It Rating ★★★★★

CURIOSITY CAVERNS Busch Gardens has turned the clock upside down in this habitat for nocturnal creatures. By leaving the lights on at night, they are able to allow visitors a rare glimpse into the habits of several species of bats and nocturnal reptiles. Dad can play Batman, and you'll learn why bats may be the environmental answer to mosquito control.
Worth-It Rating ★★★★ Add 1 if bats don't give you the creeps.

MYOMBE RESERVE Just call this "Gorillas in Our Midst," although the mist is here, too—a cool fog covers the place. At this one-of-a-kind colony of African gorillas, glass walls offer the kind of views of these animals previously available only to Jane Goodall. With its educational audio-video narrative, this is definitely worth a visit.
Worth-It Rating ★★★★★

BITES The **Kenya Kanteen** is the area's fast-food stop, right next to the elephants and the petting zoo.

THE AFRICAN VELDT AND THE SERENGETI PLAIN

Busch Gardens' zoological park features literally thousands of species with over 40 on the National Wildlife Federation's endangered list. Lions and tigers and bears, oh my! You'll find camels, giraffes, water buffalo, elephants, antelope, and much more—it's a jungle out there! Three rides offer different views of this magnificent attraction.

MONORAIL By far the best way to see the animals is on this aerial adventure. The narration gives you details about the habitats and habits of every species along with occasional anecdotes about landmark births in captivity. Unlike the other rides that traverse the park, the monorail lets you off right back where you started.
Worth-It Rating ★★★★★

SKYRIDE This cable car ride takes you over the Serengeti to Stanleyville, the park's thrill center. It also offers an aerial view of the whole layout and makes for spectacular videos.
Worth-It Rating ★★★★ Subtract 1 if the line is too long, as it often is.

CROWN COLONY

We've already covered the monorail and skyride, each of which you can access here. But there's more.

CLYDESDALE HAMLET Anheuser-Busch's Clydesdales are stabled here. Trainers are on hand to tell you about them.
Worth-It Rating ★★★★ Add 2 if you have a horse lover like our Tiffany in tow.

BITES The second-story **Crown Colony House**, with its great picture windows, gives you an excellent view of the Veldt; it's the park's fancy restaurant and has a wine list that's impressive for a theme park. The best deal we've found is on the excellent fried chicken. Seating is first come, first served.

EGYPT

AKBAR'S ADVENTURE TOURS Simulator rides are obligatory at theme parks. This newcomer, a tour of Egypt starring actor/comedian Martin Short, is supposed to be not only exciting, with the usual quota of bumps and crashes, but also funny. But Akbar's is just opening as this book is going to press, so I can't give you a firsthand report in this edition. Stay tuned.
Too new to rate.

SAND DIG Proving Busch Gardens as among the most kid-friendly of theme parks, this simulated excavation—a sandbox with an ancient theme—lets tykes dig, and dig, and dig.
Worth-It Rating ★★★

KING TUT'S TOMB There's no curse on this reproduction of Tut's three-room tomb, spectacularly detailed, right down to the burial chamber containing Tut's sarcophagus, as it looked to Professor Carter's ill-fated expedition in 1923. It's a must-see, if only because everyone should visit their mummy.
Worth-It Rating ★★★★★

MONTU You start with your legs dangling over a pit of live crocodiles! If that's not enough, cars on this inverted coaster hang from the track rather than sit on top of it, and reach speeds over 60 mph with a G-force of 3.85, as it flips you topsy-turvy. It's the world's largest coaster of its kind.
Worth-It Rating ★★★★★

chapter 6
THE MAGIC KINGDOM
Walt Disney World

Take I–4 to Exit 25B, labeled for the Magic Kingdom/U.S. 192.

Add 1 if you have children under 10. Subtract 1 if you've been there before and a return makes you skip another park you've never seen.

When they think of Central Florida theme parks, most people think first of the Magic Kingdom. It was the first of the Florida Disney parks and is still loved by millions. Opened in 1971, nearly five years after the death of Walt Disney—whose dream it was and who acquired all the land—it has changed little in its more than a quarter of a century. It was patterned after California's Disneyland, the first true American theme park. But although the Magic Kingdom is similar to Disneyland, there are many differences. Disneyland occupies 80 acres, the Magic Kingdom over 100. Disneyland is surrounded by businesses owned by others; of the 45 square miles that surround the Magic Kingdom, much is wilderness and all is owned by the Disney company.

While most of Disneyland's rides and attractions are also at WDW, they are not all in the Magic Kingdom. Star Tours,

AstroOrbiter, **6**
Barnstormer at Goofy's Wiseacres Farm, **13**
Big Thunder Mt Railroad, **31**
Carousel of Progress, **8**
Cinderella's Golden Carrousel, **17**
Country Bear Jamboree, **29**
Diamond Horseshoe Revue, **27**
Dumbo The Flying Elephant, **18**
Extraterrorestrial Alien Encounter, **4**
Frontierland Shootin' Arcade, **28**
Frontierland Stunt Show, **32**
Grand Prix Raceway, **11**
Hall of Presidents, **26**
Haunted Mansion, **23**
It's A Small World, **21**
Jungle Cruise, **36**
Legend of the Lion King, **19**
Liberty Square Riverboat, **25**
Mad Tea Party, **14**
Main Street Cinema, **2**
Mike Fink Keel Boats, **24**
Mr. Toad's Wild Ride, **15**
Peter Pan's Flight, **20**
Pirates of the Caribbean, **35**
Skyway to Fantasyland, **9**
Skyway to Tomorrowland, **22**
Snow White's Adventures, **16**

82

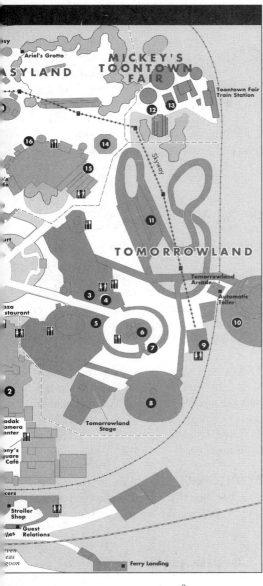

Space Mountain, **10**
Splash Mountain, **32**
Swiss Family Treehouse, **37**
Take Flight, **5**
Timekeeper, **3**
Tom Sawyer Island, **30**
Tomorrowland Transit Authority, **7**
Toon Park, **12**
Tropical Serenade, **34**
WDW Railroad, **1**

first built at Disneyland, is in Disney–MGM Studios theme park at Walt Disney World.

The Magic Kingdom's biggest drawback is its age. The concepts for many of its attractions were originally devised by Walt Disney over 50 years ago. Audio-Animatronics, the computer-controlled system of hydraulics responsible for animating many of the robots you see in WDW, were dazzling in the mid-1950s, when they debuted. But they're almost nostalgia pieces now. For little kids, the Magic Kingdom is still the number one WOW! inspiring place on this earth. For those of us with a little more life experience, it may seem dated.

TIMING I usually average an attraction every 45 minutes. But even if you hit two adventures an hour, it takes more than two days to see this park—when it's open extended hours.

EATERTAINMENT Our family tries to eat outside the gates, where meals cost half as much. But sometimes we have to eat in the park. A couple of restaurants in the Magic Kingdom require reservations, including a character meal in Cinderella Castle; to book, call 407/WDW–DINE.

SHOPPERTOONITIES If your schedule is really jam-packed, you may not have time to shop elsewhere. And some things are simply not available outside the gates. The highlight of many vacations is the photo of the family (in mouse ears) in front of Cinderella Castle. Don't blow the whole effect just to save the $5 a head on these hats.

PARADES AND PYROTECHNICS In addition to attractions, the Magic Kingdom has lots of street entertainment and a few sit-down shows. There are also several parades, which start in Town Square, head down Main Street, then meander through Frontierland; our favorite viewing spot is from the Mile Long Bar in Frontierland—you're right next to the parade route and you can sit, munch, and sip and still see it all. When buying your ticket, you get a list of parade and show times. Or you can pick one up at City Hall or call 407/ 824–4321 in advance.

The Daily Parade: Even the least of these is as exciting as any parade anywhere. The floats are dazzling, the characters are the ones you know and love, and the music jams. Whatever the theme, start time is 3 PM, weather permitting. Between Thanksgiving and New Year's, you'll see Mickey as Santa instead of the daily parade.★★★★★

SpectroMagic: In this fabulous nighttime light parade, millions of lights adorn dozens of Disney characters and floats as they parade down Main Street. Outside peak seasons, you can see it as early as 6:15; in peak seasons, it runs at 8 and 10 or 9 and 11.★★★★★

Fantasy in the Sky Fireworks: A rousing soundtrack accompanies fireworks above Cinderella Castle—one of the world's largest and most dazzling displays. In the early days, it was an occasional thing. I remember seeing local news coverage and going out to the park just for the fireworks. Over the years, the show has become increasingly important to the daily schedule. You can see it from virtually anywhere in the park. My most memorable viewpoints are all up high: the top of the AstroOrbiter, the Monorail, and the Skyway. Whether or not you are in the right place at just the right time is purely a matter of luck. Start time is as early as 7 (later during busy periods).★★★★

THE LAY OF THE LAND In the Magic Kingdom, there are seven lands with more than 50 attractions. Main Street USA leads from the entrance turnstiles and an area known as Town

Square to the so-called Hub, in the shadow of Cinderella Castle. Ranged around the Hub are Adventureland, Frontierland, Fantasyland, Mickey's Toontown Fair, Tomorrowland, and Liberty Square. Each has theme attractions, shows, eateries, and shops.

THE FAST TRACK In other parks, I advise you to travel clockwise. This is for the simple reason that most people are right-handed and bear right wherever they go. My theory is to go the way other people don't. Because of the design of the Magic Kingdom, with Cinderella Castle in the middle, many people head straight into Fantasyland. Others head left into Adventureland. The least conspicuous route is the walkway into Tomorrowland, and this is where I suggest you begin. Since you always want to start with a busy ride so that you miss the longest lines, head first for Space Mountain or Alien Encounter. Then tour counterclockwise, ending in Adventureland, seeing attractions in the order below.

Another strategy of ours is to take the Walt Disney World Railroad straight to Mickey's Toontown Fair. Then we head into Fantasyland, followed by Liberty Square, Frontierland, Adventureland, and, finally, Tomorrowland.

Choose what you want to see carefully. Wait times are posted near attractions' queue areas, and message boards parkwide list entertainment and character appearance times.

MAIN STREET USA

This old-fashioned street full of shops is busiest right before and after parades and at the end of the day.

WALT DISNEY WORLD RAILROAD Real antiques dating from the turn of the century, these little engines pull you around the perimeter of the Kingdom, with stops at Main Street, Frontierland, and Mickey's Toontown Fair. In a way, this train planted the seed that started the whole theme-park concept: It was Walt's desire to expand the ride-on scale-model train he had built at home for himself and his daughters that inspired him to create Disneyland. Here, when there's not much of a line, the train is a quick way into the heart of the Magic Kingdom. It is also a great place to videotape most of the park in one easy step. You can shoot a quick flick, stop at Mickey's Toontown Fair (the only place where you're guaranteed a photo op with the reigning rodent), shoot the kids with Mickey, then come back to the station and drop your camera in a locker.
Worth-It Rating ★★★★

MAIN STREET CINEMA *Steamboat Willie,* the first Mickey Mouse cartoon and Disney's first talkie, is featured here in an old-time movie theater. Dom Deluise leads a star-studded cast in *Mickey's Big Break,* a film about how Mickey got the part. There's no waiting and it's cool on a hot day.
Worth-It Rating ★★★ Add 1 if you're a nostalgia buff.

MAIN STREET VEHICLES Several old-time vehicles, including a vintage fire engine and trolleys pulled by gigantic horses, take you one-way down Main Street.
Worth-It Rating ★★★ Add 2 if there's no wait.

BITES **Tony's Town Square Restaurant** recreates the site of one of the most romantic moments in motion picture history, the passionate spaghetti kiss in *Lady and the Tramp.* Naturally, the cuisine is Italian. The decor is Italian-caricature, all stained glass and ceiling fans. Reservations are essential. At snack time, hit the **Main Street Bake Shop,** for Toll House cookies, or the **Plaza Ice Cream Parlor** for two scoops. I wish I could count the times I've stopped at **Casey's Corner** for a hot dog and Casey at the keyboard. It's right on the corner as you turn off Main Street toward Adventureland. At the **Plaza Restaurant,** at the Hub end of Main Street, the theme is turn-of-the-century and the food is deli-style. Reservations are recommended. The **Crystal Palace,** probably the best dining deal in the park, serves an all-you-can-eat lunch and dinner buffet with carved meats, hot vegetables, and a salad bar; characters are on hand then and at breakfast. Over the years one of the most common questions I've been asked about the Magic Kingdom is "What's in Cinderella Castle?" The answer is **Cinderella's Royal Table.** You'll find steak and seafood at lunch and dinner and Disney characters (plus early admission to the park) for breakfast. Reserve ahead (tel. 407/WDW–DINE).

ENTERTAINMENT The **Dapper Dans,** Main Street's rib-tickling barbershop quartet—complete with straw hats—sing your favorites in tight harmonies. The brass-and-drum **Walt Disney World Marching Band** plays old-time and contemporary music. The **Rhythm Rascals** (come on and hear, come on and hear) are an old-fashioned ragtime band. Finally, on the Magic Kingdom's main stage, below Cinderella Castle, you'll often find the **Kids of the Kingdom** singing and dancing up a storm.

BUYS Shopping is really the biggest attraction on Main Street. Little stores line both sides of the road. One thing many people don't realize is that though they all look like individual storefronts on the outside (and inside all look pretty different), they're actually open to one another inside. So on hot days, you can walk almost from one end of the street to the other in air-conditioned comfort by cutting through the stores.

The **Firehouse Gift Station** sells character toys and clothing with a firehouse theme. **Disneyana Collectibles** is where you can sign your name in the Magic Kingdom guest book. If you see the name "Michael Eisner" on the page, that's probably me. The shop features real and reproduced animation cells, figurines, and other Disney art and collectibles. The **Emporium** is the largest and most complete of the stores in the Magic Kingdom. Dominating Main Street at the Town Square end, it sells just about everything Disney. Where can you get your own monogrammed set of Mickey Mouse ears? The **Chapeau** is it! Only $5 plus tax, the hats used to be available only in basic black. Now, they come in a variety of colors and styles. Mine says "Annette" (really!). The **Main Street Camera Center,** the park's central camera store, stocks film, tapes, and accessories. They also sell and rent cameras, including video cams. You'll be surprised how much you can spend in **Disney Clothiers**—or maybe not. The **Main Street Confectionery** and **Market House** sell lots of sweets. **Uptown Jewelers,** the Tiffany & Company of the theme park, stocks Disney jewelry. How about a gold Mickey Mouse watch? I actually own one. You could easily blow the kids' college money on jewel-encrusted characters and other goodies. The **Main Street Athletic Shop** will sell you that Minnie Mouse workout suit you've been wanting. **Disney & Company** is a children's clothing and toy store. In the **Shadow Box,** silhouette artists snip portraits of your loved ones. You can watch glassblowers at work in **Crystal Arts.** Just keep a close rein on your littl'uns.

MAIN STREET USA

One of the bonuses of coming to WDW over Christmas is on Main Street, where every year shop windows display spectacularly animated tableaux depicting Disney features. It takes me back to when I was a little kid and one of the highlights of the season was a visit to the wonderful animated windows at Macy's in New York. I bring my kids here every year to re-create that experience for them.

TOMORROWLAND

For the last few years I have felt that Tomorrowland was what we used to think the 1990s would be like back in the 1950s. Now, the redesigned Tomorrowland is the freshest and brightest spot in the Kingdom—and a great place to start.

THE TIMEKEEPER Robin Williams plays the robot emcee of this time-travel experience, which combines Disney's CircleVision 360 filming technique with Audio-Animatronics technology to create an adventure in which a typical family interacts with legendary sci-fi writers and time-travel experts Jules Verne and H. G. Wells. Well done! The special effects are brilliant!
Worth-It Rating ★★★★★

EXTRATERRORESTRIAL ALIEN ENCOUNTER The story is that an interplanetary spacecraft is foolishly transporting some dangerous alien life forms. Guess what? They get loose and slime you! Universal's Terminator 2: 3D is a better execution of a similar concept. Still, this update of the hopelessly dated Mission to Mars attraction is a real romp!

The Fast Track: Try to hit this attraction when the waiting room is about half full. All seats are good. Timid children *will* be frightened—but mine love it.
Worth-It Rating ★★★★★

TAKE FLIGHT This one is not too high-tech but has nice visuals and a great soundtrack. Proving that every ride has its fans, this fairly simple little attraction is my wife Terrie's top Tomorrowland stop. You board a moving car that takes you through the history of commercial flight from barnstormers to jets. Big screens, wind machines, and tilting tracks create the feeling of flight. There's almost never a line and you can do the whole thing in a few minutes.
Worth-It Rating ★★★★

ASTRO ORBITER This is the old Star Jets, like Dumbo without the ears except here, you're extra high because the boarding area is one flight up, accessible via elevator. The high point is that it's a WDW high point—with a great view!
Worth-It Rating ★★ Add 1 if the lines are short. Add 3 if you can time your ride to catch the fireworks.

TOMORROWLAND TRANSIT AUTHORITY Once known as the PeopleMover, this little train takes you on an electromagnetic track around Tomorrowland and through Space Mountain. Very relaxing.
Worth-It Rating ★★ Add 1 if you're tired.

CAROUSEL OF PROGRESS This was originally at the 1964 New York World's Fair and has been in continuous operation since then. More people have been on it than any other ride or show anywhere, ever. The technology and concept are a little dated, but the show still holds up. You board a moving

theater in the round. As the seats move past each scene, you measure the scientific progress of humanity in this century by the changes in household appliances.
Worth-It Rating ★★★

SKYWAY TO FANTASYLAND I never could figure out why this ride was designed to take such a long route to go a short distance. Still, it's your best chance to get aerial video or still photos of the parks.
The Fast Track: The line is usually shorter in Tomorrowland.
Worth-It Rating ★★★ Add 1 if the line is short.

SPACE MOUNTAIN The world's premier roller coaster is entirely in the dark, with shooting stars overhead. It's also one of the best and most enduringly popular rides at WDW.
The Fast Track: The lines are long. Check the line to the left; sometimes it's shorter. Kids must be 44 inches tall to ride. Don't bother if you get sick easily, are pregnant, or have a weak heart or bad back.
Worth-It Rating ★★★★★

GRAND PRIX RACEWAY Cars on tracks, no race, no passing, no point. The lines are long, and it's all hot and smelly—I always say that the EPA should close it down because of the air quality. Besides, it's really dated. Go only if the kids won't let you get away. A better bet with the same idea is the Sega race course at Epcot's Innoventions. The simulators there *feel* real, and the race *is* real.
The Fast Track: Kids must be at least 44 inches tall to drive.
Worth-It Rating ★★

BITES On the days that we arrive in the Magic Kingdom hungry, the place that usually stops us is the **Plaza Pavilion**, a fast

THE MAGIC KINGDOM

foodery that serves pizza and chicken strips. The big windows offer an excellent view of Tomorrowland. Live shows at nearby Rocket-Tower Plaza make it even more enjoyable. **Auntie Gravity's Galactic Goodies,** near the Grand Prix Raceway, is a pit stop for frozen yogurt and fruit juices. At **Cosmic Ray's Starlight Cafe,** burgers and chicken headline one of the best fast-food menus in the Kingdom. The **Lunching Pad** at Rocket-Tower Plaza, a little hot-dog stand, is at the base of the AstroOrbiter, right across from Space Mountain.

BUYS **Merchant of Venus** wins my award for the most creatively named store in the park. Just outside Alien Encounter, it specializes in extraterrestrial souvenirs—trinkets with holograms, toy rockets, and other space thingies. **Geiger's Counter,** which has another one of those great names, is one of a couple of places in the Kingdom where you can get your monogrammed mouse-ears hat.

MICKEY'S TOONTOWN FAIR

This is the only place in the park where you can count on meeting up with the world's most famous Mouse. Bring your camera and your autograph book and stand in line for a minute with the Mickster. Be ready—cast members try to keep the line moving—and don't ask any tough questions. Mickey, like all Disney characters, is mute. He's allowed to nod (to say yes), shake his head (to say no), and shrug his shoulders ("huh?").

Replacing Mickey's Starland, which opened as Mickey's Birthdayland for Mickey's 60th birthday in 1988, Toontown was revamped in 1996, and, as a result, reflects Disney Imagineers' four decades of experience in creating theme-park fun. Toontown is easy to get around in and gives you a lot to do with minimum waiting.

Worth-It Rating ★★★ Add 2 if you're traveling with children under 10.

MICKEY'S COUNTRY HOUSE Mickey's cartoon world comes alive here. The furniture and Mickey's personal effects are all larger than life. You'll see the Great One's bedroom, his sports equipment, his photos, and his Goofy-remodeled kitchen. When you leave, you're headed straight for the Toontown County Fair, where you have an appointment with the Toontown Fair's chief magistrate, Judge Mickey!

MINNIE'S COUNTRY HOUSE The collection of arts and crafts, the charmingly rustic interior, and the manicured garden portray Minnie as Martha Stewart with big ears. Out back, she greets visitors in her garden gazebo.

DONALD'S BOAT In this wet little playground in the middle of the attractions area, kids can climb and slide on Donald's leaky boat. Little jets of water squirt everywhere, giving kids a chance to cool off on hot days. Personally, I'm neither too old nor too stuffy to stand in the jets myself on a hot day and soak myself well enough to stay cool for several hours. You're at Disney World—be a kid!

TOON PARK Foam animals and a padded floor are undoubtedly lower maintenance than the live animals of the petting zoo that used to be in this area (though I miss Minnie Moo, the cow with the mouse-ears shape on her hide). Kids like climbing on the large, padded animals and bouncing on the thick foam carpet.

THE BARNSTORMER AT GOOFY'S WISEACRES FARM The park has needed a ride like this for years—a kid-sized coaster that takes people who can't reach the height bars at the other thrill rides on a barnstorming flight that crashes right through Goofy's giant red barn.

TOONTOWN FAIR TRAIN STATION This is a great place to get on or off the Magic Kingdom's antique train. The station is large and spacious and you seldom have to wait.

BUYS The **Duck County Courthouse** sells souvenirs of *Duck Tales* and "Disney Afternoon." At the giant **Toontown Fair Hall of Fame,** you can send Florida citrus—or collect an autograph and photo with famous characters from classic Disney feature cartoons.

FANTASYLAND

A tribute to the early Disney cartoon classics on which the studio's feature business was based, this land is dominated by Cinderella Castle, where gingerbread architecture and cobblestone streets create a cartoon view of the medieval Europe, where fairy tales began.

MAD TEA PARTY This giant replica of the Mad Hatter's tea cups from *Alice in Wonderland* is one of my family's favorites. You spin around so fast that you get dizzy. (Okay, so it's a dressed-up carnival standard. But it's a great old carnival ride, with Disney music and decor that make it special.)
Worth-It Rating ★★★★

MR. TOAD'S WILD RIDE The car that pulls up to take you on this ride might be Mr. Toad's or Badger's or it might have belonged to another character from Disney's adaptation of Kenneth Grahame's *The Wind in the Willows*. Okay, the car is just a little kiddie car, and the ride is old and a bit dated, with silly stand-up plywood characters, but it's fun! Still one of the best of its kind! And the line moves pretty fast.
Worth-It Rating ★★★ Minus 1 if it's crowded.

SNOW WHITE'S ADVENTURES The wicked Queen used to scare the heck out of my kids—and apparently others, too, because she's nearly gone now, the victim of a refurbishing. It's still fairly low-tech, but now you see more of the dwarfs.
Worth-It Rating ★★★ Add 1 if you have kids under 10.

CINDERELLA'S GOLDEN CARROUSEL A great big old-fashioned merry-go-round with hand-carved wooden horses that go round and round and up and down to the tunes of famous Disney classics. I think a carousel is a pretty mundane ride for a place like the Magic Kingdom, but the kids really love this ride, and like everything else at Disney, it's world-class.
Worth-It Rating ★★★★ Add 1 if you like carousels.

DUMBO THE FLYING ELEPHANT This ride with elephant-shaped cabs was part of the inspiration for my exclusive Worth-It Ratings. Though Disney video has turned this ride into an icon, it's really just a short standard carnival attraction, and the wait is really long.
Worth-It Rating ★★★ Minus 2 if you don't have kids. Stay away unless your kids REALLY love Dumbo *and* the line is short.

LEGEND OF THE LION KING One of the new generation of Disney theater shows, this is just terrific. Life-size puppet figures, great costumes, and dazzling special effects bring the popular movie and its characters to life.
The Fast Track: See my tip about not lining up in Chapter 1. Or you'll have to wait in lion like everybody else.
Worth-It Rating ★★★★★

PETER PAN'S FLIGHT From the time she first spoke, my daughter Tiffany loved the story of Peter Pan. So we've spent many hours waiting to board a pirate ship for this flight from the Darling children's bedroom over Neverland. Too bad. Disney's excellent cartoon adaptation of Sir James M. Barrie's timeless tale deserves a better representation than this tired relic of 1950s technology. Also, the lines are too long, and the ride far too short. So sorry.
Worth-It Rating ★★ Add 1 if the line is short, 1 more if your kids are true Peter Pan lovers like Tiffany.

IT'S A SMALL WORLD If you're prone to having silly tunes stuck in your head, beware! (Or wear ear plugs!) You cruise the Small World's waterways as too-cute wooden children on either side of you sing their song over and over—first in English, then in every language spoken since the Tower of Babel. Subtly educational, it's also probably one of the most efficiently designed and best-run attractions anywhere. The lines move nicely, and you wait in air-conditioned comfort. Why can't all the rides work as well?
The Fast Track: Look to the left on the ramp as you go down to the boats. Yes, that's a line—and there's often no one in it!
Worth-It Rating ★★★★★

SKYWAY TO TOMORROWLAND The Skyway goes both ways (*see* Tomorrowland), but I like this Swiss wooden shingled station better than the concrete edifice at the other end (and so, apparently, do a lot of other people, because the line here is usually longer here).
Worth-It Rating ★★★ Add 1 if the line happens to be short.

BITES Wait! Check out the **Enchanted Grove.** Here's yet another place to get a frozen citrus slushy thing or an ice cream. **Hook's Tavern,** a corner booth next to Peter Pan's Flight, dispenses soft drinks. **Lumière's Kitchen,** inspired by Jerry Orbach's memorable singing candle in *Beauty and the Beast,* specializes in quick kid's meals. **Mrs. Potts' Cupboard** dishes out soft-serve ice cream, floats, and sundaes. **The Little Big Top** has cold drinks and shakes. **Pinocchio Village Haus,** overlooking It's a Small World, always seems downright convenient. Low-fat turkey dogs are the current house specialty.

BUYS Fantasyland shops are all clustered together around the Fantasyland entrance to Cinderella Castle. **Tinker Bell's Treasures** sells children's clothing, including Minnie Mouse dresses and other character outfits. **Mickey's Christmas Carol** is a Christmas store loaded with Disney-theme ornaments. **Fantasy Faire** has stuff from the latest animated releases. The **King's Gallery** is full of medieval-style items. We once bought Tiffany a flowing princess hat here. Like much of our Disney memorabilia, the hat is long gone, but the cherished photo remains. The **Aristocats** sells Disney and other clothing for grown-up children. Pop into **Seven Dwarfs Mining Co.** for anything related to the feature film that catapulted Walt to fame in 1937. It's amazing how many cute little character items there are. Many of the treasures featuring Doc, Sleepy, Dopey, Happy, Bashful, Sneezy, and Grumpy and their young surrogate mother have been staples in Disney merchandising for decades.

LIBERTY SQUARE

HAUNTED MANSION This is a spooktacular experience from beginning to end. Don't miss the funny tombstones near the entrance, with epitaphs like "Here Lies Fred/A Great Big Rock Fell On His Head!" Inside, you walk, then ride, through a collection of scary scenes that feature every special effect in the Imagineers' book. Lots of people ask, in the room that stretches, whether the ceiling is going up or the floor is going down? The answer is yes! (It's not an elevator, as many believe. The ceiling goes up—just as it seems.)

The Fast Track: Stay to the left, especially in the entrance area. Most people form a line, but actually there's just one big open area and people are expected to fill it up in a mass. Because they don't, you can often go right to the front. Even on crowded days, staffers actually have to ask people to move up. So when you do, ignore the curmudgeons scowling at you as you pass. When you get to the stretching room, walk straight across to the exit door, so that you can be the first out into the next queue. This is the line for the ride. You'll stand on a moving conveyor belt and step into a moving car. Everyone will be trying to go right; so follow my tip and pass on the left. You could win several valuable Disney minutes—redeemable at the next attraction.

Worth-It Rating ★★★★★

MIKE FINK KEELBOATS Only Elvis and the Beatles approached the popularity of Davy Crockett as he was depicted by Walt Disney on the *Disneyland* TV show in the 1960s. The episode with Mike Fink and the keelboat race, which this boat ride recalls, was one of the best shows. The Wild West scenery is basically the same as you see from the riverboats, except that your viewpoint is closer to the water. Don't do both unless you're determined to ride every ride.
Worth-It Rating ★★★ Add 1 if there's no line.

LIBERTY BELLE RIVERBOAT If you've never taken a ride on an old paddle wheeler, this is your chance! It's authentic, enlightening, and fun, especially if you do as I do: Jump on board singing "Old Man River," ignore the weird looks from the other passengers, and enjoy the scenery, which looks almost like Missouri. And they really do shout "Mark Twain!" At night the river pirates come out, so the boats stop running at dark.
Worth-It Rating ★★★ Add 1 if there's no line.

THE HALL OF PRESIDENTS Abe Lincoln and Bill Clinton both speak during this winner, which sums up American history as it was made by the nation's presidents. The enormous panoramic film is followed by a roll call of chief executives. Disney's Audio-Animatronics presidents are very realistic in every detail. Though they do not answer questions from the audience (believe me, I've asked), the show is an asset to any parent trying to inspire an interest in history.
Worth-It Rating ★★★★ Add 1 if you want to give your children a history lesson.

BITES One thing to be said for Disney: They go out of their way to accommodate every lifestyle. **Sleepy Hollow** offers vegetarians a nice fast-food menu of salads and sandwiches. My family's four-thumbs-up favorite fast-food stop in the park? **Columbia Harbour House.** Though fried fish and chicken baskets are the headliners, we go for the rich, hot clam chowder, served in a giant whole-grain bread bowl. Yummy! There's hearty fare like pot roast at the Colonial-style **Liberty Tree Tavern.** Dinner is with the characters, lunch is without, and both are by reservation only.

BUYS The **Silversmith** sells gifts and jewelry made of silver or pewter. If you've always wanted a cast pewter Mickey, go no farther. **Heritage House** offers Americana. My little Ricky, a budding Civil War buff, favors it for its excellent selection of Civil War-inspired souvenirs. **Olde World Antiques** specializes in Victorian jewelry and Annette Funicello's own Cello perfume. (Okay, so you've never heard of it. Anyway, it's here.) And remember *The Legend of Sleepy Hollow*? I do! It was spooky with that headless horseman, and it's the theme for **Ichabod's,** a magic store that also sells novelties and costume masks. Hit the **Yankee Trader** for kitchen items.

FRONTIERLAND

Because many of us grew up with Walt Disney, it's easy to forget that he was born at the turn of the last century, the end of the frontier era. Back then, Buffalo Bill's Wild West Show still toured America as the nation's most famous traveling show. The Old West was a frequent Disney theme. Its depiction in his Davy Crockett shows was one of his biggest successes.

DIAMOND HORSESHOE REVUE Step right into this saloon and have a root beer! Shows are continuous, dance hall girls sing and dance, and rowdy barkeeps tell jokes. It's a good place to mix food and fun.
Worth-It Rating ★★★★ Add 1 if you've decided it's time to buy food in the park.

FRONTIERLAND SHOOTIN' ARCADE You shoot at moving targets and playful characters in a highly animated gallery with safe, light-powered rifles. Ricky loves it, but I don't like paying extra.
Worth-It Rating ★★ Add 1 if you have kids.

COUNTRY BEAR JAMBOREE The most fun of all the Audio-Animatronics shows is this Disney version of the Grand Ol' Opry, with 20 full-size singing bears, a moose, and a bison. As many times as we've seen it (dozens), we still howl when Big Al sings "Blood on the Saddle." Lines are reasonable and the waiting air-conditioned, unless the line is out the door.
The Fast Track: Not everybody who's waiting gets into every show, so grab a spot near the doors when you get into the waiting room.
Worth-It Rating ★★★★ Add 1 if the line is extra short.

TOM SAWYER ISLAND In this re-creation of the world of Tom Sawyer and Huck Finn, a real island in the middle of the Magic Kingdom's lagoon, you can crawl through tunnels, scamper over swaying wooden bridges, and "fahr them guns at Fort Sam Clemens!" (The guns make a lot of noise, but don't really shoot anything, by the way.) There's no light on the island, so regardless of park hours, it closes at dusk.
Worth-It Rating ★★★ Add 1 if your kids are old enough to study Mark Twain.

BIG THUNDER MOUNTAIN RAILROAD The premise here is that a mine train has broken loose from the top of an old mine, and you're on a swooping, plunging, out-of-control ride through the mountains and gorges of Wild West mining country. Steam geysers and water add to the effect.
The Fast Track: Kids must be 40 inches or taller to ride. We usually beat the lines and the long waits by staying left. There are several water fountains en route; soak your head or your shirt to keep cool.
Worth-It Rating ★★★★ Add 1 if the line is short.

SPLASH MOUNTAIN This water coaster, a combination log-flume ride and Audio-Animatronics adventure that opened in 1995, is based on *Song of the South,* Disney's take on Joel Chandler Harris's Uncle Remus stories. During your ride with Brer Rabbit, Brer Bear, and Brer Fox, the biggest thrill is the 50-vertical-foot splashdown at the end, which you won't mind a bit on a hot day. The line winds through a maze in the valley beneath the mountain with a few minor sites and sounds like music in the bushes, but Disney could have done a much better job making the line part of the experience. As it is, the lines are long and the wait awful. Still, the ride is so good that the bad wait almost doesn't matter.
The Fast Track: No children under 44 inches tall.
Worth-It Rating ★★★★★

FRONTIERLAND STUNT SHOW Cops and robbers shoot it out in the street in front of the **Mile Long Bar** (a snack spot). It's a pretty good little stunt show. Check your entertainment schedule for times.
Worth-It Rating ★★★

FRONTIERLAND

BITES **Pecos Bill Café** is one of the larger fast-food stops, with a spectacular view of Big Thunder Mountain. Out on the street, a stand sells giant smoked turkey drumsticks. As for the **Mile Long Bar,** it's our favorite place to watch parades. If you arrive early, you can grab a seat under the roof, where you'll have a little shade. Unless you're really late or it's really crowded, though, you'll get a seat.

BUYS **Splashdown Photo** is the place where you can pick up the photo taken of your family as you plunged down the big drop at the end of the Splash Mountain ride. Even if you don't buy the picture, the instant replay is fun. The **Briar Patch** is also just outside Splash Mountain. It sells gifts based on *Song of the South* as well as Winnie the Pooh merchandise. **Big Al's,** just outside Country Bear Jamboree, sells take-home versions of that show's many popular characters. If you're old enough to remember coonskin caps, you'll be glad to know that they still have 'em at several shops. **Prairie Outpost & Supply** features Native American crafts and *Pocahontas* items. The **Trading Post** specializes in western accessories, and the **Trail Creek Hat Shop** sells hats from one to a full ten gallons. **Frontier Wood Carving** will put your name in oak.

ADVENTURELAND

TROPICAL SERENADE I dare you to take in this show, also known as the Singing Tiki Birds, and leave without its silly melody lodged in your neuro-pathways for the rest of your life (as happens to almost everyone at It's A Small World). Dating from 1963, it was the first Audio-Animatronics experience at

Disneyland. My family gives it mixed reviews. My wife thinks that the idea of watching mechanical parrots sing and tell bad jokes is for the birds. I love it, as do the kids. Lines are usually short, and it's air-conditioned and fun. At this writing, it's closed for refurbishing. But by the time you read this, it should be back on line and updated, better than ever.
Rehab too new to rate.

PIRATES OF THE CARIBBEAN Also from Disneyland, this is another welcome spot on a hot day. The lines wind through a fake dungeon that's damp, cool, and full of interesting details that stay with the theme. Then you board a pirate boat that takes you on a wild adventure, through an artillery battle and scenes of a drunken carousing (the pirates, not you).
The Fast Track: Here, even the wait is great. But time after time we skip the entire line just by keeping left.
Worth-It Rating ★★★★★

JUNGLE CRUISE One of the original Disneyland rides—I remember watching the film of its construction on Walt's TV show back in the mid-50s. The jungle props, plaster pachyderms, and amazing menagerie of other motorized mammals still hold up well after all these years. An open-sided, gas-powered steamer takes you along the Nile and through Southeast Asia, South Africa, and the Amazon rain forest, not necessarily in that order. Watch out for the squirting elephant. Some of the skippers drone, but when they take their comedy seriously, their monologues can be a hoot!
The Fast Track: The winding queue is well concealed and can be the park's worst wait on a hot, muggy day. Before committing yourself to an hour of sweat, park a family member in line while you check out the waiting time. If it's too long,

ADVENTURELAND

come back in the evening when it's cooler. If the park isn't open late, ride as early as possible.
Worth-It Rating ★★★★ Subtract 1 if the line is long.

SWISS FAMILY TREEHOUSE Disney's film *Swiss Family Robinson* has enjoyed a revival thanks to exposure on the Disney Channel and on video to a whole new generation of kids. So you may want to check out this replica of the house high in a banyan tree that appeared in the motion picture. In my family, we're all afraid of heights, so the steep open climb isn't our cup of tea. Even apart from that, I don't think it's worth the wait. You don't do anything and neither does the tree house—you just look at it. It's closed for a rehab at this writing. Will the new version shine any brighter? Stay tuned.

BITES At **Aloha Isle,** the offerings are fruit-juice-based, and shakelike. This is what the tropics are for! In **El Pirata y el Perico,** there's a pirate theme and Mexican fast food like tacos. **Sunshine Tree Terrace** serves more frozen juice concoctions—these made of indigenous citrus.

BUYS Most shops cluster in an ersatz bazaar. Stop at **Bwana Bob's** after you find that you just can't live without a stuffed tropical bird. **Elephant Tales** sells safari-theme gifts and clothing, **Traders of Timbuktu** things African. The **Tropics Shop** is your source for Hawaiian shirts and other cliché tropical attire. And check out the **Zanzibar Shell Co.** for sea shells and shell crafts like wind chimes. **House of Treasure** has a pirate theme. I wish I had a nickel for every nickel I spent here during Ricky's pirate period. (And there's more of the same at the **Treasure Chest** and **Lafitte's.**) **Plaza del Sol Caribe Bazaar,** just outside Pirates of the Caribbean, expands your tropical options.

chapter 7

EPCOT CENTER

Walt Disney World

Take I–4 to Exit 26B, labeled for Epcot and Rte. 536.

Drop 1 if you have children under 6.

Epcot Center is a breathtaking, first-class attraction loved by millions. The name is an acronym for "Experimental Prototype Community of Tomorrow," a title said to have been chosen by Walt Disney to herald a planned community similar to Celebration, the new town Disney is finally building in Kissimmee. Insiders know that the initials really stand for "Every Person Comes Out Tired" from this, the biggest of all the theme parks. I love that joke, because for years, this was my least favorite park.

But a funny thing happened while I researched this book. As I went back again and again, the place won me over. Maybe my idea of what a theme park should be was too limited. Perhaps I missed the point by simply looking for rides. Perhaps, being so conscious of value and price, I was overly annoyed by what I perceived as blatant commercialism. Or perhaps my vision was clouded by one too many trips with children who were too young to appreciate it—children who are only now old enough to be excited by the experiences it offers.

Now it's clear to me: Epcot is a place filled with wonder. It may be the only place anywhere that parents can take their children on an instant trip around the world, albeit a fantasy trip, and learn about the cultures of every continent. One can only guess how many future scientists, researchers, and doctors might find, at Epcot, the first spark that ignites their lifelong passion. The bottom line is that Epcot has too many spectacular attractions and wonderful cultural experiences to be ignored.

It is also huge. As a result, it seldom feels congested, regardless of the day or the season. If you hate theme-park crowds, or if the crowds at the other parks start to get you down, the size may be a plus. And it's ideal on rainy days. Crowds thin out when it rains. And with the right clothes and the right attitude, you could have the park mostly to yourself.

WHAT'S NEW? I included GM's new Test Track in last year's book, but due to technical difficulties, it failed to open on time. If it opens this year, you're in for a treat.

TIMING One September weekday, when crowds were thin, I went to World Showcase. Mind you, I wasn't even trying to include Future World. Nor did I have kids or family to slow me down. I did not finish before closing time. You won't either. So choose what you want to do carefully. There's far too much at Epcot for a single day.

EATERTAINMENT AND SHOPPERTOONITIES Particularly in World Showcase, food and shopping are an integral part of

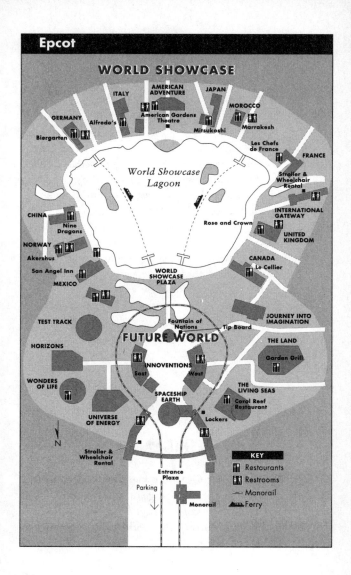

the experience. So to take advantage of many of Epcot's best features, you have to spend more money than in any other park.

THE LAY OF THE LAND Epcot is like a barbell. You enter on the bottom, in Future World, facing Spaceship Earth, Epcot's signature geosphere. Just beyond it, the pavilions of Future World are arranged roughly in a circle around a large, central plaza. Beyond this plaza lies the World Showcase Lagoon, which is ringed by a a promenade punctuated by the pavilions of World Showcase. The American Adventure pavilion is directly opposite Spaceship Earth across the lagoon.

THE FAST TRACK Because Future World opens first, I suggest you begin there. Lines will be long if you haven't arrived early. So do the things that don't have lines, such as Innoventions. Head to World Showcase a little before it opens, even if you're not finished in Future World. Start in Mexico and work clockwise to Canada. Remember, the earlier you get to World Showcase, the thinner the crowds will be. (Conversely, crowds thin out at Future World later in the day.)

Future World

SPACESHIP EARTH

SPACESHIP EARTH RIDE Question: Have you ever wondered what's inside that geosphere, the giant aluminum golf ball that is the symbol of Epcot? Answer: A great ride, which squeezes in a brief history of the world from dinosaurs to spaceships.

The Fast Track You'll often find short lines, particularly late in the day. If you arrive early and it's crowded, skip it and come back before you leave.
Worth-It Rating ★★★★★

INNOVENTIONS EAST AND WEST

What's new in the world? This is where you can see the latest in gimmicks and gadgets and try out nifty new things like virtual reality.

Stop in for a multimedia trip through the history of innovation and invention with Bill Nye the Science Guy. Then try out a new wrist telephone from AT&T. Check out the latest software, and play animator on a Silicon Graphics workstation. Have your camcorder handy: At the GE exhibit there's a nifty spot where you can be interviewed by Jay Leno through the magic of electronic special effects. My son, Ricky, would be completely happy to spend the entire day at Sega's exhibit. Its full-size road race is everything the Magic Kingdom's Grand Prix raceway always wanted to be—a wild, jolting simulator where you can pass, skid, spin out, and actually compete to win against other drivers. Too bad it costs an extra four bucks.

Also check out the leaping fountain and live entertainment from **Future Corps**. Everything is high-tech, even the entertainment. Check out **Future Corps** band, the **Kristos Acrobats,** the talking **EpBOTS** robots, and the impromptu, cacophonous, comedic **Jammitors**. Mickey, Minnie, and other characters show up in metallic, space-age outfits. Signs throughout the park list where they'll be.
Worth-It Rating ★★★★★

FUTURE WORLD

BITES Go for sandwiches and chicken at the **Electric Umbrella**, or pasta and pizza at the **Pasta Piazza Ristorante**. **Fountain View** serves espresso and baked goods.

THE LIVING SEAS

The giant aquarium in the middle of the pavilion is not keeping the folks at Sea World up at night, but you'll see a fairly impressive collection of undersea life, including sharks and manatees, as well as aquatic exhibits and a ride "through the ocean depths."
Worth-It Rating ★★★

BITES Gazing through the 8-foot glass windows at the popular **Coral Reef Restaurant** is almost like being inside the aquarium. Seafood is on the menu. And if you've ever wanted to see Mickey Mouse underwater, this is the place; he plays diver during the restaurant's character breakfast.

THE LAND

LIVING WITH THE LAND One of those infectious Disney sound tracks follows your craft as you glide along a waterway filled with high-tech gardens that are actually used to grow some of the food you eat in the park. It's fun and informative if you have school-age children.
Worth-It Rating ★★★★

GREENHOUSE TOUR They use hydroponics and other high-tech tricks to grow their own veggies and other things in the greenhouses here; on this 45-minute guided walk, you see how. Whether or not this is worth the trouble depends entirely in your interest in the science of agriculture. Make reservations when you get to the pavilion.

THE HARVEST THEATER In the *Circle of Life,* the harmless film that plays here, the *Lion King* gang talks about taking care of Mother Earth.
Worth-It Rating ★★★

FOOD ROCKS This show is like It's a Small World with singing veggies. Little kids love it.
Worth-It Rating ★★★★

BITES The **Garden Grill**, a revolving full-service restaurant, overlooks some of the scenery you see in the Listen to the Land boat ride. Reserve ahead. The **Sunshine Season Food Fair,** an elaborate food court, gives you home-style cooking with natural and organic ingredients. Try the vegetable lasagna at the **Cheese Store.**

JOURNEY INTO IMAGINATION

This pavilion explores the nature of the creative process.

MAGIC EYE THEATER *Honey, I Shrunk the Audience!,* which plays here, is the best show at Epcot and my pick for second-best 3D show in the world (after Universal's Terminator 2: 3D). A 3D sequel to the films, *Honey, I Shrunk and/or Blew*

FUTURE WORLD

Up the Kids and/or the Baby, it gets actor Rick Moranis to shrink the entire audience. You're subsequently menaced by giant reptiles. Don't miss it.
Worth-It Rating ★★★★★

THE IMAGE WORKS A cool creative playground featuring hands-on experiences with "creative playthings" that demonstrate technology ranging from computer graphics to static electricity.
Worth-It Rating ★★★★

JOURNEY INTO IMAGINATION RIDE Spend a mildly amusing 13 minutes with Figment, the purple dragon who's Epcot's quasi-mascot, and his bearded pal, Dreamfinder.
Worth-It Rating ★★★

TEST TRACK

TEST TRACK RIDE Only Disney creates the kind of combination thrill ride and visual experience that you find at Splash Mountain and the other adventure coasters. This new one, not yet open as I write, promises to be the best, longest, and fastest ever. The high drama derives from bad weather, hazardous road conditions, and high speed.

Too new to rate.

WONDERS OF LIFE

One of our favorite stops at Epcot, this has a large center court full of activities that remind me of Innoventions. But here the themes are life, health, and fitness.

BODY WARS A simulator ride, like Star Tours at Disney–MGM Studios, except that you're on an imaginary trip into a human being. Your simulator is shrunk and injected into a person (much as Martin Short is in the movie *Inner Space*). The special effects are thrilling and original, but the family and I agree that this one is a little too rough.
The Fast Track Children under 48 inches, people with heart and back problems, and women who are pregnant or think they might be are advised not to ride. Avoid it if you don't want to get roughed up. Unfortunately, there's no way to get around the lines except by showing up early or late.
Worth-It Rating ★★★★

CRANIUM COMMAND This absolutely charming and wonderfully funny film and Audio-Animatronics show takes you inside the brain of a 12-year-old boy. The star-studded comic cast includes favorite TV actors as operators of vital organs. One of the best shows at Epcot.
The Fast Track The entrance is hidden at the back of Wonders of Life, so many people miss the show and lines are often short. Before you get in, you'll be routed into a holding area with a movie. There, look for the doors to the show's theater and get as close to them as you can. All seats are good, but the front is the best.
Worth-It Rating ★★★★★

THE MAKING OF ME After you've seen this movie about how babies develop, you may want to start that little "birds and bees" talk with your kids. Or maybe not. In any case, be prepared. This Martin Short film is fairly explicit, and the fetus footage is graphic.

Worth-It Rating ★★★ Add 2 if you want Martin Short to explain the facts of life to your children.

THE CENTER COURT There are all kinds of great activities here. At the **Coach's Corner,** you can evaluate your golf, tennis, or baseball skills. Your swing is videotaped, then reviewed by pros. **Wondercycles** give a quick little workout (you—not me), along with an instant analysis of the calories burned in various thrilling simulated situations. In the cartoon/live action **Goofy about Health** show, the great Goofy demonstrates why you should get your potato off the couch. The **Anacomical Players** improvise skits about health. The **Lifestyle Revue** gives you the chance to rate the healthiness of your lifestyle (or in my case, the lack thereof). Finally, the **Fitness Fairground** lets you test your six senses (the sixth being your sense of humor). One of the activities is sticking your hand into a hole in a box, then trying to figure out what you're touching. Most people guess wrong.

BITES Pure and Simple has health-smart fast food such as waffles, yogurt, sandwiches, and salads.

UNIVERSE OF ENERGY

We love this attraction a little more every time we come! It's even better since it was completely revamped in 1996. Now it

features Jamie Lee Curtis and Bill Nye the Science Guy, with a cameo appearance by the late Albert Einstein, in a simulated game of *Jeopardy!*. The entire auditorium moves on a track through a primeval forest filled with life-size Audio-Animatronics dinosaurs. It's a multimedia extravaganza that's funny, informative, and absolutely spectacular.
Worth-It Rating ★★★★★

World Showcase

This group of pavilions is Disney's ongoing, permanent world's fair, where, in a single day, you can capture Kodak moments in front of most of the world's major landmarks.

Not every country in the world is included. Don't look for politics, either. Even though national governments actually participate in the planning and running of the attractions (perhaps *because* they do), all political content has been removed for your protection.

SHOPPERTOONITIES AND EATERTAINMENT Even if you don't buy anything, take time to browse in the shops. Nowhere else in the world will you find such a diverse sampling of international offerings in a single place. And each pavilion features the country's native cuisine in fast fooderies and great sit-down restaurants. As in all parks, the food is pricey. But the presentations are world-class, so the overall experience is memorable. Reservations are almost always required (tel. 407/824–4321 for information, tel. 407/939–3463 to reserve).

STREETMOSPHERE Streetmosphere is what Disney calls those roaming costumed characters who help set the mood. Stop now and then to watch them; they're one of the best parts of the park. **World-Class Brass** performs pop music with a little comedy throughout World Showcase. Ditto for the **Junkanoo Bus,** a wildly painted Caribbean contraption that not only plays music but has an on-board bar that serves tropical drinks! (You'll find it in Future World, too.)

THE UNITED KINGDOM

You'll see what's so great about Britain in this miniature replication featuring formal English gardens, a great traditional English herb garden and maze, and a cobblestone street lined with Tudor homes and Victorian buildings. Phone home: The old-fashioned red telephone booths really work (and make a nice photo-op).

BITES At the **Rose & Crown,** you'll find traditional British fare, both in its restaurant section and in the adjacent pub. Here's your big chance to try kidney pie (or stick with fish and chips and the obligatory British brews).

BUYS The **Toy Soldier** sells British toys. **Lords and Ladies** is all perfume and tobacco, the **Tea Caddy** all teas and teapots. **Pringle of Scotland** stocks Scottish woolens. Ever since Ricky saw *Braveheart,* he's been fascinated with Scottish culture. Each clan has its own plaid, and the selection here represents most of them. You'll also find real bagpipes, practice pipes to learn on, how-to tapes, and piper music. The **Magic of Wales** and the **Queen's Table** sell decorative items.

STREETMOSPHERE Check out the **World Showcase Players.** Guests help with the skits. And look for the roving bagpipers. When I told one of them that Ricky wanted to learn to play, we were treated to a 15-minute concert with instruction—wonderful!
Worth-It Rating ★★★★

NORWAY

The ornate architecture of a 14th-century Norwegian fortress and a 12th-century stave church make this one of the most visually entertaining spots in World Showcase. The church houses Norwegian art and artifacts.

MAELSTROM My daughter Tiffany's favorite ride in World Showcase is a stormy trip in a Viking ship with great Audio-Animatronics bears and more. But the ending is abrupt; one minute you're in the middle of a stormy northern sea, the next you're climbing out of your boat.

BITES It should come as no surprise that they do a good smorgasbord at **Restaurant Akershus,** with good hot and cold entrées and more herring dishes than you'd ever want. You'll feel like a Viking at the rough wooden tables inside the stone walls of what looks like an ancient Norse castle. Reserve ahead.

BUYS The **Puffin's Roost,** just outside Maelstrom, sells clothing, toys, and candy, including the very popular Freia's Non-

Stop, resembling M&Ms. There's also one of the world's most extensive selection of plastic, wood, and ceramic trolls.
Worth-It Rating ★★★★★

CANADA

Indian totem poles in a scene straight out of the old Northwest Mountie movies welcome you to the Great White North! Framed by a Disney version of Canada's Canadian mountains are a sparkling waterfall and a replica of Ottawa's imposing stone Château Laurier. In the foreground, Disney has re-created British Columbia's spectacularly floral Butchart Gardens.

O CANADA! This movie contains a lot of purple mountains' majesty. I love these CircleVision 360 movies. You're completely surrounded by curved screens, which literally put you in the center of the action. But there are no seats, and nothing but a guard rail to lean on. I'd like the thrilling toboggan ride, the powerful audio, and the spectacular views a whole lot more if I didn't have to stand.

BITES With its big, low stone arches, **Le Cellier** looks like a fancy cellar restaurant, but the hearty prime rib, turkey, and shepherd's pie are served cafeteria style, along with salads and desserts. It's my kind of place—and not a bad deal.

BUYS **Northwest Mercantile** is like a log cabin stocked with Native American crafts. **Le Boutique** sells French-Canadian jewelry, fragrances, and novelties.

STREETMOSPHERE Canada is another place where Ricky can find bagpipes—look for both the **Caledonia Bagpipes** and the **Pipes of Nova Scotia.** You may also run into the **Canadian Comedy Corps,** who remind you how funny Canadians can be.

Worth-It Rating ★★★

FRANCE

Here you enter a charming French neighborhood from the 1600s. The Eiffel Tower, which is also here, may be the park's best photo-op. (It's claimed that the real McCoy is the world's most photographed structure. Who can argue?)

IMPRESSIONS OF FRANCE During this 18-minute widescreen tour of France, you ride, slide, and fly through Paris and the French countryside to the strains of music by classical French composers, played over an excellent sound system. (See, you *can* sit down at an Epcot movie.)

BITES Wouldn't you expect great French food here? At **Les Chefs de France,** take the spiral staircase to the second floor, where three world-class chefs (Paul Bocuse, Roger Vergé, and Gaston Lenôtre) offer dishes like duck à l'orange and snapper with scallops and crab that are truly awesome. **Bistro de Paris** is our favorite Epcot restaurant. My wife, Terrie, loves the French onion soup, and we both endorse the rack of lamb for two. At **Au Petit Café,** you can just pop in and grab a quiche, a croissant, or a chunk of French bread and cheese. And the pop-up children's menu is adorable. If you arrive late in the

WORLD SHOWCASE

evening, the meal comes with a reasonable view of IllumiNations from a comfortable seat. Reserve for all.

BUYS Pâté anyone? Check **Le Mode Français.** For fragrances, it's **La Signature,** for cosmetics the **Guerlain Boutique,** for wine **La Maison du Vin. Plume et Palette** has art and crystal (watch the kids—"you break it, you bought it" is the motto). With youngsters, you're better off in **Galerie des Halles** (or maybe not—it sells toys and candy). Look for the *Hunchback of Notre Dame* booth. Where else would it be?

STREETMOSPHERE **Gordoon,** a clown with a Maurice Chevalier accent, improvises with children and seltzer. It's wet, wild, and wonderful. And although gypsies aren't French, France does have gypsies, as portrayed in *Hunchback.* The **Tzigantzi** troupe performs their songs and dances, and Left Bank portrait artists nearby paint you while you wait.

Worth-It Rating ★★★★

MOROCCO

This is a finely detailed reproduction of the cities of North Africa, based on Fez and Marrakesh, only a lot cleaner than the real thing. Fez House and the Nejjarine Fountain are both replicas of famous structures from ancient Morocco, and there's an interesting (if a little sparse) exhibit of Moroccan art. But where's Rick's American Café?

BITES North Africans consider lamb to be the best of all meats. At **Restaurant Marrakesh,** beef, chicken, and fish also go into the couscous, but it's never as good with the substitutions. While you dine, the **Casablanca Fez Belly Dancers and Musicians** gyrate. You'll need reservations.

BUYS Carpets, clothing, and crafts spill out the doors and into the street in true bazaar style. **Marketplace in the Medina, Casablanca Carpets, Tangier Traders,** the **Brass Bazaar, Medina Arts,** and the **Berber Oasis** are great places to pick up handcrafted Moroccan brass and leather goods. At the pavilion's edge, clever Disney marketers have taken advantage of the Mideast connection to set up an *Aladdin* shop.

STREETMOSPHERE Keep your ears open for the folk musicians accompanied by belly dancers. Wow! The aforementioned **Houzali Troupe** performs in the courtyard by the lagoon—four drums, a flute, and one very nice belly.
Worth-It Rating ★★★ Add 1 if you plan to shop here.

JAPAN

In the real Japan, land is scarce and highly prized, and the gardens precious. So the centerpiece of Epcot's Japan is a spectacular re-creation of a classic Japanese garden. You'll also see a replica five-story pagoda dating from the 8th century, Nara's Temple of Horyuji. An art exhibit is housed in a looming reproduction of an antique stone castle surrounded by a moat. Don't miss the life-size statues of mounted samurai on your way out.

BITES In the **Teppanyaki Rooms,** you sit at tables that wrap around big grills where chefs chop up meat and veggies before your eyes, faster than a samurai. If you've been to Benihana, you know the drill. **Tempura Kiku** specializes in batter-fried fare. Reserve for both of these. **Yakitori House** serves Nipponese fast food. The teriyaki beef and chicken dishes, the yummy red bean dessert, and the children's menu rate a mention. And it's surprisingly inexpensive.

BUYS One of Japan's leading merchants, **Mitsukoshi**, offers the best of the wares from its department stores—great kimonos and Japanese dolls as well as lacquerware, fabrics, karate outfits, samurai swords, jewelry, carvings, paintings, and about a zillion little knickknacks.

STREETMOSPHERE **One World Taiko** consists of two drummers beating out those great old Japanese tunes. **Matsurizi**, a larger group, also performs Japanese percussive music. The bizarre troupe known as **Cirikili** is made up of "stilt birds"—Japanese actor/acrobats on high stilts who wear mechanical bird contraptions that make them look like warriors astride giant metallic ostriches. Think *Shogun* meets *Star Wars*.
Worth-It Rating ★★★ Add 1 if you plan to eat here.

THE AMERICAN ADVENTURE

The focal point of this pavilion is a magnificent Colonial-style structure that's a little like Philadelphia's Independence Hall and Williamsburg's Governor's Mansion in one, with touches of the White House and the Capitol. The beautiful rose garden outside, inspired by the one at the White House, features varieties named for U.S. Presidents and historical figures. Shaded by stately magnolias and sycamores, the grounds look and feel like colonial Virginia—particularly impressive when you remember that you're in tropical Florida.

THE AMERICAN ADVENTURE SHOW This really is the best show in the World Showcase, and I'm not just being patriotic. Audio-Animatronics Ben Franklin and Mark Twain host this dazzling musical half hour. It's Disney's best Audio-Animatronics show, period. The figures are so lifelike that at times they look and sound like real actors. The montage of familiar and poignant scenes from America's recent past may moisten your eyes, as they do mine.

BITES No funny stuff at the **Liberty Inn.** Strictly American burgers, hot dogs, and fries.

BUYS Hit **Heritage Manor** for cutesy American country-style gifts. The selection of American flag novelties (I collect 'em) is one of the best I've seen anywhere, even in Philadelphia and Washington, D.C.

STREETMOSPHERE The **Voices of Liberty** sing a capella in the show waiting area. Or try to catch the **Sons of Liberty,** a traditional fife and drum corps. The **American Gardens Theater,** across the promenade from the pavilion, features concerts and celebrity appearances; check the schedule near the stage.
Worth-It Rating ★★★★★

MEXICO

A carving of the serpent-god Quetzalcoatl presides over the steps of this imposing reproduction Maya temple. Inside, there's an impressive display of pre-Columbian primitive art. And in the plaza in the pavilion's center is a large, open shopping area crammed with Mexican novelties. In perpetual twilight, the plaza is always cool and dark—excellent on hot, muggy afternoons. The front steps are one of the better places to see IllumiNations.

EL RIO DEL TIEMPO The pavilion's main feature is this ride (the name translates as "river of time"), which takes you through representations of the history of Mexico from ancient cultures to the present. It's cool, refreshing, and pleasant, nothing more, so move on if the wait looks long.

BITES The setting of the **San Angel Inn Restaurant,** overlooking the River of Time ride, is one of the park's most romantic. Lavish margaritas enhance the mood. On the menu, along with predictable Mexican-American enchiladas and tacos, are unexpected selections like mahi-mahi and grilled shrimp. I call the **Cantina de San Angel** "Taco Tinker Bell" (get it?). Its waterfront veranda is a good viewpoint for IllumiNations, and the kids like the churros—crispy, cinnamon-coated Mexican sweets. I highly recommend the generously sized margaritas. Ricky says that the watermelon juice, which you can buy by the cup, is the best he's ever had.

BUYS Deep in the interior of the pavilion is the **Plaza de los Amigos,** a faux Mexican street market where you can walk among carts filled with castanets, handmade Mexican dolls, pottery, jewelry, ponchos, straw hats, leather goods, even tequila. At **Artesanias Mexicanas,** Mexican glass blowers make tiny animals and characters in glass as well as big, ornate, overpriced, overblown doojamahickees that are definitely not for kids. You can also buy pottery, candles, and other less easily destructible crafts.

STREETMOSPHERE Mariachi Cobre, a 10-piece horns and string ensemble, serenades guests on the veranda and in the pavilion with the kind of music most of us best remember from old gunslinger and bandito movies. **Huitzilin,** a native American drum and wind group, involves guests in stories, dances, and songs.

Worth-It Rating ★★★★

ITALY

An ornate fountain and a tall brick tower dominate the classic plaza, a reproduction of St. Mark's Square. Faithful re-creations of Venetian bridges lead to gondolas that are permanently moored on the lagoon.

BITES If you've never had fettuccine Alfredo perfectly prepared, you should try it at the elegant **L'Originale Alfredo di Roma Ristorante,** a branch of the restaurant that invented it. Strolling musicians serenade under the spectacular chandeliers, and the fresh pasta is made right before your very mouth. Not a pizza in sight! Reservations a must.

BUYS Il Bel Cristallo sells Venetian glass, jewelry, leather, and Capodimonte ceramics—those large, shiny ceramic objects covered with pink flowers and angels made famous by the Home Shopping Network. **La Cucina** stocks Italian edibles, wines, and cooking implements. **Delizie Italiane** sells Italian sweets. Pinocchio anyone? His shop is here, too.

STREETMOSPHERE In the piazza look for **I Cantanapoli,** a street quartet from Naples, playing all your Neapolitan favorites.

Worth-It Rating ★★★★

GERMANY

A statue of St. George slays a statue of a dragon in the main square, surrounded by the gingerbread rooftops.

BITES The raucous **Biergarten** has an all-you-can-eat buffet—look for me! The wurst is the best! Roast chicken, dumplings, kraut, and potato salad round out the spread. Imported beers in quart steins that look like pitchers are served to revelers at long, wooden tables. And there's nonstop live oompah music, plus yodeling, a glockenspiel, giant alpine horns, and a serenading saw. **Sommerfest** serves German fast food. Try a brat with kraut, mein frau!

BUYS German shops ring the courtyard. Look for German sweets, beer steins, cuckoo clocks, hand-carved wooden nutcrackers, and other Christmas items. A nutcracker nut from an early age, Ricky certifies the selection as the best he's seen (I certify that it's not the cheapest). Check out **Der Bücherwurm** and its beautiful hand-painted eggs; the stuffed stuff and dolls at **Der Teddybär;** and the fine German crystal at **Kunstarbeit in Kristall.**

STREETMOSPHERE The **Alpine Trio**—guitarist, tuba player, accordionist—appear frequently in the square.

Worth-It Rating ★★★ Add 1 if you want to eat a lot.

CHINA

A garden-ringed Temple of Heaven dominates this pavilion. There's a fine display of ancient imperial art, largely from the collection of Beijing's Palace Museum and San Francisco's Avery Brundage Collection.

THE WONDERS OF CHINA This CircleVision 360 movie skips the sweat shops. But it's Chinese torture to endure this 20-minute show with no seating—everyone stands, with only rails to lean on. I understand the concept—it's easier to spin around while standing. I just don't like it. But if you don't mind, you may enjoy this lavish production with its wide view of the varied cultures and breathtaking geography of this enormous country.

BITES The beautifully appointed **Nine Dragons** serves regional dishes from all over China. **Lotus Blossom Café** is the place to pick up a quick egg roll, stir-fried beef, or wonton soup. Prices are reasonable, and the food is very good.

BUYS **Yong Feng Shangdian** is China's own Macy's. Much of what you see is predictable—lots of silk and knickknacks. Other offerings are surprising, including the Chinese furniture and several pieces only Michael Eisner could afford.

STREETMOSPHERE In the courtyard, both the **Pu Yang Acrobats** and the **Flying Dragon Variety Troupe** perform feats of balance and agility. **China Si Zhu** is the warmup for *Wonders of China*: A performer tells stories of Chinese history while playing the flute, zither, or dulcimer.

Worth-It Rating ★★★★ Subtract 2 if you care about human rights.

WORLD SHOWCASE

ILLUMINATIONS

Mark Fisher, designer for Rolling Stones, Tina Turner, and Pink Floyd shows, has made this night show faster and hipper, with more lights, music, and fireworks than ever before. The pyrotechnics are amazing, even by Disney standards. It definitely wows the crowds. Unfortunately, the presentation can't overcome the venue's limitations. No matter where I am, I always feel I'm missing most of the show. When you can see it, what you see is fireworks up high and down low on barges on the water and laser lights dancing on Spaceship Earth, turning it into a giant globe, playing on other Epcot buildings, and lighting up the lagoon, all to the accompaniment of a rousing sound track. I can't even imagine how great it would be if I *could* see everything.

chapter 8
DISNEY–MGM STUDIOS THEME PARK
Walt Disney World

Take I–4 to Exit 26B, marked for Route 536 and Epcot.

It's very nice, but not quite Universal.

D isney has done an excellent job of reinventing the movie park, a genre invented by Universal Studios. Although both movie parks try to capture the spirit of the studios of Hollywood's Golden Age, the 1930s and 1940s, Disney–MGM is not so much a replica of an old-time Hollywood studio as a caricature of one—specifically, the one Disney created so successfully for the film *Who Framed Roger Rabbit*.

The park is wonderfully detailed. As you enter, you'll pass a filling station surrounded by vintage cars, oil cans, gas pumps, and spare parts dating from the 1940s. Across the plaza is an old-looking Hollywood-style bungalow, complete with front porch, presided over by a costumed character known affectionately as Sid Cahuenga. A rotating Mickey stands astride an Art Deco globe designating Disney–MGM's Crossroads of the World; beneath the marvelous mouse's marker, the streetscape features rows of reproductions of famous Hollywood facades.

What does Disney have to do with MGM? Almost nothing: There's never been a Disney–MGM film. But at the time that corporate raider Kirk Kerkorian was disassembling the old MGM in the 1980s, scattering its parts to the winds, Disney was in need of some extra concept material for its movie park, and the rest is history.

Comparisons are inevitable when you write about two movie parks in the same book. Many of the rides and shows at Disney–MGM are similar to those at Universal Studios Florida, but toned down, with the result that Disney–MGM comes across as Universal-Lite. Catastrophe Canyon on the Backstage Studio Tour at Disney–MGM, and Universal's Earthquake: The Big One, are almost identical. But the explosion and flood at Catastrophe Canyon, which take place outdoors in a good-sized area, are not nearly as terrifying as those at Universal, which take place indoors. Disney–MGM's Star Tours and Universal's Back to the Future are both simulator rides. But the Back to the Future screen, 90 feet tall, is bigger than a drive-in theater's; the Star Tours screen seems smaller than the one at your local mall's multiplex.

The strengths of the Disney park are its cartoon and children's attractions. Those themed around the late Jim Henson's incredibly popular Muppets and the movie *Honey, I Shrunk the Kids* make the park a must-see for families. Disney's animated films—*Aladdin, Pocahontas, The Lion King, Toy Story, Hunchback of Notre Dame,* and now, *Hercules*—are all brought to life with wonderful stage shows, seen in Orlando only at this park. These shows are among the best in any theme park, with production values that are Broadway class or better. Another highlight is the streetmosphere, strolling character actors pretending to be silent film stars,

DISNEY–MGM STUDIOS THEME PARK

starlets, agents, and other vintage Hollywood types; interacting with guests, they add immeasurably to the sense of place.

TIMING You can't quite do it all in a day, but it's going to be fun to try! Choose carefully.

EATERTAINMENT Eating out here makes for some terrific themed experiences. Though you can sometimes just drop in, you should really make reservations way in advance (tel. 407/939–3463 or 407/WDW–DINE).

SHOPPERTOONITIES If you remember my rule to shop in the parks only for what's unavailable elsewhere, you'll look for movie memorabilia, from autographs to animation cells. Prices range from "Wow, what a deal!" to "If you really want it honey, I guess we could sell the house."

PARADES AND FIREWORKS The Studios' parade is always a celebration of the latest major animated flick, and brings its characters to life—big, bright and bold, right in the middle of the street. **Sorcery in the Sky,** the wonderful fireworks show, is based on the Sorcerer's Apprentice sequence from Uncle Walt's *Fantasia*. It climaxes with a giant inflated Mickey in his sorcerer's hat, towering over the park like the world's biggest conehead!

TV SHOW TAPINGS The **Production Information Window,** at the main entrance, dispenses information and tickets for shows that require an audience. But it's best to call ahead and schedule your time accordingly. (*See* my advice on attending tapings in Chapter 3.)

DISNEY–MGM STUDIOS THEME PARK

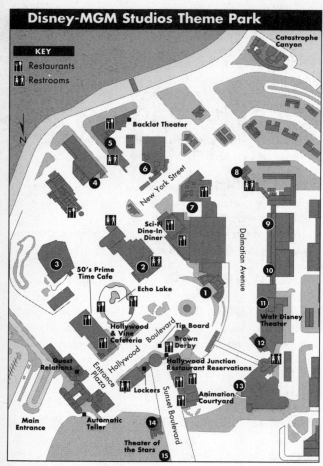

American Film Institute Showcase, **8**

Backstage Pass to "101 Dalmatians," **10**

Backstage Studio Tour, **9**

Beauty and the Beast Stage Show, **14**

Great Movie Ride, **1**

Honey, I Shrunk the Kids Movie Set Adventure, **7**

Indiana Jones Epic Stunt Spectacular, **3**

Jim Henson's Muppet*Vision 4D, **6**

Magic of Disney Animation, **13**

Star Tours, **4**

Studio Arcade, **5**

Superstar Television, **2**

The Making of...., **11**

Twilight Zone Tower of Terror, **15**

Voyage of the Little Mermaid, **12**

134

THE LAY OF THE LAND As you enter, you walk straight down Hollywood Boulevard. Sunset Boulevard is off to your right, Echo Lake to your left. Ahead, New York Street is roughly on the left, Mickey Avenue slightly to the right.

THE FAST TRACK My advice is to do all the attractions that involve walking first. The Magic of Animation, the Backstage Studio Tour, and the *Honey, I Shrunk the Kids* adventure playground are much more enjoyable without sore feet. Plus, most people run for the rides right off the bat, so they're less crowded later in the day.

HOLLYWOOD BOULEVARD AND ECHO LAKE

A replica of Grauman's Chinese Theater, the scene of most of the major Hollywood premieres in those days, is straight ahead, dominating the park's skyline. On your left as you face the theater is a small lake, around which the park has re-created Hollywood's Echo Park, famous as a location for movie shoots.

THE GREAT MOVIE RIDE The lobby of this Disney version of Hollywood's most famous landmark is full of memorabilia—most notably Dorothy's original ruby-red slippers. Inside, a tram takes you through scenes from the *Wizard of Oz, Mary Poppins,* and other great films, featuring perfectly detailed Audio-Animatronics replicas of screen idols such as John Wayne, Jimmy Cagney, and Edward G. Robinson. I won't spoil it for you except to say that it really *is* a great movie ride. *The Fast Track* The line here varies more than most others, by turns nonexistent and very, very long. My advice: Never

wait. If it looks like you'll have to, walk away and come back later.
Worth-It Rating ★★★★★

INDIANA JONES STUNT SPECTACULAR I was picked! Many volunteer, but few are chosen, and I was actually chosen to go down on the tarmac and play a bad guy in the redo of the exploding airplane scene in *Raiders of the Lost Ark*. I didn't do much, but what a view! This tightly choreographed demonstration of stunt magic and acrobatics includes the race with the giant boulder from the same movie. The wait is long and boring. Be patient.
Worth-It Rating ★★★★★

SUPERSTAR TELEVISION This one is similar to Universal's Hercules and Xena. But here, instead of a single experience, there are three separate attractions, one just for kids. Superstar Television demonstrates visual effects with clips from TV series such as *I Love Lucy, Cheers, Home Improvement,* the *Tonight Show with Johnny Carson,* and the *Late Show with David Letterman.* To show how the audio is created, **ABC Sound Studio** gets seven guests to try their hands at overdubbing movies. The results are a lot like badly dubbed foreign films, and they're always comical. Arrive early for both attractions, because before each show a producer chooses the most enthusiastic spectators as participants. The new hands-on **SoundWorks** section allows kids to add those wacky sound effects to cartoons, an idea similar to the interactive area at The Funtastic World of Hanna Barbera at Universal Studios.
Worth-It Rating ★★★★ Add 1 if you really know nothing about TV. Deduct 1 if you've been inside a studio before.

DISNEY–MGM STUDIOS THEME PARK

STAR TOURS Okay, I keep saying it's a lot smaller than Universal's Back to the Future. But it's still a great ride. And it's not as rough. As the story goes, your shuttle to the moon of Endor is piloted by a rookie robot of monumental ineptitude—and that's where the thrills begin. The waiting area is part of the experience; it's pure *Star Wars,* a high-tech workshop littered with space junk and assorted 'droid parts from a long time ago in a galaxy far, far away. Plus, it's air-conditioned. Have your camera ready as you leave, because Chewbacca often hangs out in the exit area.

The Fast Track Be on the lookout for a second line. When you first enter, you'll see a robot and spacecraft repair area with a steep ramp. Apparently, it's not obvious to everyone that there are usually two lines.

Worth-It Rating ★★★★★

BITES Every showbiz eatery worth its salt has caricatures on the walls, and why should the **Brown Derby** be an exception? The setting is stylish and faintly deco, and the presentations are impressive; the menu is straightforward American steaks, seafood, and pastas. Book ahead or come early. **Starring Rolls,** near the Brown Derby, invites you to ignore your diet. The **Prime Time Cafe** makes you wonder: Is it dinner time or show time? A woman claiming to be your mother brings you meat loaf and insists that you eat your veggies, as tableside TVs play clips in beautiful black and white. My wife, Terrie, had a huge peanut butter and jelly sandwich. The gleaming stainless steel and Formica around us took us back to that modern age, the 1950s. I have been seated unannounced, but it's best to come with reservations. **Hollywood & Vine Cafeteria,** next door, is your typical 1950s cafeteria—convenient and reasonably priced. Ricky, my son, loves the ribs. It's a big place, so lines are usually manageable. At the **ABC Commis-**

HOLLYWOOD BOULEVARD AND ECHO LAKE

sary, between the Great Movie Ride and the Sci-Fi Dine-In (*see* below), the food is nowhere near as bad as it is at the feeding troughs for which it is named. Look for burgers, fries, and chicken sandwiches.

On the shore of Echo Lake, you'll find **Dinosaur Gertie's Ice Creams of Extinction**, cleverly shaped like a dinosaur whose nose appears to smoke—courtesy of the cold air in the freezer. **Min & Bill's Dockside Diner** is another giant prop you just can't miss, an old gray junk freighter where you'll find snacks like yogurt, frozen fruit, and juices.

Backlot Express is another fast foodery. Or how about dinner in a '57 Chevy convertible served by a car-hop at the drive-in theater? The venue is the **Sci-Fi Dine-In Theater**, where tables are set up inside fake cars. Terrie goes for burgers, fries, and a shake. I love the wonderful seafood-topped pasta. **Pizza Planet** was a place Ricky anticipated the minute he saw it in *Toy Story*. It's a pizza place and an arcade, just like in the movie but it's tiny and underwhelming. As important as it is to the story and as big a hit as the movie was, this should be better.

BUYS Disney never misses a chance to put merchandise in your face. **Movieland Merchandise** and **Crossroads of the World** sell movie-theme souvenirs—and lots of candy in film cans. Look to the left as you enter the park, and you'll see **Sid Cahuenga's One-of-a-Kind**, a virtual Hollywood museum. You might even see Sid, dressed in his safari outfit, rocking on the porch of his shop. My daughter Tiffany's favorite movie, *Peter Pan,* was well represented by original posters here, some in foreign languages, that were surprisingly reasonably priced. The selection constantly changes—be on the lookout for private letters, autographed pictures, and personal keepsakes from some of the biggest stars of all time.

DISNEY–MGM STUDIOS THEME PARK

Many of these items cost more than your entire vacation. Some cost more than my net worth. And others you can take home for a song (well, almost). Just to your right as you enter the park is **Oscar's Classic Car Souvenirs & Super Service,** the reproduction gas station. It's stocked with trinkets and toy-size classics like the famous '57 Chevys and Ford's great T-Bird. **Darkroom,** nearby, handles photo supplies, rentals, and emergencies.

Heading down the Boulevard, you pass **Mickey's of Hollywood, Pluto's Toy Palace, Disney & Co,** and **LA Cinema Storage,** which sell Disney and Disney–MGM logo merchandise—and it ain't just T-shirts and mouse ears anymore. At **Cover Story,** you can have your picture put on the cover of a fictitious magazine. **Celebrity 5 & 10,** a takeoff on a vintage Woolworth store, fascinated my children as an example of how it was way back when Dad was a kid. **Keystone Clothiers** is stuffed with Beverly Hills-style outfits (with prices to match), all to give you that vintage Tinseltown look. **Lakeside News** stocks magazines—including many showbiz titles.

Returning from Endor, you pass through **Endor Vendors,** which is loaded with *Star Wars* souvenirs and space toys. We found Ricky's light saber with sound effects here, and my own Darth Vader mask. Ricky loves the **Indiana Jones Adventure Outpost** stand, which offers rubber snakes, many variations on Indy's trademark hat, and more.

NEW YORK STREET

A technique called "forced perspective" lets filmmakers fake big-city skylines right on the lot. New York Street, used in *Dick Tracy,* is the perfect example.

JIM HENSON'S MUPPET VISION 4D This is a great show! Spectacularly silly, it's complete with exploding walls, rain from the ceiling, pies in the face, and other slapstick. You'll see all the Muppets you know and love along with a weird flying character created especially for this show.
The Fast Track If you sit too close up, you'll miss the best laughs (look for the two old guys in the box seats!).
Worth-It Rating ★★★★★

STUDIO ARCADE Here you'll find whatever's the latest in video games and other diversions—but prepare to part with a bag of quarters. My personal opinion is that arcades take too much of your money too quickly.
Worth-It Rating ★★

HONEY, I SHRUNK THE KIDS MOVIE SET ADVENTURE This free-form playground is a great place to cool off on a hot day. You climb and slide on giant grass and trash, just like in the movie but with water squirting everywhere.
Worth-It Rating ★★★★ Add 1 if the line is short, as it often is.

BITES Mama Melrose's Ristorante Italiano fits the New York theme perfectly, with designer pizzas baked in a brick oven, pasta, steak, and seafood. You need reservations.

MICKEY AVENUE AND THE ANIMATION COURTYARD

Here are Disney's working soundstages, where shows and/or films may be in progress.

BACKSTAGE PASS TO "101 DALMATIANS" On the site of what used to be the Inside the Magic special effects tour, you can explore the props and special effects used in the live-action release about the famous spotted puppies and the sinister she-devil (Cruella DeVil—get it?) who wanted to turn them into a fur coat. Did you know that not all the pooches were real? Here you'll see a mechanical dalmatian puppet that was used in the film, along with the facade of the mansion that the memorable Glenn Close character called home.
Worth-It Rating ★★★★

VOYAGE OF THE LITTLE MERMAID Ariel and Sebastian lead an all-starfish cast in this live adaptation of the Disney cartoon feature. Glowing, floaty, black-lit characters, a cool mist emanating from the ceiling, and a gee-whiz bubble machine make you feel truly sub-marine. Remember back in 1992 when a 21-year-old college student named Leanza Cornett, playing the heroine at the time, went from Ariel's throne to win the Miss America pageant? The stars are still that good.
Worth-It Rating ★★★★★

BACKSTAGE STUDIO TOUR Ironically, this is more like the original Universal Studios Hollywood tour than anything at Universal Studios Florida. It's part self-guided walking tour, part tram ride through production, wardrobe, props areas, a soundstage, and an exhibit area or two. You cruise a residential street lined with the homes of Beaver, the Golden Girls, the Empty Nest gang, and more—but there are no buildings behind the facades. The Catastrophe Canyon section features an exploding gas truck and a flood similar to the one at Universal's Earthquake: The Big One but not nearly as scary. However, it's a more impressive production with an in-depth

MICKEY AVENUE AND THE ANIMATION COURTYARD

explanation of the earthquake/explosion/flood effect that Earthquake lacks.
The Fast Track Lines are long. Do it early or late. The wait may be shorter, and the heat of the blast is really miserable in afternoon heat.
Worth-It Rating ★★★★★

THE MAGIC OF DISNEY ANIMATION You see artists working on future animated films on this self-guided multimedia tour of the artistic cornerstone of the empire. I was fascinated by the original multiplane camera, the Walt Disney invention that gives his early animation such unequaled realism. On display are original drawings and cells from Disney classics.
Worth-It Rating ★★★★★

THE AMERICAN FILM INSTITUTE SHOWCASE See actual costumes, props, and sets used in current hit movies. No lines.
Worth-It Rating ★★★

THE MAKING OF . . . The Walt Disney Theater screens short, usually fairly interesting films that cover the special effects and the actors in the most recent Disney hit (*Flubber* at this writing).
Worth-It Rating ★★★

BITES The **Soundstage** food court—decorated with props, giant movie lights, rigging, and other film artifacts—is the park's largest eatery, serving pizza and pasta, burgers, chicken, and salads. Character breakfasts and buffet lunches fill up fast, so book ahead. Above, you can sip (alcoholic) drinks high in the rigging at the **Catwalk Bar**. On a real movie set, such an activity would be high-risk. **Studio Catering**, across from the studio tour entrance, near the corner of Mickey Avenue and New York Street, has snacks.

BUYS Under the Sea, a souvenir stand just outside the Voyage of the Little Mermaid, is good for mermaid merchandise and movie memorabilia. Outside the Backstage Studio Tour and behind Catastrophe Canyon, you'll hear the roar of the explosions as you shop at **Studio Showcase,** surrounded by a variety of movie-theme gift items.

SUNSET BOULEVARD

TWILIGHT ZONE TOWER OF TERROR At around $95 million, this is the world's most expensive ride. It's actually two rides, back to back. A Rod Serling double tells the attraction's story, supposedly that of an episode that never aired, about a 1930s elevator crash caused by a lightning storm that shut down the magnificent Hollywood Hotel. Fascinating detail abounds, from the hotel's crumbling vine-covered facade to the dusty, moldy queue area inside, littered with the TV show's most memorable props. After you board an elevator in the mansion's spooky sub-cellar, a 13-story ride up with a quick outdoor view of the park is followed by a free-fall that includes a few seconds of actual weightlessness. Then, suddenly, you repeat the elevator ride and its sequel. The long wait is definitely part of the experience.
Worth-It Rating ★★★★★

BEAUTY AND THE BEAST STAGE SHOW This amazing production was so well done that it was successfully adapted for Broadway, where it is still playing to capacity.
Worth-It Rating ★★★★★

BITES **Sunset Ranch Market** is a nifty bit of Disneyana, a re-creation of a place that Walt frequented in Anaheim around the time he bought the Disneyland property. You eat outdoors on picnic tables; the fare is light, with lots of citrus. **Rosie (the Riveter's) Red Hot Dogs** is on the same theme. Legend has it that Walt used to stop at the original for a hot dog when he visited Anaheim. You can, too—for chili dogs and chili by the bowl.

BUYS The **Anaheim Produce Company** recalls the orange grove that became Disneyland. You'll find citrus to purchase. In the middle of Sunset Boulevard, **Once Upon a Time** sells character merchandise from the vintage classics. Near Hollywood Boulevard, **Legends of Hollywood** stocks books, posters, and videos of and about famous films. **Golden Age Souvenirs**, outside Superstar Television, sells goodies that recall the early days of TV. I got my Howdy Doody key chain here. (Remember, at Disney, you're traveling through another dimension—a dimension not only of sight and sound but also of stuff.) At **Tower Hotel Gifts**, pick up a Serling for the den.

chapter 9
DISNEY'S ANIMAL KINGDOM

Take Exit 25B off I-4.

Because the park is not yet complete at this writing, it is not yet rated. Given Disney's creative talent, you can expect this to be a five-star event.

During 1997, a tree grew like crazy on 500 acres of the southwestern edge of Walt Disney World near Blizzard Beach and the All-Star Resorts. Already over 14 stories high, the Tree of Life is the centerpiece of Disney's largest and most ambitious theme park yet, Disney's Animal Kingdom.

From Walt's *True Life Adventure* series to animated films featuring critters like Mickey Mouse, the Disney organization was built around our furry, feathered, finned, and fossilized friends. Disney's new Animal Kingdom, which is some five times the size of its Magic predecessor, was inspired by mankind's love for animals, or more specifically, the late Uncle Walt's love for critters. Devoted to creatures real, imaginary, and extinct, it will be the world's largest zoo, and is slated to be home to more than a thousand live animals along with Audio-Animatronics robots and classic Disney characters. Several live-animal experiences here put you face-to-face with animals who are restrained by barriers that are either invisible or cleverly disguised, so that you experience the feeling of a journey into the wild.

Like all theme parks, this one is a collection of several lands on the animal theme. At this writing, it appears that rather than wandering among the lands at will, as you do in most other theme parks, you visit Disney's Animal Kingdom more like you do a safari park—that is, you travel (by boat, on foot, and by four-wheel-drive vehicle) along a pre-delineated path. Hours of operation will be more like a safari park's as well—from dawn until dark. The enormous Rainforest Café at the entrance will begin serving breakfast at 6 AM.

WHAT TO SEE

THE OASIS You'll enter through a tropical garden with bright flowers, cool waterfalls, grottoes, and glades, where colorful creatures are abundant. Ducking under a thundering waterfall, you'll pass through a misty cloud to get to the **Rainforest Café**, an Audio-Animatronics dining adventure that is a twin of the amazing, like-named restaurant in Downtown Disney (*see* Chapter 10).

SAFARI VILLAGE Crossing a wooden bridge that spans the Discovery River will bring you to this central crossroads of Animal Kingdom. It's in the center of the Discovery River, and it's the starting point of all journeys through the Animal Kingdom. Dominating the village is the towering **Tree of Life**, nearly 200 feet above the ground and 50 feet around, with hundreds of hand-carved animals growing from its trunk. Inside it is a spectacular multimedia 3D theater that screens *Bugs,* a look at life from a bugs-eye view, based on the new film from America's foremost computer genius, Steve Jobs, and Pixar, the people who brought you *Toy Story.* Nearby, you can begin a **Discovery Cruise** up the Discovery River, past the dreaded Dragon Rocks, with views of steaming geysers, prehistoric beasts, and amazing fantasy creatures en route.

DINOLAND U.S.A. The new axiom among theme park designers seems to be "You can't go wrong with dinosaurs." I envision this part of Disney's Animal Kingdom as Gatorland with dinosaurs (*see* Chapter 15). Dinoland's **Boneyard** is a paleontological dig site-cum-playground where kids will search for buried "fossils," slide down the bones of T-Rex, and play with a triceratops and a 50-foot-tall brachiosaurus. **Countdown to Extinction,** a multimedia simulator adventure, will use Audio-Animatronics and cars on tracks to complete the effect of total chaos. You'll journey 65 million years into the past to a smoky, primeval world where you'll barely escape a close encounter with dinosaurs, just before a comet collides with the earth, wiping out all of the dinosaurs forever. Along the considerably calmer **Cretaceous Trail,** a nature walk, you'll be reminded that many of today's plants and some animals have been with us a long time: Cycads, palms, ferns, and a few reptiles and amphibians have all survived from the age of the dinosaur. The **Theater in the Wild** will be the site of live stage shows based on animal themes, hosted by none other than the Lion King. Mickey and Minnie will preside over a character greeting area here, similar to Mickey's Starland.

AFRICA At the town of Harambe, on the edge of the African savannah, herds of zebras, giraffes, lions, and elephants, including several endangered African species, will roam a land-

WHAT TO SEE

scape of rich forests, tropical rivers, and wide open plains. **Kilimanjaro Safari** will be set in the African wilderness during monsoon season. When your safari encounters a band of nasty poachers in the midst of evil doings, you'll cut to the chase over washed-out roads and through landslides and flash floods before finally crossing a crocodile-infested river by way of a collapsing bridge. **Gorilla Falls Exploration Trail**, another nature walk, will take you through the habitat of the lowland gorilla, with underwater windows in their tank-cum-lagoon to give you a unique view of bathing hippos. The trail will also steer you into a walk-through aviary filled with exotic birds. Your Disney's Animal Kingdom safari ends aboard the **Wildlife Express** across the African savannah to the **Conservation Station,** the Animal Kingdom infirmary, where you'll meet trainers and experts in an interactive and educational experience that focuses on the battle against extinction.

chapter 10
DOWNTOWN DISNEY

From I–4, take Exit 26, marked for Route 536. Head on Epcot Center Drive to Buena Vista Drive, then turn right. Although you'll drive a longer distance than if you come via Exit 27, marked for Route 535, but you'll actually spend less time, because there's so much more traffic on 535.

You can't do everything here in Orlando, but if Downtown Disney is one of your choices, you won't regret it!

Downtown Disney, now a destination attraction in its own right, is the complex made up of the Disney attractions in the Lake Buena Vista area between Routes 535 and 536. These include longtime favorites Disney Village Marketplace and Pleasure Island as well as the former Hotel Plaza, plus an all-new and totally spectacular addition to Disney's nightlife and shopping scene—the West End.

There must be a bunch of reasons for so many people to come here, and there are! From fine dining to fast food, from fine art to knickknacks, there's something for everyone, every age and every taste.

TIMING Come during the day for lunch and some leisurely shopping, or come at sundown to party until 2 AM.

THE LAY OF THE LAND Downtown Disney runs parallel to I-4 between Route 535 on the north and Route 536 on the south. If you enter as I suggest, from the south via Route 536, you'll take Exit 26B, marked for Epcot, off I-4, then turn north on Buena Vista Drive. The first left turnoff you come to is for Disney's West Side; then, also on your left, are turns for Pleasure Island and finally the Marketplace, near Route 535.

THE FAST TRACK This enormous complex is currently suffering from too much success. Traffic is terrible! On the last several trips, I have allowed myself an extra half hour for traffic, parking, and walking from a distant parking spot, and it has never been enough! My favorite end-run, at this writing, is outlined above. I avoid much chaos this way. As you'll soon see for yourself, the Disney traffic planners have their own ideas about how you should get around and have set up the signs to direct you to Route 535, which feeds you right into a snarl that includes the entrance to Hotel Plaza. Still, even though their signs don't always tell you that Route 536 takes you to Downtown Disney, they have done a good job marking the road itself.

Once inside, crowds flow counterclockwise, so once again, my advice is to go against the flow.

Here are some other tips:

- Though many places don't require reservations, "priority seating" is often available. (This is something like a reservation—the restaurant won't have a table waiting, but your name will go to the top of the list when you arrive.) Go for priority seating wherever you can. You'll be competing with thousands of others for each pricey experience, so take any advantage you can get.

- Come early—traffic peaks in the complex at around 8 PM, so the earlier you arrive the better your chance to get ahead of the mob.
- Don't count on valet parking. Depending on where you're going, you may be able to park closer by looking for a regular spot. And on my last trip, lines of cars waiting for attendants were backed up worse than the traffic to get into the lots.
- If you're coming from elsewhere on Disney property, you may want to leave your car and use complimentary Disney transportation—it's faster and easier, and gets you closer. And you'll appreciate a bus or boat even more when you're leaving.
- WDW hotel guests should remember that they can have purchases made in the shops delivered directly to their rooms—see, you *can* go clubbing and shopping in a single night.
- For more information, call Guest Relations for Downtown Disney at 407/828-3058.

The West Side

This complex of clubs, concert halls, and restaurants with a scattering of shops is the biggest and best part of Downtown Disney. Although the pay-as-you-go policy can make the experience pricey, everything you find is brand-spanking-new and state-of-the-art, and should be high enough in quality to justify your outlay (although many of these attractions were not sufficiently complete at the time of this writing for me to rate them).

CIRQUE DU SOLEIL Montreal's Circus of the Sun gives two shows a day in the 1,600-seat state-of-the-art theater and concert hall inside a brightly colored and extravagantly illuminated circus tent. The circus acts are amazing, the costumes spectacular, the music sparkling, and the choreography no less than dazzling. A must-see.

Too new to rate.

HOUSE OF BLUES This theme restaurant from Dan Aykroyd, Jim Belushi, and pals may be the biggest and best of all the theme restaurants owned by celebrities—and there are several around town. Its multilevel concert hall regularly hosts the big names in blues, soul, and rock. The food served there and in an adjacent restaurant is Cajun-style with plenty of barbecue and carbohydrates, and overly generous desserts. Jambalaya, étouffée, gumbo, and bread pudding are the specialties. Walls are covered from floor to ceiling with American folk art. On Sunday, the main event is the all-you-can-eat gospel brunch, an experience unduplicated in our area that is definitely a Worth-It. Advance tickets are usually required along with a specific seating time.

Worth-It Rating ★★★★★

DISNEYQUEST This high-tech 100,000-square-foot pay-for-play fun center is the prototype for a series of mini-Disney Worlds coming soon to a city near you. Entering its Ventureport, the gateway to the complex, brings you to four virtual worlds. The Explore Zone takes you riding raging rapids, visiting ancient lands, and speeding through outer space. The Score Zone pits you against superheroes in battles of skill and daring. The Create Zone is your own private Imagineering studio, where you can create art and concoct special effects. And in the Replay Zone, billed as a "Carnival on the Moon,"

classic games meet outer space in a wacky send-up of the old-time midway. Because you pay for each activity, DisneyQuest may be a relatively expensive way to spend two or three hours.
Too new to rate.

VIRGIN MEGASTORE In its three stories, the ultimate multimedia superstore from tycoon Richard Branson houses over 200,000 titles of music, video, and printed products, 300 listening booths, 20 movie preview stations, an indoor-outdoor café, a video wall, a satellite-uplinked TV studio, and, above the entrance, an elevated stage that regularly hosts some of the biggest names in entertainment and where we recently saw our favorite band, Sister Hazel.
Worth-It Rating ★★★★★

WOLFGANG PUCK CAFE Okay, Orlando is full of restaurants owned by stars, but where do the stars eat? In Hollywood, one of their favorites is Spago, owned by restaurateur Wolfgang Puck. Here, Puck is producing fast food at surprisingly reasonable prices—creative pizzas, grilled fish and vegetable spring rolls. Plus, there's a sushi bar and, upstairs, a really good fancy restaurant with ambitious cuisine. Priority seating is available and is a good idea for dinner; call 407/939–3463.
Worth-It Rating ★★★★ +

GUITAR GALLERY BY GEORGE'S MUSIC A local music store, George's Music takes its place on the world stage in this double-decker showcase of music accessories, books, clothing, and learn-an-instrument packages. Many of the collectible guitars on display are replicas of instruments that have been owned and played by the world's most famous practitioners. Although they range in price from a few dollars to tens of thousands, it costs you nothing to gawk at the daz-

THE WEST SIDE

zling stainless steel surroundings, spectacular neon, and the startling props (like the 30-foot-high guitar strummed by an animated hand).
Worth-It Rating ★★★★★

BONGOS CUBAN CAFE When you count restaurant-owning stars, don't overlook Gloria Estefan and her producer husband, Emilio. Inside the sky-high pineapple dominating the Downtown Disney skyline, they preside over a set that invokes the famous Copacabana. You almost expect to see Desi Arnaz and Xaviar Cugat as you sway to the Latin music they loved on a 16,000-square-foot dance floor. The cuisine is every bit as Latin as the live nightly entertainment, and the Cuban coffee as strong as nearby NASA's shuttle fuel. Unfortunately, the food is below average, the portions small, and the prices high. Priority seating is available (tel. 407/939–3463).
Worth-It Rating ★★★★

AMC 24 THEATER COMPLEX Billed as the largest theater complex in the Southeast, this has 24 theaters and over 6,000 seats. There's Sony Digital Sound throughout; seating is plush and, in 18 theaters, it's terraced and arranged stadium style, with 6 feet of legroom and love seats for two. Two theaters are huge and balconied. It's a great place to catch a movie you'd want to see anyway.
Worth-It Rating ★★★★★

PLANET HOLLYWOOD Inside the globe that dominates the Downtown Disney scene, I ate Thai shrimp, and my son, Ricky, the rib expert, gave a thumbs-up to the generous portion of extra-tender St. Louis-style BBQ. Four jam-packed levels feature the world's largest and most amazing collection of Hollywood costumes, props, art, and memorabilia. The

multimedia show on several giant screens around the room is newsreel, movie trailer, home video, and corporate hype rolled into one spectacular bit of razzle-dazzle. The experience is overpoweringly intense. Come early and plan to wait, and wait, and wait.
Worth-It Rating ★★★★★

DISNEY'S CANDY CAULDRON Snow White's nemesis, the Wicked Witch, and her many costumed helpers, invite you to step into their delightfully dark, dank dungeon to take a bite of the candy apple. While you're there, try the fresh fudge, the cotton candy, or any of the other confections that are made right before your watering mouth.
Worth-It Rating ★★★

FORTY THIRST STREET Even when you just stop for coffee or juice in Downtown Disney, it's a total sensory experience. This coffee bar-gone-fantastic features a multiscreen laser light show with surround sound and fiber optics everywhere. Your coffee is made from freshly ground beans, roasted before your eyes.
Worth-It Rating ★★★

CELEBRITY EYEWORKS STUDIO Beneath your feet is a replica of Hollywood's Walk of Fame. Overhead, a video crew on a catwalk is shooting for an upcoming production. Check the monitor—you're the star! In Downtown Disney, the local frame shop is like that. The eyewear is trendy, from glasses to shades, and displayed amidst photos of celebs in glasses—Hollywood's greatest "spectacles!"
Worth-It Rating ★★★

DAVID COPPERFIELD'S MAGIC UNDERGROUND The celebrated magician, escape artist, and showman has assembled a giant collection of magic tricks and illusions, exotic gifts, and exclusive signature clothing for sale to both beginning magicians and expert practitioners of the art of hocus-pocus.

Too new to rate.

HOYPOLOI The waterfalls and decorative items here will all give you good feng shui (feng shui being a Chinese discipline that seeks to create an environment harmonious to both nature and the human spirit).
Worth-It Rating ★★★★

MAGNETRON A store created just for people who collect refrigerator magnets? Here is the world's largest and most extensive collection of "attractive" gifts, souvenirs, and other items that do more than just hang around.
Worth-It Rating ★★★★★

SOSA FAMILY CIGARS Although government is fighting tobacco in all its forms, cigar smoking is newly fashionable. My family remains opposed, so I will not rate this collection of cigars, humidors, and smoking accessories from a famous name in tobacco.

STARABILIAS If you have been dying to re-create that Cracker Barrel look in your very own den, make a beeline for this store, a jumble of old metal advertising signs and other collectibles ranging from autographs to nickel Coke machines. Everything is for sale, including the life-size Colonel Sanders I saw on my last visit, but it's fun just to browse.
Worth-It Rating ★★★★★

Pleasure Island

Pleasure Island is essentially a handful of nightclubs with a single, joint admission price and fairly uniform drink prices. Whether or not you enjoy any given club depends on your own tastes—so I've just given you one overall rating for the whole shebang. Is it worth your time and money? Admission is just under $20, and drinks start at around $3 for domestic beers, with specialty mixed drinks in the $10 and up range, about the same as at other nightlife attractions. You can save money by getting your evening's pass included in a Disney length-of-stay pass or by asking for discount tickets—sometimes available at Disney restaurants and hotels. Regardless, if a nightlife attraction is what you're looking for, this one is first-class.

Once you've bought the general admission ticket, you can come and go as you wish, entering and leaving any of the clubs at will.

Note that Portobello, Fulton's, and the AMC Theaters are open to the public, without the Pleasure Island cover charge.

Worth-It Rating ★★★★★

WEST END STAGE Every night at midnight, the folks at Pleasure Island remind you that tomorrow is the first day of the rest of your life with a New Year's celebration complete with fireworks. Major concert artists, from country, rock, and pop to R&B, jazz, and rap, also perform. Call 407/824-4321 for schedules.

THE BET SOUNDSTAGE Black Entertainment Network operates this club featuring R&B, soul, jazz, blues, rap, and hip-hop. Here, you won't forget that African-American entertainers like Chuck Berry and Little Richard also invented that thing called rock-and-roll.

COMEDY WAREHOUSE The place to catch stand-up and improv from house comics and the occasional national performer. The place is usually packed, and there are no reservations. So if this is your choice, start your evening here. Personally, the last time I was here, I did not feel that the comedy was worth the wait.

8TRAX Remember John Travolta as Tony Manero in *Saturday Night Fever?* You'll see lots of guys doing those steps over the same pulsating, translucent rainbow dance floor. A too-loud sound system completes the totally tacky effect.

MANNEQUINS DANCE PALACE The biggest draw on the island features contemporary music with a state-of-art sound and video setup, a live DJ, professional dancers, and a dazzling light show. The dance floor revolves, and the beautiful young people who generally fill the place are a show of their own.

ADVENTURERS CLUB I say, old chap, this place simply defies simple description. In one of its spooky rooms, primitive masks suddenly start to talk; in the salon, adventurers regale guests with tall tales. If you're like me, you'll enjoy the chance to jump in and play with the actors (one night I plan to dress up and pretend I'm one of them). If you're like my wife, Terrie, you'll sit back, sip your drink, and watch an old man make a fool of himself. A hoot!

ROCK & ROLL BEACH CLUB This three-story surf bar must have been designed by someone who went to the old Ocean Pier in Daytona to see the Beach Boys with me. When you climb the funky old stairs, you'll hear music that's just like you remember it, too—early-garage-band. The night isn't complete without a rousing sing-along to "Louie, Louie"! Anybody for "Wild Thing"?

PLEASURE ISLAND JAZZ COMPANY This place has all that jazz, from swing to fusion, from New Orleans to experimental improv, courtesy of name musicians and talented locals. The room is laid-back and comfortable, invoking the spirit of Thelonius Monk.

WILD HORSE SALOON Ricky won't miss the Fireworks Factory, the restaurant that occupied this space, where he burned his mouth so badly on Dad's hot sauce that he couldn't eat any dinner. Its replacement is from Chicago's Levy Restaurants and the Nashville Network (TNN). TNN is providing the country music talent, Levy the great barbecue. There's also a country-and-western store.

The Marketplace at Downtown Disney

Previously known as Disney Village Marketplace, Walt Disney World Shopping Village, and a a handful of other names, this is the oldest part of Downtown Disney, with a wide selection of shopping and dining.

FULTON'S CRAB HOUSE This replica of a paddle-wheel riverboat, the former *Empress Lilly,* is now an excellent seafood restaurant that serves some of the best crab cakes anywhere. There is also a daily character breakfast (tel. 407/WDW–DINE).

PORTOBELLO YACHT CLUB This sleek, stylish restaurant serves pasta, chicken, veal, and other northern Italian specialties we've always enjoyed. Reservations suggested (tel. 407/934–8888).

RAINFOREST CAFE As you enter from the West End, it's hard to miss the 65-foot active volcano that marks the entrance to this restaurant–store–attraction. Outside, you may encounter an animal trainer introducing his cockateel to visitors. Inside, you can wander more or less freely; it's a total-immersion experience, complete with robotic animals and special effects including a "thunderstorm" (every 20 minutes—actually only a refreshing mist). There's an eternal line for a table, where the patient chow down on traditional steaks as well as exotic dishes like blackened meat loaf, which is absolutely nothing like anything Mama used to make. Exotic drinks and desserts are both enormous and excellent.

THE ART OF DISNEY Disney animation art and collectibles have skyrocketed in value over the years. So it's not only excellent as decoration but may be a good investment as well.

2R'S READING & RITING A Disney book store featuring current best-sellers, children's books, reading accessories, and a few toys, along with the now-obligatory cappuccino bar.

TEAM MICKEY'S ATHLETIC CLUB Sports clothing and equipment with the Team Mickey and other college and pro-club logos, along with sports memorabilia of all kinds.

WOLFGANG PUCK CAFE Sharing the building with Team Mickey is the second of Puck's two Downtown Disney locations. (*See* above.)

RESORTWEAR UNLIMITED Lancôme beauty products, designer casual wear, and bathing attire for the country club crowd.

AUTHENTIC ALL-STAR GEAR The retail end of the All-Star Café, the celebrity sports–theme restaurant at Disney's Wide World of Sports, sells sports gear from boxer shorts to hockey pucks, plus tons of T-shirts.

CAP'N JACK'S OYSTER BAR The nautical setting and lagoon view are pleasant but, considering how casual it all is, prices may be a bit high, even for the excellent chowder, fine jumbo shrimp cocktail, and fabulously pink strawberry margaritas.

SUMMER SANDS Check out the straw hats and canvas bags, summery clothing and jewelry, and shades, not to mention the loads of wonderfully tacky Floridiana.

GOURMET PANTRY It's an eatery on one side, a retail store on the other, both packed with delectable delights: deli goodies, wines, kitchen gadgets, cookbooks, and culinary aids. A cornucopia of kitchen kitsch!

HARRINGTON BAY CLOTHIERS Aw, shucks, you left your favorite Ralph Lauren outfit at home! Tell Buffy not to worry! You can pick up a replacement here.

THE MARKETPLACE AT DOWNTOWN DISNEY

TOYS FANTASTIC When we saw this all-Mattel store, my daughter, Tiffany made a beeline for the Barbies—the selection was bountiful. (Not so of the boys' toys.)

DISNEY'S DAYS OF CHRISTMAS A year-round Christmas store with the Disney characters (what else?) on ornaments.

GHIRARDELLI SODA FOUNTAIN & CHOCOLATE SHOP You'll find chocolates, ice cream, and soda-fountain specialties at this branch of San Francisco's famous chocoholic fantasy. Bring your sweet tooth.

EUROSPAIN Crystal is cut and glass is blown before your eyes here. The results are for sale, along with other art in glass, ceramics, jewelry, and European collectibles. Although most items are fairly pricey, some are surprisingly reasonable.

DISCOVER Learning toys, books and accessories, scientific stuff, environmentally aware animal toys, and other imagination-sparking items for kids of all ages keep company with a large selection of Disney character items in the same vein. It's hard not to like a place like this.

WORLD OF DISNEY The world's largest Disney store is actually 12 huge boutiques filled with everything Disney. Stuffed animals? There are thousands, along with jewelry, books, videos, toys, clothing, even intimate apparel—Minnie's Secret, anyone? The selection is awesome.

LEGO IMAGINATION CENTER At this Lego superstore—one of only two in the entire world at this writing—the awesome Lego structures on display include an amazing interactive outdoor playground and a 30-foot LEGO sea serpent. The frequent demonstrations of Lego art are fascinating. For Lego fans, this is a must-see.

STUDIO M A photo-op with the world's most famous mouse, plus Mickey photos and frames.

MARKETPLACE ACTIVITIES

BOATIN' AND FISHIN' While shopaholics search out the perfect Mickey golf balls, the rest of us rent the little sporty two-person boats known as Water Sprites at **Cap'n Jack's Marina.** Although you can rent them on many Disney waters, this marina is the most convenient place to rent 'em if you're staying off-property. (Note: You must be 14 to drive.) The marina is also a departure point for guided fishing trips in search of Florida's famous largemouth bass. And you can rent cane poles for angling off the dock—you'll catch shiners and maybe a bass. All fishing is catch-and-release only. For information, call 407/828-2461.

FUN, FOUNTAINS, AND SAND Water jumping out of the sidewalk from these water features cools young and old alike on hot Florida days. You're in Disney—so have some fun, scream, and get wet! Nearby, right by the waterfront, is **Sand Street Station,** a giant sandbox and playground with a kids' train ride, a cute little diversion on a busy Disney day. Or just kick back at secluded **Sunset Cove,** with a beach chair and an ice-cold drink; it's also by the water.

MCDONALD'S McDonald's at Disney—it was inevitable. What, you didn't come all this way for a Big Mac? Near Lego and Studio M.

SHOWS For years we have come to the **Dock Stage** for the annual Christmas shows. There are also seasonal concerts and special shows of all kinds, some of them excellent. Check with Guest Services at 407/824–4321.

chapter 11

UNIVERSAL'S CITYWALK

To get there, follow the directions to Universal Studios Florida in Chapter 3. From the parking garage (the world's largest), a moving sidewalk transports you to CityWalk's central plaza, and everything all around you.

Since this facility is not yet complete, I haven't been able to rate CityWalk. But as at Downtown Disney, the merchants and participants here are world-renowned in their own right. So there is every reason to expect that this will be one of the premier dining and nightlife areas in the world.

This giant entertainment complex, which should look something like a modern baseball stadium except with buildings where the seating would be, is to be the hub of the new Universal Florida. It will be home to half a dozen high-profile theme clubs and restaurants, with their attached shops—each one a separate attraction in its own right, with a separate admission. A large waterway through CityWalk's center will be spanned by two bridges and traversed by boats and Venetian-style gondolas. The eastern shore of the waterway will be dominated by the gigantic new Hard Rock Live concert venue, a spectacular re-creation of Rome's Colosseum.

TIMING Everything is open daily. You can come by day for shopping, and have a meal in one of the clubs, or wait until dark for the nightlife and do your shopping between music stops. Count on spending four or five hours—but it will depend on what you plan to do.

THE FAST TRACK If you plan to go at night, find out what's on in advance and make your reservations as far in advance as possible.

THE LAY OF THE LAND Individual destinations here are arranged in a semicircle. Entries below are arranged in geographic order, starting on the left as you get off of the moving sidewalk and heading clockwise through the complex.

THE SCENE

NASCAR CAFE The scheme is to detail the racing theme here right down to the pit-crew uniforms of the wait staff, the seating in rows of gleaming race cars, and the eating utensils, which look like mechanic's tools. So in some ways, it should be similar to I-Drive's Race Rock, one of our family favorites. However, this place will be much larger, with two levels, and it will be NASCAR-sanctioned. A video wall will show clips, and you'll see memorabilia and rare NASCAR artifacts and collectibles at every turn. In the kids' arcade, all the games are on NASCAR themes. To eat? Heaps of barbecue, fried chicken, and good ol' American meat and potatoes. When races are in town at Disney's Walt Disney World Speedway, count on catching NASCAR legends when they stop in to grab a bite and sign autographs.

UNIVERSAL CITY CINEMA Want to catch a movie? Catch this cutting-edge showcase for the newest films from Universal and other studios with giant screens, high-fidelity surround sound, and stadium seating. The 16-screen, 5,000-seat complex will also house several eateries, cafés, and shops.

E! ENTERTAINMENT TELEVISION PRODUCTION CENTER Just as Nickelodeon broadcasts from Universal Studios Florida, the E! Entertainment Network originates its daily programming from this glass-fronted production center. You can watch tapings and live celebrity interviews, and offer your own opinions on *Who's Hot—and Who's Not!* on the show of that name—to millions of E! viewers every day.

MOTOWN CAFE The "Temptations" and the "Supremes"—two house groups faithfully commemorating the classic stars—take turns performing onstage at this club inspired by the music of the Detroit recording label that gave us those legendary acts as well as the Jackson Five, the Four Tops, and almost every other seminal R&B entertainer of the last 30 years. The menu offers soul food and such, including sweet-potato fries, meat loaf, and a range of large and gooey desserts. On display all around are photos, life-size statues, and memorabilia from some of Motown's most popular artists. The obligatory on-premises shop sells everything from souvenir T-shirts to gold records and collectible 45s from Motown's golden era, the 1960s.

BOB MARLEY In an authentic replica of reggae star Bob Marley's own Jamaican house and garden, you'll get the chance to soak up Jamaican culture along with Jamaica's food, spirits, and music. Marley's extended musical family, including his singer/songwriter son, Ziggy, are all involved in the operation and occasionally stop by to entertain. You can try Jamaica's national dish, curried goat, or go for more familiar entrées, along with island beers and rums.

PAT O'BRIEN'S The landmark New Orleans speakeasy, which calls itself the birthplace of dueling pianos as entertainment, is also the birthplace of the Hurricane—one of the world's most famous specialty drinks and the granddaddy of all specialty drinks. CityWalk's Pat O'Brien's has everything you find in the New Orleans original, right down to the fabled flaming fountain—a spectacle of fire and water.

JIMMY BUFFETT'S MARGARITAVILLE Most of the renowned Florida troubadour's best material concerns food and drink, so it's no wonder that he will now be inviting parrotheads (as his fans call themselves and the rest of us to have a "cheeseburger in paradise" or simply "waste away again in Margaritaville." Remember the line, "Smell of shrimp, they're beginning to boil?" You can expect plenty of such Key West specialties, including several dishes based on native conch, and Key lime pie colored the proper yellow (no, it's not supposed to be green!). Late nights at CityWalk's Margaritaville, you should be able to catch performances by the best of Florida's many guitar-strumming Buffett impersonators and even, on occasion, by the "Son of a Son of a Sailor" himself.

CITY JAZZ This promises to be a hotbed of jazz, with an acoustically perfect, state-of-the-art concert hall, designed for jazz, as its centerpiece. Flanking the hall on one side will be *Downbeat* magazine's Hall of Fame, where jazz legends, living and otherwise, will be inducted into immortality amidst the world's largest collection of jazz memorabilia, under the supervision of the definitive authorities, the editors of *Downbeat* magazine. Opposite the Hall of Fame you'll find the Thelonius Monk Institute of Jazz, where jazz greats are slated to train up-and-comers and guests are invited to listen.

EMERIL'S OF ORLANDO "BAM!" Here, fans of wacky TV Food Network chef Emeril Lagasse, soon to be a *Good Morning America* regular, will recognize that trademark exclamation and the high-energy hubbub in the open kitchen of the master chef's only venture outside New Orleans. Even if you don't know Lagasse from his show, you may want to sample what he calls his "kicky cuisine"—which features slightly crazed dishes like pistachio-orange-crusted scallops.

MARVEL MANIA Like the Marvel-theme island in Universal's upcoming Islands of Adventure, this new Marvel-theme fast-food restaurant is going to be more than another place to get burgers, fries, and such. It will also bring to life Spider-Man, X-Men, the Fantastic Four, and other members of the 4,000-strong cast of Marvel characters in a multimedia experience complete with light and sound effects and onstage action that will transport you straight into the Marvel Universe.

HARD ROCK CAFE As large as the famous giant guitar-shape building at Universal Studios was, it was still not big enough to house the enormous crowds drawn. So the HRC moves to an even larger home, appropriately modeled after Rome's Colosseum. Although no slaves or gladiators are on hand, as in the original, you will find no shortage of rock memorabilia, Save the Planet T-shirts, and other souvenirs, not to mention the trademark pig sandwich—the best pulled-barbecue anywhere.

THE SCENE

HARD ROCK LIVE Not to be outdone by House of Blues, Wild Horse Saloon, and other theme-joints-come-lately, the original celebrity restaurant has created a concert hall. The permanent home for its nationally televised *Hard Rock Live* television show, it will feature rock veterans and up-and-coming stars in nightly concerts. *Schedules: tel. 407/351–7625.*

chapter 12
MORE EATERTAINMENT
Tooth Picks, Plus a Little Night Music

The world's number one vacation destination will never lack places to eat and make merry. But beware: With over 40 million visitors each year, who needs repeat business? That's why you have me around. I describe a few of my favorites below. Unless otherwise noted, all accept major credit cards and are open daily. The range of prices listed at the end of each review is for dinner entrées.

My Short List

BOSTON LOBSTER FEAST This is Orlando's best deal on a meal! It is also my favorite buffet anywhere! All-you-can-eat steamed lobster with hot butter is the Maine attraction at this restaurant adjoining the Florida Mall, along with crab, shrimp, oysters, clams, and fresh fish. I love the calamari salad, the lobster bisque, and the New England clam chowder. (Plenty for landlubbers, too, including a fine London broil.) Salads and tasty desserts round out the deal. And the price is even better with my exclusive coupon! It's at the intersection of Sand Lake Road and Orange Blossom Trail. *8204 Crystal Clear La., Orlando, tel. 407/438-0607. $24.95 adults, $15.95 children under 12. No reservations.*

OUTBACK RESTAURANT AT BUENA VISTA PALACE By far, the best family dining on Disney property is at the Buena Vista Palace, the premier resort at Downtown Disney. The Outback—*not* part of the national chain—comes complete with a stuffed crocodile in a rushing stream, aboriginal weapons and costumes on the walls, a dugout canoe hanging from the ceiling, and a general out-in-the-wild feel. A superb steak will be prepared before your eyes on the "barbee" (Aussie for barbecue), or you could go for seafood, most notably the enormous, excellent, and reasonably priced lobster (around $10 a pound). *1900 Buena Vista Dr., Lake Buena Vista, tel. 407/827-2727. Entrées $13-$32.*

PONDEROSA GRAND BUFFET I rate this as Orlando's absolute best family buffet. True, Ponderosa is a national chain, but I've been all over the country and I've never seen any like the Ponderosas here. They're the cleanest and best anywhere, colorfully decorated and with a fabulous, attractively presented selection of over 100 fresh, tasty, all-American dishes, both hot and cold, at every meal. *Orlando: 5535 S. Kirkman Rd., tel. 407/345-0200; 6362 International Dr., tel. 407/352-9343; 8510 International Dr., tel. 407/354-1477; and 14407 In-*

ternational Dr., tel. 407/238-2526. Kissimmee: 7598 W. Irlo Bronson Memorial Hwy., tel. 407/396-7721; 5771 W. Irlo Bronson Memorial Hwy., tel. 407/397-2477. Entrées $8–$15.

SLEUTH'S MYSTERY DINNER THEATER This year's top pick as Orlando's top dinner show goes to Sleuth's. It's the best food and show combination in town! Your choice of chicken, lasagna, or prime rib is accompanied by ample side dishes and lots of beer or wine. The show is a hilarious, interactive whodunit with audience participation that always includes kids. Ricky stole the show when he questioned a certain short suspect on his platform shoes. It's just off I-Drive. *7508 Republic Dr., Orlando, tel. 407/363-1985. Shows nightly at varying times. $34.95 adults, $22.95 children 2–11, children under 2 free.*

SUNDAY BRUNCH AT THE RENAISSANCE ORLANDO Kudos for Central Florida's best brunch go to the spread at this resort next to Sea World, at the southern end of I-Drive. The 150 items on the buffet vary slightly week to week but may include—as on our latest visit—succulent lamb, perfect eggs Benedict, and a lavish selection of seafood, sushi, and much more. The champagne keeps coming. *6677 Sea Harbor Dr., Orlando, tel. 407/351-5555 or 800/327-6677. $29.95 adults, $14.95 children 4–12, under 4 free.*

CHARACTER MEALS

These events in restaurants in local hotels and theme parks put you and your kids in direct contact with your favorite characters—Mickey, Minnie, Cinderella, Woody, and the gang. The breakfasts we have attended have become some of our family's most treasured memories. Figure out which characters you want to see and choose your meal based on what's available.

If the one you choose is in a theme park, you will be admitted before the park opens to the public, when it is nearly empty and the magnificent landscaping is at its most beautiful as the cast members ready the grounds for the new day. Prices vary, but are surprisingly reasonable. Plan on around $15 per adult and $8 per child 3–12 (children under 3 free).

As early as possible (up to 60 days in advance), call 407/WDW–DINE for reservations, which are usually a must. At Universal, call 407/224–6339.

Worth-It Rating ★★★★★

THEME RESTAURANTS

The first celebrity-owned theme restaurant, the **Hard Rock Cafe**, started out in London, but the concept really has taken root in Orlando, and, in fact, founder Robert Earl now calls Orlando home. The HRC moves to giant new quarters with the opening of Universal's CityWalk. There, you'll also find **Bob Marley**, in a re-creation of the reggae star's Jamaican home and **Jimmy Buffett's Margaritaville** (*see* Chapter 11). In Downtown Disney, Jim Belushi and Dan Aykroyd have built the **House of Blues**, Gloria Estefan brought the Latin beat with **Bongos**, and NASCAR has sanctioned the **NASCAR Cafe**; these join the longtime draw, **Planet Hollywood**, in the riveting blue globe on the edge of Downtown Disney (*see* Chapter 10). And at Disney's Wide World of Sports, Andre Agassi, hockey's Great Gretzky, Ken Griffey, Jr., Joe Montana, Shaquille O'Neal, and Tiger Woods have funded the

Official All-Star Sports Café (*see* Chapter 14). All of these are dazzlingly stuffed with theme memorabilia from floor to ceiling, as is my current favorite of them all:

RACE ROCK This one is from stock car king Richard Petty, Indy racer Michael Andretti, and several of their fast friends. You're served by uniformed trophy babes and pit crew under awesome race cars and boats, suspended from the ceiling; you'll find loads of racing memorabilia and race car simulators, too. But the highlight is the food, mainly mildly spicy Tex-Mex with some great barbecued ribs and chicken. In the lobby, an open-sided tractor-trailer sells all kinds of racing-logo shirts and souvenirs. *8986 International Dr., Orlando, tel. 407/248–9876. Entrées $7–$18.*
Worth-It Rating ★★★★★

CHURCH STREET STATION AND DOWNTOWN

When promoter Bob Snow came to Orlando back in the early 1970s, he wanted to revitalize its shabby downtown by turning it into a dining and shopping attraction with a historic flavor. Although problems had dogged his efforts to do the same thing in Pensacola, he was wildly successful in Orlando in this complex of restaurants and night spots occupying local landmarks like Orlando pioneer Stanley Bumby's hundred-year-old hardware store. For years, until Disney created Pleasure Island, his Church Street Station was synonymous with Orlando nightlife in the minds of tourists. And it's still a great spot. Bob Snow and his successors scoured the world and filled the complex with 19th-century metal ceiling tiles, hand-carved woodwork, church pews, chandeliers, and

MY SHORT LIST

stained glass. Vintage flying machines from hot-air balloons to biplanes are suspended from the ceilings, and the stuffed game animal heads adorn the walls. Rare and expensive antique vehicles are parked in the street, including a highly prized 1939 Duesenberg; a 1912 steam engine and old Pullman cars are stopped on the old train tracks. It's an eclectic visual tour de force.

Be prepared for a good time. Church Street Station is a loud, rowdy, in-your-face place to party hearty. There are four main nightclubs, three with scheduled sets; showtimes are staggered so that you can take in a set in each during an evening. **Rosie O'Grady's** is a New Orleans–style jazz club where you can snack on a burger to the strains of an enthusiastic Dixieland band. Waiters and waitresses even dance on the bar. The **Orchid Garden Ballroom,** done up in Victorian style with rich woods and decorative glass, has a high-powered 50s-style rock band for dancing. And many major country stars have performed in the **Cheyenne Saloon and Opera House,** a Western music hall featured on numerous national TV shows. Intricate carved woodwork encloses several levels of balconies, and you can order Wild West fare—buffalo, beef steaks, chicken, and ribs (entrées $12.50 and up). **Phineas Phogg's Balloon Works,** the fourth club, is a non-stop modern dance and rock club, mostly for Gen X-ers. It's full of vintage balloonist's paraphernalia. There are also a couple of restaurants.

After 6 PM, you have to pay a cover charge to enter these Church Street Station clubs, and food and beverages are extra and pricey. You're expected to buy a drink or two, at around $4 a pop, in each of its night spots. So for a couple, it's easy to go through a couple of hundred dollars in an evening. But if you don't want to spend the bucks, you can have a great time soaking up the streetmosphere and taking in the restaurants with no cover.

In turn-of-the-century-style **Lili Marlene's Aviator's Pub and Restaurant,** the prime rib comes in generous portions au jus or blackened. Entrées are about $20. The very casual **Crackers Oyster Bar,** which reminds me of the old fish camps that still dot Florida, does a more than respectable job with fresh Florida seafood, and serves everything from raw oysters to a nice lobster-and-clam bake. The specialty is a tangy Pensacola clam chowder, but I like the chef's chili—loaded with gator meat. This place doubles as a sports bar. Entrées cost between $9.95 and $25.

Lunchtime, when Church Street Station levies no cover, is also great for soaking up the atmosphere without paying. There's also an excellent Sunday brunch buffet at Lili Marlene's ($12.95). And tours of the complex are available. The area is also home to several other excellent clubs and restaurants.

Church Street Exchange, the shopping part of Church Street Station, has over 50 specialty stores, many of them locally owned and operated. A flight-ready biplane hangs from the ceiling on the second floor, where there's also an excellent food court and **Commander Ragtime's Midway,** possibly Orlando's most extensive arcade, with about a zillion video games and claw machines. The fabulous **Buffalo Trading Company,** in the building that used to house Stanley Bumby's famous old hardware store, has all kinds of western items including copies of an autographed picture of Butch Cassidy and the Sundance Kid and many, many fringed buckskin jackets. The **Bumby Emporium,** also huge, sells Church Street souvenirs and lots of old-timey stuff. Out on the street, jugglers, magicians, bagpipers, and other musicians entertain day and night.

MY SHORT LIST

Church Street Market is just across the courtyard from Church Street Station, and if you didn't know the politics of the place, you'd think it was part of the same complex. Actually, it was cleverly created by another developer to cash in on Church Street's popularity and its advertising. Still, it has a number of worthwhile shoppertoonities. If you've never been to a **Sharper Image** store, you can visit one here. It's an attraction in itself, stocked with whatever is the state of the art in virtual reality, personal digital assistants, or electronic doodads that work underwater. **Brookstone** sells fancy hardware. And, of course, there's food: The politically incorrect **Hooter's,** a sports bar, features spicy chicken wings served by scantily clad young women. And **Jungle Jim's** has family prices and a cute jungle theme the kids will love.

The Fast Track: Church Street shows are timed so that you can catch them all in an evening by going from one to the next. So that's what everybody does. Before you start out, pop your head into each of the three music spots to see which is least crowded, and start there. Then you'll be moving from venue to venue with the smallest group. *129 W. Church St., 407/422–2434 (ext. 427, to find out about tours of the complex). Cover $17.95 adults, $11.95 children 4–12. Church Street night spots open daily 11 AM–2 AM, shops open 11–11.*

Worth-It Rating ★★★

SAPPHIRE SUPPER CLUB Orlando's emerging rock scene has produced such nationally famous acts as Matchbox 20, Sister Hazel, the Backstreet Boys, My Friend Steve, Von Ra and many others. For most groups, it begins at this spot, the area's premiere showcase of new music. Several Mexican entrées and an outstanding New York steak in peppercorn sauce headline a surprisingly reasonably priced menu and a modest but nicely priced wine list. Cover charges, ticket prices, and reservation policies vary by event, but usually $5 gets you in. *54 N. Orange Ave., Downtown Orlando, tel. 407/246–1419.*

DISNEY'S BOARDWALK

My wife, Terrie, and I fell in love with this place at first sight. Designed in classic New England style to re-create the old boardwalks built along the northeastern beaches just after the turn of the century, this area has shopping, dining, lodging, and entertainment. Admission to the whole complex is free, and—here's the best part—there are no cover charges at any of the clubs! (The **BoardWalk Inn** and the **BoardWalk Villas** are both part of the Disney Vacation Club's time-share operation, but you don't have to be a time-share owner to stay there or party at their bars and clubs.) The boardwalk overlooks a lagoon facing the Yacht and Beach Club, their lighthouse, and the pirate ship at their mini-water park. Epcot is to your right, and you can see the Eiffel Tower in the distance, rising just above the BoardWalk's gazebo. Away from the water are a handful of shops and an arcade with pinball and video games (I hate arcades—Ricky, my son, hits the arcade and bang, that's the end of 20 bucks and we haven't even done anything).

What keeps us coming back to the BoardWalk are the clubs. The **Atlantic Dance Club** recalls the ballrooms that broadcast swing music in the 1940s. The **ESPN Club** is the ultimate sports bar, with monitors everywhere—all tuned to ESPN, of course. **Jellyroll's** is a big, rollicking night spot with two piano players at dueling grand pianos. It's the kind of place where you'd expect a cover, but there is none. In the **Belle Vue Room**, a lakeside lounge, the elegant decor and formally attired waiters make you feel like the Great Gatsby. **Big River**

MY SHORT LIST

Grill and Brewing Works is Disney's own microbrewery; it serves British pub fare like sausages and meat pies. At **BoardWalk Bakery,** bakers bake a lot of bread right before your eyes, along with pastries and sweets. The **Flying Fish Café** serves fresh seafood. A house specialty is scallops with black truffle risotto. Reservations are accepted. Besides its highly entertaining show of pizza-twirling, **Spoodles** has a Mediterranean menu that includes some very good grilled lamb chops and a Moroccan vegetable platter, among other fairly exotic dishes. (Reservations are a good idea.) The bars in the BoardWalk Inn and BoardWalk Villas are every bit as atmospheric and fun. Terrie and I love all the old Atlantic City pictures displayed in these hotels—wonderful bits of nostalgia that date back to what the kids haved dubbed the "gray-and-white days." There's even a picture of Atlantic City's famous diving horse.

And what would a boardwalk be without taffy? Hit **Seashore Sweets.** On our last visit, a boardwalk magician delighted the children with a show during which he was able to extract a variety of exotic objects from their ears. All in all, the BoardWalk is charming, nostalgic, and entertaining—as well as being the home of some of the best deals on Disney property. *2101 N. Epcot Resort Blvd., Lake Buena Vista, tel. 407/939–3420; 407/WDW–DINE for restaurant reservations. Clubs open daily 7 PM–2 AM, shops open daily 9 AM–1 AM.*
Worth-It Rating ★★★★★

DINNER THEATERS

These spectacular productions, an institution in a town where everything must have a theme and entertainment value, cost literally millions of dollars to produce. Beer and wine are served.

MORE EATERTAINMENT

CAPONE'S You have to know the password to get into this speakeasy featuring a Runyonesque musical comedy set in gangland Chicago in the 1930s. What the food may lack in quality, the buffet more than makes up in quantity. Costumed and in character, the servers keep the hooch coming. It's a good show and a good time. *4740 W. Irlo Bronson Memorial Hwy., Kissimmee, tel. 407/397–2378. Shows nightly at 7:30. $31.99 adults, $16.99 children 3–12, children under 3 free.*
Worth-It Rating ★★★★

HOOP DEE DOO REVUE The long-running Wild West musical revue in WDW's Fort Wilderness features frontier guys and gals in gingham, jeans, and buckskin singing, dancing, and pratfalling their way into your heart. Small children think the slapstick's hilarious, and it's hard not to have a good time. Plus, the chicken, ribs, and country fixin's are downright good! *Fort Wilderness Campground Resort, Walt Disney World, tel. 407/WDW–DINE. Shows nightly at 5, 7:15, and 9:30. $37 adults, $19.50 children 3–11, children under 3 free.*
Worth-It Rating ★★★★

KING HENRY'S FEAST Jesters, jugglers, acrobats, and magicians are all on hand. You might call this medieval lite—not as grand or as intense as Medieval Times (*see* below), but still a good show. The food is pretty good, too. *8984 International Dr., Orlando, tel. 407/351–5151. Shows nightly at 7 and 9:30. $34.95 adults, $21.95 children 3–11, children under 3 free.*
Worth-It Rating ★★★★

LUAU AT SEA WORLD Disney's Polynesian Luau may be the Orlando's original, but this one's better and costs less. It's a full-fledged Polynesian presentation, with singers, musicians, and dancers doing the hula and the fire dance. *7007 Sea World*

MY SHORT LIST

Dr., Orlando, 407/363–2559. Shows nightly at 6:15. $29.95 adults, $19.95 children 8–12, $9.95 children under 8, under 3 free.
Worth-It Rating ★★★★★

MEDIEVAL TIMES The area's most successful dinner show re-creates a joust and tournament complete with knights on horseback, sword fights, falconry, and more—accompanying a feast of chicken, barbecued ribs, soup, sangria, beer, and soda. The food is better than competitors', the pageantry majestic, the plot romantic, the trained animals amazing, and the fights exciting and realistic. There is truly something for everyone. Though my family goes often, we always enjoy the show; it's always slightly different and seems better than the time before. It sells out early, so reserve well ahead. *4510 W. Irlo Bronson Memorial Hwy., Kissimmee, tel. 800/229–8300. Shows nightly at 8 (also at 10 in peak seasons). $34.95 adults, $22.95 children 3–12, children under 3 free.*
Worth-It Rating ★★★★★

MURDERWATCH MYSTERY DINNER THEATER You'll have to be good to figure out whodunit at this show at the Grosvenor Hotel, a real killer! And the buffet is excellent. It's only on Saturday night. *1850 Hotel Plaza Blvd., Lake Buena Vista, 407/827–6500, ext. 6103. Shows at 6 and 9, Saturday only. $33.95 adults, $17.95 children under 9, children under 3 free.*
Worth-It Rating ★★★★★

OHANA Though the pay-one-price meal that goes with this show at Disney's Polynesian Village Resort is not officially all-you-can-eat, nobody ever refused us seconds. I kept ordering more of the super-jumbo skewered-and-grilled shrimp. You get a Polynesian name and a chance to participate in the show. It's great fun and great food, both at an appealing price. *Polynesian*

Village Resort, Walt Disney World, tel. 407/939–3463. $19.95 adults, $14.95 children 12–16, $8.95 children 3–11, under 3 free.
Worth-It Rating ★★★★★

PIRATES DINNER ADVENTURE A life-size pirate ship sails seas of real water in the center of the cavernous arena that houses this huge production just off I-Drive. Circus acrobats swing overhead as you swig beer and sangria. The chicken and ribs are not as good as the food at Medieval Times, but they're not bad, and the show is very entertaining. *6400 Carrier Dr., Orlando, tel. 800/866–AHOY, 407/248–0590. Shows Tues.–Sun. at 6:30. $33.95 adults, $19.95 children 3–11, children under 3 free.*
Worth-It Rating ★★★★

POLYNESIAN LUAU South Seas islanders perform the hula, the fire dance, and other feats of skill and artistry at this mainstay of WDW's Polynesian Village Resort. The feast features roast pork, poi, and other delicacies. One of WDW's trademark events, it still seems fresh, even after all these years. Reserve way ahead. *Polynesian Village Resort, Walt Disney World, tel. 407/WDW–DINE. Shows daily at 4:30 and 6:45. $37 adults, $19.50 children 3–11, under 3 free.*
Worth-It Rating ★★★★

WILD BILL'S This redo of Buffalo Bill's Wild West Show has horseback riding, native American dancing, western dancing, sharpshooting, knife throwing, rope tossing, and just plain general hoopla! Good food, good show. *5260 W. Irlo Bronson Memorial Hwy., Kissimmee, tel. 407/351–5151. Shows nightly at 7 (sometimes also at 9:30). $33.95 adults, $19.95 children 3–11, under 3 free.*
Worth-It Rating ★★★★

MY SHORT LIST

SUSHI AND SEAFOOD

THE CRAB HOUSE Stuff yourself on crab, shrimp, and shellfish at the great all-you-can-eat buffets here. At dinner, there's a good selection of straightforward seafood entrées as well. *8496 Palm Parkway, tel. 407/239-1888, and 8291 International Dr., tel. 407/352-6140, both in Orlando. Buffets $9.99 at lunch, $17.99 at dinner (adults and children). No reservations.*
Worth-It Rating ★★★★

KOBE JAPANESE STEAK HOUSE I'm a regular at the two locations of this local chain that still offer all-you-can-eat sushi nights—although neither is in the attractions area. The sushi is all fresh, handmade to your order. It's not a nightly thing, so call ahead. You'll also find the area's best teppanyaki Japanese restaurant, featuring a dazzling samurai chef at every table. And the price is right. The Colonial Drive location is at least 30 minutes from U.S. 192, at least 20 minutes from I-Drive. The Altamonte Springs location is just off I-4, 30 minutes from Exit 25A/U.S. 192, 20 minutes from the main I-Drive exits at Kirkman and Sand Lake. *2110 E. Colonial Dr., Orlando, tel. 407/895-6868; 468 W. S.R. 436, Altamonte Springs, tel. 407/862-2888. $18.95 adults and children.*
Worth-It Rating ★★★★

OFF THE BEATEN PATH

PETE'S BUBBLE ROOM At this landmark 20 miles north of Universal, every day is Christmas circa 1955 and it's always Howdy Doody time; every table is a display case crammed with toys from my childhood (Ovaltine premiums, Hopa-

long Cassidy lunch boxes, etc.). The prime rib is the biggest I've seen outside of Omaha. Rich, rich, rich red velvet cake (in a slice that's big enough for two) is my favorite of the famous dessert selection. One of a kind and worth the trip. *1351 S. Orlando Ave. (U.S. 17/92), Maitland, tel. 407/628–3331. Entrees $14–$26.*
Worth-It Rating ★★★★★

chapter 13
WATER PARKS

n Central Florida you'll find more aquatic thrills than anywhere else on the planet. The Orlando area alone boasts five major water parks. There's just no reason not to get in the swim.

At each, you'll find flumes, slides, pools, tubing courses, and kiddie areas. **Flumes** are tubular, curved slides greased with a trickle of water. You race through the tube, speed through the turns, then shoot out into a shallow pool at the bottom. In some flumes, you ride on mats or in inner tubes; most are ridden bare-back. In family flumes, up to six people ride together in flexible rubber tubs. **Water slides** are always open-sided and not as curvy as flumes. The key difference among them is the vertical drop, the number of feet between the highest and lowest elevations. You'll also find **tube courses**, where you float on a meandering stream. Most parks also have **wave pools**, simulating ocean action. Still others have totally unique features—the reef at Typhoon Lagoon, where you swim with live sharks, and Water Mania's Wipe Out, where you can try surfing a wave.

TIPS AND BASICS Because free tubes are usually in short supply at water parks, rentals are available, along with lockers and towels. Fast food is everywhere but pricey. Picnics are allowed; glass containers and alcoholic beverages are not (nor are overly revealing bathing suits). Independent parks charge for parking; Disney water parks do not. Also remember:

- Your best value is later in the day—after 3, 4, or 5 PM, depending on park, crowd, season, and weather—when temperatures drop, early sunburns thin the crowds, and some parks offer half-price admissions.
- Never, ever leave children unsupervised. Make sure that someone is watching each child at all times. Wave pools can be chaotic.
- Don't wear anything around your neck, wrists, or ankles—it could snag and cause serious injury. If you have long hair, pull it back or keep it tied up, and keep your head up when sliding!
- Use sunblock and watch your sun time. A bad sunburn can ruin your whole vacation.
- Ladies, take note: all parks have a high-speed water slide with a giant vertical drop, five to 12 stories. Guys often wait at the bottom to watch women lose their tops. Gentlemen they are not.

ORLANDO AND KISSIMMEE WATER PARKS

WET 'N WILD My pick for the best-value water park, this one on I-Drive is the original water thrill park and still offers more ride per buck than any other wetland, particularly if you follow my recommendation and purchase the Orlando FlexTicket. You'll find the thrills in the giant wave pool; on the Bomb Bay and Der Stuka, both with 76-vertical-foot-drops; in the Black Hole, a slightly terrifying flume in the dark (not for the claustrophobic); in the Bubba Tub and the Surge, two rides where your whole family can flume together; and on the Fuji Flyer, a speeding downhill raft that seats four. The new Hydra-Fighter, which seats 8 to 12 lunatics, moves them around as they fire a water cannon at their fellow guests. The Lazy River, a tube-in-the-ol'-stream ride, is one of the few mellow experiences here. This high-energy park is usually crowded from late morning until late afternoon. We always found the kiddie area inconveniently distant from the other rides. The folks at Wet 'n Wild told me that they made it this way on purpose, to keep the kids safe from high-energy traffic. They do have a point, but it's a trade-off. *Exit 30A off I–4. 6200 International Dr., near Kirkman Rd., tel. 407/351–9453. Open daily 10–6, until 11 in summer. $25.95 adults, $20.95 children 3–9, children under 3 free (½ price after 3, or after 5 in peak season).*

Worth-It Rating ★★★★★ Make that 5+ if you purchased your ticket as part of the Orlando FlexTicket.

WATER MANIA This park opposite Disney's Celebration in Kissimmee is unfortunately not keeping up with the quality of other area attractions. Still, most of the regular water park stuff is right here: a giant wave pool, multiple flumes, several tube rides, high-vertical-drop slides, and a tubing course. The surfing attraction is one-of-a-kind: The simulated ocean waves are so realistic that actual surfing competitions have been held here. Moreover, food and rental prices are usually better than in any other park; tickets are more heavily discounted; and discounted tickets more abundant than for other water parks. *Exit 25A off I–4. 6703 W. Irlo Bronson Memorial Hwy., tel. 407/396–4994. Open daily 11–5, with earlier openings and later closings in busy seasons and warm weather. $23.95 adults, $17.95 children 3–12, children under 3 free (½ price after 3).*

Worth-It Rating ★★★ Add 1 if you get a free ticket, if you're staying on U.S. 192, of if you have small children. Subtract 1 if you pay full price.

DISNEY WATER PARKS

Disney has successfully made water parks into total themed fantasy experiences, not duplicated anywhere else. If that's what you're looking for, you will probably decide that the Disney parks are worth the money. And if you're staying on Disney property and really want to do a water park, proximity and availability of Disney transportation make one of these attractions an obvious choice. For ticket prices, *see* Chapter 2.

TYPHOON LAGOON The landmark of this attraction near Walt Disney World Village is a ship that was tossed atop a mountain during a terrible storm (or so the story goes). Forget the fact that there aren't any hills here in Florida—this is Disney, where anything is possible. Highlights include the world's largest wave pool, a pair of incredible vertical slides, three white-water raft rides, and a river ride, which takes you easily from place to place and to the well-equipped tykes' area called Ketchakiddie Creek. The unduplicated specialty of the house is a tropical snorkeling adventure where you actually swim with small live sharks (safely; I've done it, and I'm not brave. The hardest part for me was the icy water). *Exit 26B off I–4, tel. 407/560–4141. Open daily 10–5 (until 7 or later in summer).*

Worth-It Rating ★★★★ Add 1 if you're doing it on a Disney pass.

BLIZZARD BEACH Did I say Typhoon Lagoon's theme is farfetched? Disney has abandoned all pretense of plausibility in this park. Here's the story: the weather turned freakish; a snowstorm blanketed Florida; Disney tried to cash in by building a ski resort; the sun returned; and Blizzard Beach was born.

Mount Gushmore, at its center, is the source of multiple flumes. The high-vertical-drop slide is the world's tallest at 120 feet (12 stories). A radar unit clocks your descent on a big digital display at speeds of up to 60 mph. The chairlift is a nice touch. So is Tike's Peak, a conveniently located, kid-size version of almost all the rest of the water park. At the Blizzard Beach Ski Patrol Training Camp, you can try to jump across floating simulated ice floes without falling in. The result looks sort of like *Baywatch* on ice. *Exit 26B off I–4, west of World Dr. on Osceola Pkwy., opposite the Disney All-Star Resorts, tel. 407/560–3400. Open daily 10–5 (until 7 or later in summer).*

Worth-It Rating ★★★★★ Make that 5+ if you're doing it on a Disney pass.

RIVER COUNTRY From the beginning, Disney has billed this park as a "re-creation of the ol' swimmin' hole." It's a good one. While no longer Disney's premier water park or even a state-of-the-art water attraction by today's standards, it holds up well for what it is, a rip-roarin' chance to feel like Huck Finn on the mighty Mississippi! And admission is lower than for other Disney water parks.

Spreading out from its own sandy beach on the shore of a natural Florida lake, River Country has old-time rope swings, flumes, raft rides, and a smallish kiddie section (not particularly convenient). There are nature trails and a playground and, for those who may not like the feel and aroma of Florida lake water, an oversize heated and chlorinated swimming pool.

Water launches to River Country leave regularly from both the Magic Kingdom and Disney's Contemporary Resort. *Exit 26A off I–4 (follow signs to Fort Wilderness), off Fort Wilderness Tr. tel. 407/824–2760. Open daily 10–5 (until 7 or later in summer).*

Worth-It Rating ★★★ Add 1 if you're a Mark Twain fan. Subtract 1 if you like your water chlorinated.

chapter 14

THE WIDER WORLD OF SPORTS

Orlando visitors often remark that everything here seems to be its own "World." In addition to Walt Disney World and Sea World, there's Bargain World, Boat World, even Flea World—a flea market, not a dog kennel. Now that Disney owns ABC and its sister network ESPN, Disney has entered the wide world of sports in a very big way. Add the area's already broad base of golf and other sports activities, and Orlando may soon be Sports World.

DISNEY'S WIDE WORLD OF SPORTS

"If you build it, they will come," we learned in the fantasy baseball movie *Field of Dreams*. Disney is betting heavily that there are enough sports nuts—tourists and locals—to support an Orlando field of dreams on 200 acres at the southwest corner of Disney property, near Blizzard Beach. The sprawling yellow complex, designed to house events televised on Disney's own ESPN, conjures up images of the mostly vanished baseball parks that helped to define the sport in the first half of this century. But there's much more than baseball here.

Here, you can visit a Basketball Hall of Fame; watch the Atlanta Braves in spring training or the Harlem Globetrotters in exhibitions; or take in Amateur Athletic Union national track-and-field events, and several events of the 1999 Senior Olympics. And you'll find any number of opportunities to learn, practice, and refine your skills in almost any sport imaginable.

SPECTATOR SPORTS FACILITIES The largest structure in the complex is the **Fieldhouse**. Inside are six basketball courts and facilities for martial arts, table tennis, weight lifting, wrestling, boxing, fencing, gymnastics, handball, and even badminton. Baseball is also a big deal. The **Ballpark** is particularly charming and old-timey. The Atlanta Braves have spring training here, and farm teams are scheduled to play here at other times. The Ballpark is part of the **Baseball Quadraplex,** which includes three additional ball fields of major-league dimensions, one fully lighted. The Ballpark can seat nearly 10,000; these accommodate just a few hundred. And watch out, Williamsport. With their permanent bleachers, scoreboards, and dugouts, these two **Youth Baseball Fields** were designed for major events like the Little League World Series, which currently takes place in that western Pennsylvania town. Softball anyone? The four regulation softball fields in the **Softball Quadraplex** are lighted for night play. In addition, there are four white-sand beach **volleyball courts,** a spiffy **track and field complex,** four **soccer fields** with international specifications, and a **tennis complex** with 11 fast-dry courts (the United States Tennis Association's Men's Clay Court Championships are slated to take place here annually in spring). This is all in addition to the **Velodrome** built for the Centennial Olympics in Atlanta, which the Imagineers had disassembled, shipped to Orlando, and reassembled, steel girder by steel girder, on this site. Call Disney's Sports Line as you firm up your travel dates to see what's on (tel. 407/363–6600), and schedule accordingly. And do this as far ahead as you can, since Disney events regularly sell out. Also look into sports-vacation and event-related packages, available through Walt Disney Travel Company Sports Reservations (tel. 407/939–7810).

THE NFL EXPERIENCE On a regulation football field here at Wide World of Sports, National Football League-trained pros supervise visitors who want to try their hand at any of 10 different events.

OFFICIAL ALL-STAR SPORTS CAFÉ This sports bar with a difference comes to you courtesy of tennis star Andre Agassi, hockey's Great Gretzky, Ken Griffey, Jr., Joe Montana, the Orlando Magic's former star Shaquille O'Neal, current local resident Tiger Woods, and Orlando's own Robert Earl, who founded both the Hard Rock Cafe and Planet Hollywood. Rooms are filled with videos featuring live events along with taped highlights from every major sport. You chow down on all-American steak and seafood.

GOLF

Along with its many other distinctions, Central Florida is the number-one golf destination in the world, with more holes of golf than almost any other part of the United States. I'm not a golfer but for those of you who are, here's my take on what's out there.

DISNEY'S 99 HOLES The passionate golfers all know that Walt Disney World, taken as a whole, is one of the largest and best golf resorts, anywhere, with its six very good courses with very good facilities. These are in three locations on property—near the Magic Kingdom, at the Armed Forces R&R station known as Shades of Green; near Downtown Disney; and near Fort Wilderness. Each area has complete facilities, everything from a PGA-staffed instructional program to a pro shop, locker room, snack bar, and restaurant.

In theory, all courses are open to the public. However, guests at resorts on Disney property and those with hotel reservations can make reservations up to 60 days in advance with a major credit card (tel. 407/WDW–GOLF, or 939–4653), and Disney's own guests may have an edge in getting a tee time when the getting is tough.

Near the Magic Kingdom: The **Palm**, designed by Joe Lee, is the toughest Disney course, cut through the dense pine forest. The **Magnolia**, another Joe Lee test, is the longest course at WDW. Extra long fairways challenge the most powerful drivers, along with 11 water hazards and 97 sand bunkers; the one on the sixth looks remarkably like the well-known silhouette of a certain mouse. Directly adjacent is **Oak Trail**, a nine-hole, par-36 walking course with relatively short fairways and fast greens. The smallest of Disney's courses, it makes a perfect little golf outing on a tight family vacation schedule.

Near Fort Wilderness: **Eagle Pines** was created by Pete Dye, with a low profile and roughs of pine needles and sand. **Osprey Ridge,** designed by Tom Fazio, is links-style, with elevated greens and tees, nine water holes, and over 70 bunkers scattered through pine forests, palmetto scrub, and marshy stands of Florida cypress.

Near Downtown Disney: **Lake Buena Vista,** another Joe Lee design, is the oldest of the Disney courses, with an island green on the seventh hole.

HEADS UP, DUFFERS! The average player can't go far wrong on almost any of the dozens of area courses, many fairly inexpensive. Several are worth a detour, though. **Arnold Palmer's Bay Hill Club and Lodge** (9000 Bay Hill Blvd., Orlando, tel. 407/876–2429), near Universal Studios Florida, is the home of Arnold Palmer's home course, and as you would expect, is consistently top-ranked by *Golf Digest* magazine. Nearby, in the shadow of the area's tallest and most beautiful hotel, **Mariott's Orlando World Center** (1 World Center Dr., Orlando 32821, tel. 407/239–4200), are 18 more holes of perfectly manicured golf. The hotel is also the home of Nick Faldo's Golf School. The 45-hole Jack Nicklaus layout at the **Hyatt Regency Grand Cypress Resort** (1 N. Jacaranda, Orlando, tel. 407/239-1234), directly behind Downtown Disney, is a faithful re-creation of historic Scottish courses; PGA-certified pros at its golf academy video your strokes.

chapter 15
GRAND OLD FLORIDA ATTRACTIONS AND OTHER DIVERSIONS

Entrepreneurs from all over the world flock to Orlando in the belief that where there are millions of tourists, there are millions of dollars to go around. One company spent a small fortune on a theme park that would have featured a levitating hotel designed to hover four feet above the ground, supported only by psychic energy. (I am not kidding.) Such places come and go pretty quickly. Some attractions are real survivors—vintage Florida landmarks that predate Walt Disney World, and even Disneyland, by decades. These are good enough to merit a mention, perhaps even a visit. I cover the best of them all in this chapter, along with WDW destinations—like Disney Institute and Discovery Island—that are real alternatives to a day in the parks.

Should you bother at all? Obviously some of what you'll find is unique to the area. As for the rest, I advise you to think twice before you spend your time on the kinds of attractions you'll find at home: In Central Florida, with its huge pool of visitors, they'll probably be bigger, better, newer, and nicer—but they won't not necessarily be a good deal. If you read my Chapter 1 and took the time to calculate the hourly cost of your vacation—or even if you just use my hypothetical $33.82 per hour—you know that it's costing you at least $30 to $40 per waking hour just to be here. When you add that figure to the cost of, say, go-cart rides at $3 or more a lap, you are easily spending $50 to $60 an hour on go-carting.

Or look at it this way. If you can expect to see about one ride or show every 45 minutes in a theme park, a reasonable estimate, you can do about 16 rides during a 12-hour day. If a theme park ticket costs you around $40, the cost works out to $2.50 a ride. Some of the smaller attractions I describe below, like Paintball World, are full-day experiences that you may well want to choose instead of one of the theme parks. Most, however, will set you back about $10 each, or 4 times as much as a single theme-park ride. To duplicate a theme park day, with its 16 adventures, you would be spending an average of $160 per person per day.

Obviously, you don't want to do that. However, you might be mixing some time by the pool with shopping and a couple of other fun things, and that's where these attractions come in. So, if your family includes a real go-cart fan or miniature golf fanatic, or if you have an hour or so to kill on an afternoon, don't let me stop you. I'm just here to help you decide what's worth it and what's not. As an attractions connoisseur, I can tell you that, within categories, the biggest difference is location. Don't waste gas driving to Kissimmee if you're staying on International Drive.

Here are my top picks, with my favorites listed first in each category.

GRAND OLD FLORIDA ATTRACTIONS AND OTHER DIVERSIONS

GRAND OLD FLORIDA ATTRACTIONS

SILVER SPRINGS In 1996 while we were all congratulating Disney on bringing the theme park to Central Florida 25 years ago, Silver Springs quietly celebrated its 100th birthday. Although it takes an hour and a half to get there, my family visits this 350-acre park at least once a year. It's built around crystal-clear Mammoth Spring, the world's largest natural artesian spring formation and the source of Florida's awesome Silver River. Glass-bottom boat tours give you a perfect view of dugout canoes on the river bottom, where they sank before the arrival of Columbus. There are also concerts by big-name entertainers, a narrated cruise down the unspoiled tropical river, and a jeep trip through a dense cypress and live oak forest, where you'll see sloth, exotic deer, and antelope. And, usually in June, July, and August, the springs are opened for swimming. The drive here is through Florida's magnificent horse country, as significant to Thoroughbred racing as Kentucky's bluegrass. The park is just off I-75, a mile east of Ocala on Route 40. The all-in-one ticket is a great value. Tip: Bring insect repellent—would you believe that in an attraction with insects the size of house cats, there is none to be found in the entire park? *5656 E. Silver Springs Blvd., Silver Springs, tel. 904/236–2121 or 800/234–7458. $27.95 adults, $18.95 children 3–9, children under 3 free. Open daily 9–5:30, longer during school vacations.*
Worth-It Rating ★★★★

GATORLAND Back in 1949, when Owen Godwin founded the self-proclaimed Alligator Capital of the World, Florida had dozens of alligator parks. But only Godwin had the foresight to put his just a few miles from the piece of land that

later caught the eye of a Californian named Walt Disney. Today, alligators are so thick they are literally on top of each other. There are three shows here: **Gator Jumparoo** pits a hungry gator against a chicken in a leap for lunch—that is, a trainer holds a raw chicken above the water and a hungry gator leaps to retrieve it. (This show is best first thing in the morning, when the gators haven't eaten since supper.) **Gator Wrestlin'**, an old Florida tradition, pits a full-size man against a man-size gator in an honest-to-goodness wrestling match. The goal of the man is to end up on top, while keeping the gator's powerful mouth clamped shut. The goal of the gator is not clear. And in **Snakes of Florida**, you'll see deadly Florida rattlesnakes, water moccasins, and coral snakes in cages and in demonstrations. You can also ride an old-time narrow gauge choo-choo through some genuine Florida swampland through undeveloped park areas or go for a walk in the same terrain. (But beware: The swamp wildlife is real and some of those reptiles have no respect.) Back in the center of the park at **Pearl's Smokehouse,** you can actually see a man eating gator—women and children can eat some, too. Fried gator nuggets taste a lot like chicken. (Wouldn't you have guessed?) Gatorland is also one of the world's largest commercial alligator farms. The thousands of gators on the grounds are not just there for your entertainment. They are also destined to serve humankind as shoes, belts, luggage, and meat. So if you're shopping for gator goods, the gift shop here is the place. Be prepared to hold your nose. Like all wildlife parks, this can be stinky, especially in the hot sun. *14501 S. Orange Blossom Trail (U.S. 441), between Orlando and Kissimmee, tel. 407/855–5496 or 800/393–5297. $11.95 adults, $8.95 children 3–9, children under 3 free. Open daily 8–6.*
Worth-It Rating ★★★★

GRAND OLD FLORIDA ATTRACTIONS AND OTHER DIVERSIONS

HOMOSASSA SPRINGS STATE WILDLIFE PARK The main attraction at this 174-acre state park is an underwater viewing area in a natural spring that is home to Florida's famous endangered sea cow, the manatee. There are also ranger tours and nature trails. It's three hours from Orlando via U.S. 19. *9225 W. Fish Bowl Dr., Homosassa Springs, tel. 352/628-2311. $7.95, $4.95 children 3-12, children under 3 free. Open daily 9-5:30.*
Worth-It Rating ★★★★ Add half a star if you're in the area.

WEEKI WACHEE SPRINGS CITY OF MERMAIDS I have to admit that back in the 1960s, when I first saw the ads for an underwater show featuring "live mermaids," I thought the idea was bizarre. It is. But it's still entertaining to see these "live mermaids"—young women performing a gracefully choreographed submarine spectacle, complete with narration and music. (They pause frequently to sip air from bubbling hoses around the set.) The current production is of Hans Christian Andersen's "The Little Mermaid," a story also used by another theme park whose name escapes me just now. Other attractions at this park 45 minutes north of Tampa include a wilderness river cruise, exotic bird shows, and a petting zoo. Adjacent **Buccaneer Bay** is the state's only water park at a natural springs. *6131 Commercial Way (U.S. 19 and Rte. 50), Weeki Wachee, tel. 352/596-2062 or 800/678-9335. $16.95 adults, $12.95 children under 10, children under 3 free. Open daily 9:30-5:30, longer during school vacations.*
Worth-It Rating ★★★ +

BOK TOWER GARDENS Speaking of bizarre, who knows what moved an eccentric 1920s millionaire, *Ladies Home Journal* founder Edward Bok, to create one of the world's

GRAND OLD FLORIDA ATTRACTIONS

premier carillon towers in the middle of nowhere. Now a National Historic Landmark, 279-foot Bok Tower has recitals daily at 3 PM, and the bells ring every half hour beginning at 10. The adjoining botanical garden contains 36 species of indigenous plants that are rare or endangered. The complex is 3 miles north of Lake Wales. *Burns Ave. and Tower Blvd. (on U.S. 27 and Route 60), Lake Wales, tel. 941/676–1408. $4 adults, $1 children 5–12, children under 5 free. Open daily 8–6.*
Worth-It Rating ★★★ Add 1 if you're in the neighborhood anyway.

CYPRESS GARDENS Nowadays, theme-park water-ski shows are almost as common as parades. But the first were staged by Dick Pope, Sr., at the 200-acre garden complex he established in 1936, and they are still world-class. Sparkling lakes and ancient cypress swamps surround the park, which is home to 8,000 varieties of plants and flowers from 90 different countries. You can tour the gardens on your own, with a guide, or on a scenic boat ride. Other attractions include circus acts, an ice-skating revue, reptile and birds of prey shows, Floridiana, shops and restaurants, children's rides, and the spectacular Butterfly Conservatory, with thousands of species. Don't miss the Southern Belles, the park's famed hostesses, who wear showy antebellum dresses. Just one question: How do they handle those huge hoops in the heat? *Off U.S. 27, about 22 mi south of I–4, near Winter Haven, between Orlando and Tampa, tel. 941/324–2111, 800/237–4826, or 800/282–2123 in Florida. $29.50 adults, free to all under 17. Open daily 9:30–5:30, longer in peak seasons.*
Worth-It Rating ★★★★

MARINELAND OF FLORIDA Would you believe that this is not only the original marine-life park but Florida's first movie park as well? Back in the 1920s, Cornelius Vanderbilt Whitney opened an underwater studio to provide stock footage for the fledgling motion picture industry. Public tours were an afterthought, inspired by Carl Laemmle's tour of California's Universal City Studios. Whitney went on to fund Marineland's Marine Studies Institute, still a leading research facility. Although the attraction has not kept pace, it can be fun if you're nearby. It's about 80 miles from Orlando, on the East Coast's gorgeous ocean highway, between St. Augustine and Daytona. The adjacent Quality Inn is one of Florida's undiscovered beach resorts—and a real bargain. *101 U.S. A1A, Marineland, tel. 800/824-4218. $14.95 adults, $9.95 children 13–17, $7.95 children 3–12, children under 3 free. Open daily 9–5:30.*

Worth-It Rating ★★★

INSIDE WALT DISNEY WORLD

DISNEY INSTITUTE A pet project of Disney CEO Michael Eisner, this is Disney's answer to Chautauqua, western New York State's venerable learning retreat. In a lush, wooded setting on WDW property, near Downtown Disney, the Disney Institute offers 60 programs in eight areas of interest, ranging from film and the performing arts to cooking, gardening, and sports. Programs are conducted by highly qualified instructors and visiting celebrities. There are evening programs and performances (ballet, films, comedy, and beyond) in an outdoor amphitheater, a small movie house, and an even smaller theater. Fees start at about $81 per person for a single day for adults and children over 7, including 2 learning sessions, use of the fitness facility, and admission to that

evening's performance. A complete program for kids aged 10 to 17 and a day camp for kids from seven to nine make the Institute family-friendly. *Tel. 800/282–9282.*
Worth-It Rating ★★★★★

DISNEY'S FANTASIA MINIATURE GOLF The biggest and best miniature golf course I've ever seen is a must-see for miniature golf enthusiasts. Enchanted broomsticks, dancing elephants, and other characters from *Fantasia* are the obstacles; musical fanfares from the film reward successful putts. If you have time to play only one miniature golf course in Orlando, it should be this one, which is next to the Swan and Dolphin hotels, near Epcot. *Buena Vista Dr., tel. 407/560–8760. $9 adults, $8 children 3–11. Open daily 10 AM–midnight.*
Worth-It Rating ★★★★

DISCOVERY ISLAND Walt Disney had a special place in his heart for this attraction on an 11-acre island across Bay Lake and the Seven Seas Lagoon from the Magic Kingdom. It is said that when he picked the original parcel of land that was to become Walt Disney World, he earmarked the island as a wildlife sanctuary.

The result is now a zoological park accredited by the American Association of Zoological Parks and Aquariums, home to 250 plant species, not to mention over 100 species of animals, many threatened with extinction. Discovery Island is also the site of one of the world's largest walk-through aviaries, and there are small shows, including "Animal Encounters," "Feathered Friends" (with parrots), the "Birds of Prey" show, and "Reptile Relations." Times vary; shows may be canceled if it rains or storms.

You can get there via WDW transportation from the Magic Kingdom, the Contemporary Resort, and Fort

Wilderness; if you're driving, use the Fort Wilderness exit off I–4 and follow signs to Fort Wilderness, where you can catch a launch to the island. Special nature programs are available; call 407/824–3784 for information. *See* Chapter 2 for fees.
Worth-It Rating ★★★ Add 2 if you love nature.

ELECTRICAL WATER PAGEANT On view several times a night all year long, this is like a floating version of the Magic Kingdom's nightly SpectroMagic parade. You can watch it from the beach at the Polynesian Village Resort, where it starts nightly at about 9 PM. Then it moves to the Contemporary, the Grand Floridian, and Fort Wilderness. You can also see some of it from the Magic Kingdom's turnstiles area near the ferry and monorail. Ask at Guest Relations in City Hall for times. There's no charge.
Worth-It Rating ★★★★★ How can you not love something that's dazzling, this entertaining—and free!

INTERNATIONAL DRIVE AND ORLANDO

ORLANDO SCIENCE CENTER AND LOCH HAVEN PARK Most big cities have a hands-on children's museum. As you would expect in the city with neighbors like the Walt Disney Company, Lockheed-Martin, and NASA, Orlando's is terrific. It's enormous, with a planetarium and observatory at the top, towering over Orlando's lovely old Loch Haven Park. Exhibits change monthly but are always professionally mounted, with lots of high-tech razzle-dazzle. The planetarium regularly presents laser light shows.

Loch Haven Park is also home to the city's art museum, which exhibits many kinds of art from primitive to contem-

porary. The **Orlando Historical Museum** is the local archive; most artifacts are from the early part of this century. The **Central Florida Civic Theater** and **Children's Theater** are also here; shows change monthly. Loch Haven Park itself is a lovely, shady, lakeside preserve where you'll find kite fly-ins, balloon meets, and model-boat club meetings. This is the real Orlando, with an exotic mix of the Old South and big money. *Science Center: 810 E. Rollins St., Orlando, tel. 407/ 896–7151. $6.50 adults, $5.50 children 3–11, children under 3 free. Open Mon.–Thurs. and Sat. 9–5, Fri. 9–9, Sun. noon–5; laser shows Fri. and Sat. 9, 10, 11, and midnight.*
Worth-It Rating ★★★★★

RIPLEY'S BELIEVE IT OR NOT! One of the best photo-ops in town, this must-see building was intentionally designed to look like it's falling over into one of Florida's many famous sinkholes. Inside you'll find a collection of oddities gathered by explorer/writer/cartoonist Robert Ripley and his successors, including some weird stuff such as two-headed animals. When my Ricky was six, he got so spooked that he ran out of the place. *8201 International Dr., near Sand Lake Rd., tel. 800/998–4418. $9.95 adults, $6.95 children 4–12, children under 4 free. Open daily 9 AM–midnight.*
Worth-It Rating ★★★★★

MOVIE RIDER If you're a simulator junkie who just can't get enough of this kind of ride, this stand-alone attraction may be the quick fix you need! Bigger than *Star Tours,* but only about half the size of *Back to the Future,* its main appeal is the length of the experience—about a half hour in the careening chair. Trivia: This attraction is from Iwerks Entertainment, the company founded by Ub Iwerks—Walt Disney's original partner. *8815 International Dr., tel. 407/352–0050, and 5390 W.*

GRAND OLD FLORIDA ATTRACTIONS AND OTHER DIVERSIONS

Irlo Bronson Memorial Hwy., Kissimmee, tel. 407/396–4185. $8.95 adults, $6.95 children under 12 (those under 42" tall free). Open 11–11 weekdays, 10 AM–midnight on weekends.
Worth-It Rating ★★★★

TRAINLAND TOY TRAIN MUSEUM This spectacular toy-train display in Goodings Plaza includes one of the world's largest model-railroad layouts. And the price is right. *8255 International Dr., tel. 407/363–9002. $6 adults, $4 children 3–13, children under 3 free. Open Mon.–Sat. 10–10, Sun. 10–6.*
Worth-It Rating ★★★★

AIR ORLANDO Helicopter rides and a view of scenic Orlando, for a price. *8990 International Dr., tel. 407/352–1753. $20–$395 adults, $20–$225 children 2–12, children under 2 free. Open Mon.–Sat. 10–8, Sun. noon–8.*
Worth-It Rating ★★★

CONGO RIVER GOLF & EXPLORATION CO. A giant waterfall, simulated mountains, and jungle props simulate high adventure at this mini golf course near Wet 'n Wild. The humongous waterfalls cool you off, even on hot days. There are tunnels, ramps, and rocks, and plaques tell stories at each hole. This one has a twin in Kissimmee. But, as I said, Fantasia's tops. *6312 International Dr., tel. 407/352–0042. $6.95–$9.95, children under 4 free. Open daily 10 AM–11 PM.*
Worth-It Rating ★★★

PIRATE'S COVE ADVENTURE GOLF At these pirate-theme miniature golf layouts, the giant waterfalls are inexplicably full of blue food coloring. This is our next-favorite miniature golf layout, after Fantasia. *8601 International Dr., Orlando, tel. 407/352–7378; Crossroads Center, I–4 Exit 27, Lake Buena*

INTERNATIONAL DRIVE AND ORLANDO

Vista, tel. 407/827–1242. $6.50–$7 adults, $5.50–$6 children 4–12, children under 4 free. Open daily 9–11:30.
Worth-It Rating ★★★

TERROR ON CHURCH STREET This big haunted house in downtown Orlando near Church Street Station is full of things that go bump in the night. Most of it is in the dark, with black light for effects. It all may be too intense for little kids. *135 S. Orange Ave., tel. 407/649–3327. $13 adults, $11 children 3–17, children under 3 free. Open daily 7 PM–midnight.*
Worth-It Rating ★★★ Add 2 if you're visiting with teens.

AROUND KISSIMMEE

MEDIEVAL LIFE Actors portray typical villagers in this re-creation of a medieval town, demonstrating falconry and crafts such as carving and weaving. Check out the dungeon and torture chamber. It's free when you attend Medieval Times, the area's big dinner show. *4510 W. Irlo Bronson Memorial Hwy., Kissimmee, tel. 800/229–8300. $8 adults, $6 children 3–12, children under 3 free. Open daily 4:30–8.*
Worth-It Rating ★★★★★ That's if you see it before or after attending Medieval Times. Otherwise, subtract 2.

PAINTBALL WORLD If your vacation isn't complete without a paintball war in the Florida sun, don't miss this unique experience off U.S. 192 at its eastern end, behind Old Town. In the paintball world, this is the most famous playing field, appearing on ESPN's Annual International Paintball World Championships. In the games here, platoons of make-believe soldiers armed with real guns shoot at each other with ex-

ploding balls of red paint. Many families come to work out their aggressions. You can shoot your spouse here, legally! This is a grown-up version of Capture the Flag—definitely not kid stuff (and in fact, children under 10 are not allowed to play). There's a spectator area for noncombatants. *2701 Holiday Trail, tel. 407/396–4199. Pump gun $18.95, semiautomatic $25 for the day 20-min games with 10-min breaks weekends 10–4 and on some weekdays in peak seasons; closed most weekdays.*
Worth-It Rating ★★★★★

GREEN MEADOWS FARM This warm-and-fuzzy attraction, 5 miles off U.S. 192, combines a petting zoo and a tour of a working farm with hayrides, cow-milking, and more. *1368 S. Poinciana Blvd., tel. 407/846–0770. $13, children under 2 free. Open daily 9:30–5; last tour at 4.*
Worth-It Rating ★★★★ Add 1 if you're bringing little city kids who've never had another chance to see a farm.

OLD TOWN A lot bigger than it looks from the street, this has always been a family favorite, with rides and shopping, on a re-created brick main street, for mostly nostalgic items—one nifty store specializes in things for Jimmy Buffett fans. The kart track and arcade are excellent. And the Old Town Photo Gallery, where you dress up to have antique-style photos taken, is one of the largest such operations in the U.S. *5770 W. Irlo Bronson Memorial Hwy., Kissimmee, tel. 407/396–4888. General admission free; price for individual attractions varies. Open daily 10 AM–11 PM.*
Worth-It Rating ★★★★

CONGO RIVER GOLF & EXPLORATION CO. This spot, 3 miles east of I-4, is a twin of the Congo River Golf on I-Drive

AROUND KISSIMMEE

(see above). *4777 W. Irlo Bronson Memorial Hwy., tel. 407/396–6900. $6.95–$9.95, children under 4 free. Open Sun.–Thurs. 10 AM–11 PM, Fri.–Sat. 10 AM–midnight.*
Worth-It Rating ★★★

JUNGLELAND This animal park, which recently made national news when a lion escaped, is neither as big as Gatorland, nor as funky as Titusville's Jungle Adventure, but they're working hard to upgrade it. If you want to see some gators without committing to a day at Gatorland, this is a good bet. *4580 W. Irlo Bronson Memorial Hwy., Kissimmee, tel. 407/396–1012. $9.95 adults, $6.95 children 3–11, children under 3 free. Open daily 9–6.*
Worth-It Rating ★★★

PIRATE'S ISLAND ADVENTURE GOLF Another pirate golf (*see* Pirate's Cove, *above*). *4330 W. Irlo Bronson Memorial Hwy., Kissimmee, tel. 407/396–4660. $5.50 adults, $4 children 3–12, children under 3 free. Open daily 9 AM–11 PM.*
Worth-It Rating ★★★

chapter 16
THE SPACE COAST

The fastest route is the Beeline Expressway, Route 528. For a more scenic alternative, take I-4 east then the East–West Expressway to Route 50. This safe and modern four-lane state highway was the original route between Orlando and the coast and contains several authentic Florida attractions that I recommend.

I'm a space kid. My father's transfer with the missile program is what brought my family to Florida from Maryland in the 1950s. I'm constantly amazed by the enormous discrepancy between the number of people who plan to visit the Kennedy Space Center and the number who actually make it there. I have always attributed this phenomenon to the ever-increasing length of stays covered by the Disney passes and to Disney's apparent effort to take an ever-larger percentage of every Florida vacationer's dollar. It's a shame that so many people travel so far and get so close to the space center only to miss it—one of the truly outstanding experiences in Central Florida.

Created at the height of the Cold War, the space center is surrounded by a large buffer area, a tropical wilderness that is one of the last places where you can see the Sunshine State the way it used to be. On the way in or out, we often stop to watch alligators sun themselves on the banks of roadside streams. (Please don't get out to feed them—tourists are among their favorite foods.)

My ideal Florida vacation includes the Space Center, some of the grand old Florida attractions described in Chapter 15, and the East Coast beaches described in Chapter 17. I advise you to spend a few days seeing theme parks, and then drop in on the real Florida. If you leave early enough, you'll see the rose-colored dawn and a sunrise over the primeval wilderness just east of metropolitan Orlando. Plan an extra day and you can travel back in time to an original Florida settlement, take an airboat ride across the saw grass, and see an authentic old reptile park, all within 50 miles of Orlando.

WHAT TO SEE

JOHN F. KENNEDY SPACE CENTER VISITOR CENTER I get goose bumps here. The impact of visiting the site of the greatest scientific achievements in the history of humanity simply cannot be overstated. Brave Americans first breached the stratosphere and shot to the moon from here, and they still journey into space on a regular basis. It astonishes me that just an hour from my suburban neighborhood, I can see and touch the actual artifacts that transported all of us to the edge of reality.

Located in the U.S. Government NASA complex, this attraction is also Central Florida's best visitor value. You enter the grounds for free, park for free, and walk around for free.

The visitor center is also free. Here, exhibits showcase everything that's been in space, from pressure suits to capsules that carried astronauts aloft. Don't miss the lunar landing module and the film shot on the moon—not just the video that we've all seen a zillion times, but 16mm movies filmed and narrated by astronauts on the moon. **Satellites and You** is a 45-minute educational experience in which computer-animated scale models and video illuminate satellites and the role they play in our lives. At **Spaceport Theater** entertaining and educational documentaries are free throughout the day, including *The Boy From Mars* and *Apollo 13: Houston, We Have a Problem.* At the **Launch Status Center,** you'll receive up-to-the-minute briefings on missions in progress and get a behind-the-scenes look at what's going on at Kennedy Space Center. Outside, you can walk through the space shuttle *Explorer,* a complete, full-size spacecraft; photograph spacecraft in the Rocket Garden; and have your picture taken with Spaceman, the Space Center's own character, who wears a lunar landing pressure suit. Forget your camera? Show some ID and borrow one for free.

There is a separate charge for the films shown in two of the world's largest IMAX theaters, with screens 50 feet high (about five stories!). Some of the footage in these launch documentaries, shown nowhere else on earth, was shot in space by the astronauts using an ultra-high-resolution camera; some was taken from the Hubble telescope. ***Mission to Mir,*** narrated by astronauts Norm Thagard, John Blaha, and Shannon Lucid, contains live-action shots of *Mir,* the now-infamous Russian space station. ***The Dream Is Alive*** is an overview of the space program narrated by Walter Cronkite. ***L5: First City in Space*** is the center's first 3D IMAX film. Using data from NASA and leading scientists, the production combines live action with 3D animation to take you on a tour of a space city, through the Candor Chasm of Mars, and finally to the surface of a comet. Unless you're in training to be an astronaut, this is the closest you'll come to being in space.

You can also sign up for two guided bus tours to the launch pads for the Mercury, Gemini, and Apollo capsules, as well as those of the current shuttle program. (There is a charge for these tours.) The more popular **Red Tour,** also known as the KSC Tour, visits the Apollo launch area, the shuttle launch area, and most of the current operational sites. You'll see the mile-long device that moves the shuttle from the hangar to the pad and takes a full day to do it; a Saturn rocket like the ones that propelled the Apollo flights—the largest rocket ever built—displayed horizontally in a pavilion where you can view every inch of it; and lots of real moon memorabilia, including a lunar rock. The **Blue Tour,** sometimes called the Historical Tour, visits the old Mercury and Gemini pads with a stop at the Air Force Museum. (Note that tour itineraries do change from time to time, and the Blue Tour is not always available, particularly in slow seasons.)

What amazes me about the early space program is how low-tech it was. By current standards, we sent those people up in tin cans propelled by firecrackers. Close inspection of the rocket engines betrays pipes and fittings that would be at home on a plumber's truck and gizmos that are no more sophisticated than my lawn mower. Many of today's luxury cars have more powerful onboard computers and navigation systems than Apollo used to go to the moon. One space capsule you can actually poke your head inside left the earth and returned controlled by nothing but row upon row of on-and-off toggle switches. I could spend literally hours standing and staring, trying to imagine the courage that our astronauts must have possessed to hurtle into the void at incredible speeds in those tiny flying buckets.

The Fast Track: Buy your movie and tour tickets first, then proceed through the Visitor Center and the other attractions accordingly. Lines usually move pretty well. Except on launch days.

In peak season, roads may be so clogged that you can't even get near the place. The park may be closed without notice, and an admission charge is levied and special tickets required (which you must purchase in advance from the address below and pick up on the day before the launch in person, with photo ID). It's a lot of trouble, and there's a chance the launch could still be scrubbed. Even so, I urge you to go if the opportunity presents itself. As jaded as I am from living in the world's playground, I know of no more unforgettable experience.

Bites: In the food court, you chow down on Italian food, southern fare like fried catfish, and cold sandwiches. **Mila's**, a sit-down restaurant with old jukebox/Art Deco motifs, reminds me of Florida the way it was when I first came here. The food is like the food our moms used to fix: shepherd's pie, Salisbury steak, ham with pineapple, Yankee pot roast, and chicken pot pie. This place is neat!

Rte. 405, East Titusville, tel. 800/KSC–INFO in Florida, 407/452–2121. Admission free; launch days $10, children under 3 free (purchase tickets in advance with a credit card at 407/452–2121, extension 4343). Bus tours: $10, $7 children 3–11, children under 3 free. 3D IMAX movie: $7, $5 children 3–11, children under 3 free. Other IMAX movies: $6 per movie, $4 children 3–11, children under 3 free. Open daily 9–6, usually longer in peak seasons.

Worth-It Rating ★★★★★

U.S. ASTRONAUT HALL OF FAME One small step from the gates of the Space Center is this attraction created by the Mercury Seven Foundation, the original Mercury astronauts and their families. The astronauts have contributed memen-

tos, films, photos, and artifacts to make this a worthwhile extension of the Space Center experience. Shuttle simulators provide realistic facsimiles of astronaut experiences. This is also the home of the **U.S. Space Camp,** a summer camp that gives children and adults the chance to train for space travel on equipment used by early astronauts. It's the right stuff! *6225 Vectorspace Blvd., Titusville, tel. 407/269–6100 (Hall of Fame) or 407/267–3184 (Space Camp). $13.95 adults, $5.95 children 5–10, children under 5 free. Open daily 9–5.*
Worth-It Rating ★★★★★

ON THE WAY

FORT CHRISTMAS COUNTY PARK This absolutely free attraction, just off Route 50, is a genuine 19th-century Florida settlement that grew up around a wooden fort built during the Seminole wars. The fort's name, derived from its dedication on Christmas Day, makes the town's post office one of the busiest in the United States. Around Christmas, don't miss the historical reenactment. *23760 E. Colonial Dr., Christmas, tel. 407/568–5053. Free. Open daily dawn–dusk.*
Worth-It Rating ★★★★★ Subtract 2 or 3 if you aren't nearby.

JUNGLE ADVENTURE Roadside wildlife parks like this very reasonably priced attraction were once Florida's main attractions. Most have closed. Some like Gatorland, have grown modern and slick. Jungle Adventure is Cracker–style, recalling the old backwoods types that used to roam, hunt, and homestead Florida's swamps and forests. It contains about a zillion alligators, a petting zoo, and a small refuge for endan-

gered species, including eagles and panthers. *26205 E. Route 50, Christmas, tel. 407/569–2885. Open daily 9–6. $9.75 adults, $7.50 children 3–12, children under 3 free.*
Worth-It Rating ★★★

MIDWAY AIRBOAT RIDES Skim across the saw grass in a high-speed airboat while spotting cranes, egrets, eagles, and other local wildlife—perhaps even a gator or a water moccasin. Trips from Florida's oldest fish camp, on the Banana River, last 35 to 45 minutes. It's buggy and hot in summer, raw and windy in winter. *28501 E. Route 50, Christmas, tel. 407/568–6790. 9–4:45. $12 adults, $6 children 2–12, children under 2 free. Open daily.*
Worth-It Rating ★★★★★ Subtract 2 if swamps give you the creeps.

chapter 17
BEACH, BEACH, BEACH
Florida's Atlantic Beaches

Orlando is only about an hour's drive from the beach towns of Florida's East Coast, and each one has a unique flavor. Driving is permitted on the sand in some—catching some rays next to an active roadway can take some getting used to, so choose accordingly.

DAYTONA BEACH AND NORTH

DAYTONA BEACH At the turn of the century, people raced their cars on the hard-packed white sand at Daytona, about an hour northeast of Orlando and, because of the good highway access, one of the easiest beaches to get to. Since then, driving on the beach has been a distinguishing feature of Daytona life, though beach traffic has been severely reduced during the past year by successful protests from environmental groups fighting for the protection of endangered sea turtles. The result is that most of the Volusia Beaches, including large portions of Daytona and New Smyrna, are now closed to vehicular traffic.

Where you will still find cars, it's still dangerous—occasionally, an errant car does run over a pedestrian or two—but traffic is kept to a crawl and restricted to designated lanes, and handy motorized carts offer snacks, sodas, and even sand castle–building aids and rent beach umbrellas, boogie-boards, and motor scooters. The surf is moderate, with prime East Coast waves. Surf-fishing is allowed early morning and away from bathers. There is also good fishing on the nearby Halifax River, and you'll find plenty of deep-sea charters. To the south, **Ponce Inlet** affords spectacular fishing from shore, pier, or boat. The historic red **Ponce de León Lighthouse** makes a pleasant focal point of an outing, and several local seafood restaurants nearby serve fresh, authentic Florida fare such as shrimp, oysters, scallops, mahi-mahi, and my favorite native fish, grouper. You'll also find native Florida lobster; it has no claws and it's a lot chewier than Maine lobster, but some people actually prefer it.

More college students flock to Daytona than anywhere else in the world during spring break. So between February and May, you may have trouble finding a room, and when you do, you may find yourself sandwiched between rowdy drinking parties. The spring break reputation has made Daytona the place to see hard bodies in skimpy bathing suits the rest of the year, too.

The **Daytona International Speedway** (1801 W. International Speedway, tel. 904/254–2700) is another major player in town. Its biggest annual events are **Bike Week,** a celebration of motorcycle racing in early March, and the **Daytona 500** auto race in February. The speedway's new **Daytona**

USA includes a simulated ride in a stock car race and a racing museum. It's a must-see only for serious enthusiasts.

Because the speedway dominates local politics and because its most successful races are motorcycle events, Daytona has rolled out the red carpet for America's motorcycle gangs. Establishments offering adult entertainment, tattooing, and body-piercing have become ubiquitous. Although this makes some families uncomfortable, there has been no noticeable increase in the kinds of crimes normally associated with bikers.

Spring breakers and bikers are hard on hotels, and most of Daytona's beachfront shows the wear and tear. My rule is never get a room here without seeing it first. Still, Daytona has some lovely places to stay, including the beautiful new **Marriott** (100 N. Atlantic Ave., tel. 904/254–8200) and the **Adam's Mark Resort** (2637 S. Atlantic Ave., tel. 904/767–7350).

Information: Convention & Visitors Bureau of Daytona Beach, 126 E. Orange Ave., Daytona Beach, 32114-4406, tel. 904/255–0415. Destination Daytona, 1801 Volusia Ave., Daytona Beach 32114, tel. 904/253–8669.

Worth-It Rating ★★★ Add 1 if you're a race fan, 2 if you're a NASCAR-card-carrying fan.

ORMOND BEACH Immediately north and adjacent to Daytona, Ormond is Daytona without many of the problems—at least for the moment. Ormond is quieter and easier to get around in than its neighbor—except during spring break, race weeks, and bike week. During those times, Daytona has no city limits. Though Ormond has its ma and pa motels, like the rest of the East Coast, most properties here are more upscale.

Information: Chamber of Commerce, 165 W. Granada Blvd., Ormond Beach, 32174-6303, tel. 904/677–3454.

Worth-It Rating ★★★★

BEACH, BEACH, BEACH

ST. AUGUSTINE An hour north of Daytona is the oldest city in the United States and one of Florida's best family destinations—mellow, educational, inexpensive, and lots of fun. The St. Augustine slogan says it all: "Eight miles of beach and the rest is history." The history begins in 1513, when Juan Ponce de León discovered St. Augustine. Formally established by Pedro Menendez de Aviles in 1565 on the shores of Mantanzas Bay, St. Augustine is one of the oldest continuously incorporated cities in North America, though it has variously flown the Spanish, British, U.S., and Confederate flags. The site of de Aviles's landing is also the site of the U.S.'s oldest church, the **Mission Nombre di Dios** (San Marco and Ocean Aves., tel. 904/824–2809). But St. Augustine is loaded with other things to see and do, most accessible via two trams that let you get on and off at will.

One of the best-known sites in St. Augustine is Florida's oldest fort, the impregnable **Castillo de San Marcos** (Canal St.)—cannonballs simply sank into the spongy local coquina rock of which it was built. The original **Ripley's Believe It Or Not Museum** (19 San Marco Ave.) is also in St. Augustine, along with **Zorayda Castle** (83 King St.), a fortress built by a paranoid father to imprison his maiden daughters, and **Potter's Wax Museum** (17 King St.), an eerie collection of lifelike wax figures. There are also restorations of a home, store, and jail, and, on U.S. A1A, the world-famous **St. Augustine Alligator Farm** (999 Anastasia Blvd.), which features reptile and other wildlife shows and exhibits and is very similar to Gatorland. (I recommend that you see an alligator farm while you're in Florida, but you certainly don't need to visit more than one.)

My son Ricky's pick is the **Museum of Weapons and Early American History** (21 King St.), the life work of weapons collector Donna Lee Walton. Displaying weapons dating back to the Colonial period, this little building is simply packed with Civil War and Colonial memorabilia. Tiffany, my daughter, favors the **Oldest Wooden School House** (14 St. George St.), built in the 1700s with floors of tabby, a mortar made of indigenous oyster shell. The **Lightner Museum** (75 King St.), housed in a former hotel that's now a part of downtown St. Augustine's Flagler College, is Terrie's pick. St. Augustine came into a golden age at the turn of the last century, when railroad tycoon Henry Flagler made the city the number one tourist destination in the United States. The Lightner Museum displays the world's premier collection of Louis Comfort Tiffany's stained glass and other art and artifacts of that grand era.

Another of my favorite St. Augustine destinations is **O. C. White's Restaurant** (118 Av. Menendez, tel. 904/824–0808), in an 18th-century structure reputed to have been a pirate residence. Owner David White regales diners with tales of the home's notorious past and of its current ghostly residents (featured on TV's *Sightings*). We all love the family-priced seafood. At the other end of the historic bayfront, anchored by the Castillo de San Marcos on the north, is the restored **King's Forge Restaurant** (12 Av. Menendez, tel. 904/829–1488). Swords, antique guns, armor, and other examples of the blacksmith's craft adorn the brick walls of the building where an 18th-century blacksmith toiled. Today, you can dine on seafood, steak, and the specialty, prime rib, while enjoying the best view in town, a spectacular panorama of Castillo de San Marcos and Matanzas Bay.

Also in St. Augustine is the official Florida state play, *The Cross and Sword* (1 Riberia St.), a spectacular dramatization of the early struggles for control of the area, performed in an amphitheater carved out of the palmetto-scrub jungle. Bring mosquito repellent.

BEACH, BEACH, BEACH

St. Augustine's best beach is on beautiful **Anastasia Island.** You can drive on some stretches of it, but the nicest parts are accessible only by foot. The surf is moderate and the beach composed of rare coquina—tiny, pulverized shells mixed with dark sand. Another good beach is on a small barrier island south of St. Augustine near Marineland, a venerable Florida oceanside attraction (*see* Chapter 15); it's the site of the clean, pleasant **Marineland of Florida Quality Inn** (101 U.S. A1A, Marineland 32804, tel. 904/471–1222). Old hotels and vintage bed-and-breakfasts abound, along with chain hostelries.

Information: *Visitor Information Center, 1 Riberia St., St. Augustine, 32084, tel. 904/825–1000.*
Worth-It Rating ★★★★★

SOUTH OF DAYTONA

NEW SMYRNA BEACH The Namey family condo is immediately south of Daytona at this quiet, secluded beach. It stays that way, too, because there are no major four-lane roads from Orlando. Hotels are few and small—among them the **Holiday Inn Hotel Suites** (1401 S. Atlantic Ave., New Smyrna Beach, 32169-3113, tel. 904/426–0020) and the **Islander Beach Resort** (1601 S. Atlantic Ave., New Smyrna Beach, 32169-3199, tel. 904/427–3452). Instead, most people stay in individual condos or rentals such as the legendary **Roberto del Mar** (3619 Hill St., New Smyrna Beach 32169, tel. 407/644–3292). To the south is the northern end of the **Canaveral National Seashore** (tel. 407/867–2805), part of the buffer zone around the Space Center and the site of the last totally unspoiled Florida beach. Here, we have petted manatees, watched dolphins frolic, and picked giant conch right off the sandy shore. I sincerely hope I'm not making the area sound too appealing. We would just as soon keep this off-the-beaten-path secret to ourselves.

Information: *Chamber of Commerce, 115 Canal St., New Smyrna Beach, 32168-7003, tel. 904/428–2449. New Smyrna Beach Rentals, 4155 S. Atlantic Ave., Suite 509, New Smyrna Beach, 32169-3793, tel. 800/609–7874.*

Worth-It Rating ★★★★

COCOA AND THE SPACE COAST This is probably your best value on the East Coast. Easily accessible by the Beeline Expressway or via Route 50 east of Orlando, the beaches of Brevard County, known as the Space Coast, are family-friendly, safe, and reasonably priced. Many are part of the southern end of the Canaveral National Seashore. A Space Coast visit can be combined with visits to the Space Center and surrounding attractions (*see* Chapter 16).

Florida's biggest surfing waves are nearby, at the **Canaveral Jetties** north of Cocoa Beach. Brevard beaches have soft, white sand, with occasional patches of coquina. Driving is not allowed, but there are beach concessions and oceanfront restaurants. (Be aware that a state law makes it mandatory for all such establishments to continuously play Jimmy Buffett's "Margaritaville." If you find a beach bar that is not playing the song, you are required to report it immediately to the local authorities.)

The centerpiece of Cocoa Beach is **Ron Jon's Surf Shop** (4151 N. Atlantic Ave., tel. 407/799–8820), the largest surf shop in the world—actually a whole shopping complex occupying several city blocks, with individual sections specializing in everything aquatic from swimsuits to scuba gear. In the main store, a three-story waterfall runs through an atrium and you'll find the largest selection of T-shirts anywhere.

(That's what it feels like, anyway.) Ron Jon's blankets Orlando with more outdoor advertising than even Universal Studios Florida. Check it out.

Along Atlantic Avenue is a favorite family eating spot, **Yen-Yen** (2 N. Atlantic Ave., tel. 407/783–9512), which serves Hong Kong–style cuisine. And we often travel the 50 minutes east to Titusville from Orlando to stand in line at the popular **Dixie Crossroads** (1475 Garden St., tel. 407/268–5000), for all-you-can-eat Florida rock shrimp—they're split, broiled, and served hot, like tiny lobsters. It's not uncommon to spy an astronaut here.

At the north end of the Space Coast, north of Cocoa, is **Playalinda Beach.** It is part of the Canaveral National Seashore (although it is not connected by land to the section south of New Smyrna Beach). Playalinda often has nude or topless bathing, though its status changes with the complexion of local politics.

If you want to stay in the area, try the **Radisson Suite Hotel Oceanfront** (3101 N. U.S. A1A, Indialantic, 32903-2135, tel. 407/773–9260); the **Holiday Inn** (1300 N. Atlantic Ave., Cocoa Beach, 32931-3299, tel. 407/783–2271); the **Ramada Inn–Kennedy Space Center** (900 Friday Rd., Cocoa, 32926-3313, tel. 407/631–1210); the **Ramada Oceanfront Resort Hotel** (1035 U.S. A1A, Satellite Beach, 32937-2320, tel. 407/777–7200); or the **Ramada Inn Kennedy Space Center** (3500 Cheney Hwy., Titusville, 32780-2503, tel. 407/269–5510).

Information: Chamber of Commerce, 400 Fortenberry Rd., Merritt Island 32952, tel. 407/459–2200. Welcome Center, 1325 N. Atlantic Ave., Cocoa Beach, 32931-3220, tel. 407/783–8811. Chamber of Commerce, 1005 E. Strawbridge Ave., Melbourne, 32901-4740, tel. 407/724–5400.

Worth-It Rating ★★★★ Add 1 if you combine a visit here with a trip to the Space Center.

SOUTH OF DAYTONA

chapter 18
SHOPPERTOONITIES

In no other place in the world do you have more opportunities to buy more things bearing the likeness of Mickey Mouse. Still, although you can save money on many items by shopping outside the parks, there are many items you won't find elsewhere. This is particularly true of items themed around beloved characters like E.T., Fievel, and Shamu, which are not widely distributed ourside the parks that feature them. And remember, there's a lot more to Central Florida than characters. So many people from abroad go on shopping sprees here that export specialists have sprung up, selling everything from Levis to electronics. Read on for some of my favorite shopping destinations—all open daily.

MY SHORT LIST

Worth-It Rating ★★★★★

SPORTS DOMINATOR I have regularly seen shoes by the top brands like Reebok and at this high-volume outlet for as little as $9.95 a pair. While I can't guarantee what they'll have when you arrive, I can promise consistently amazing prices—even on official uniforms of home teams everywhere. *6464 International Dr., Orlando, tel. 407/354–2100; 8550 International Dr., Orlando, tel. 407/345–0110; 7550 W. Irlo Bronson Memorial Hwy., Kissimmee, tel. 407/397–4700.*

BARGAIN WORLD Some of the largest souvenir shops around, these have a gazillion T-shirts, toys, and trinkets as well as film, sunscreen, and even jackets—all at incredibly low prices. *6464 International Dr., Orlando, tel. 407/351–0900; 8520 International Dr., Orlando, tel. 407/352–0214; 7586 W. Irlo Bronson Memorial Hwy., Kissimmee, tel. 407/239–7733; 5781 W. Irlo Bronson Memorial Hwy., Kissimmee, tel. 407/239–0077.*

ASTRONAUT HALL OF FAME Know some kids who have seen *Apollo 13* 13 times? Here at the main entrance to the Space Center, they'll find the best selection of space-related merchandise anywhere: patches, decals, medallions, astronaut suits, model rockets, and more. *6225 Vectorspace Blvd., Titusville, tel. 407/269–6100.*

GATORLAND Yes, Gatorland. Although primarily known as an attraction, it is also one of the world's largest commercial alligator farms and sells great alligator shoes, boots, belts, wallets, and luggage at farm-direct prices. *14501 S. Orange Blossom Trail, Orlando, tel. 407/855–5496.*

RON JON SURF SHOP The world's largest surf shop, open around the clock, is a multi-block complex, announced by more billboards than even Universal Studios Florida. Check out the three-story waterfall in the lobby, the world's largest selection of T-shirts, and surf gear, swimwear, and exotic gifts galore. *4151 N. Atlantic Ave., Cocoa Beach, tel. 407/799–8820.*

WORLD OF DENIM At these huge Levis and casual wear dealers, volume keeps prices phenomenally low, and many people come to Orlando annually to stock up. *1411 Sand Lake Rd., Orlando, tel. 407/851–1773; 8255 International Dr., Orlando, tel. 407/345–0263.*

SHOPPING CENTERS, DISCOUNT MALLS

POINTE ORLANDO You can't miss the four story teddy bear in front of FAO Schwarz, which includes complete shops devoted entirely to Lego and Barbie. But Pointe Orlando is much more than that. There's an awesome example of the next generation of movie theaters, as well as over 70 terrific stores and eateries. *9101 International Dr., Orlando, tel. 407/248–2838. Too new to rate.*

BELZ FACTORY OUTLET WORLD This enormous complex right on I-Drive is two separate major malls with four smaller annexes. Remember O.J. Simpson's famous Bruno Magli shoes? One of the few places you can get them is here, along with stuff from other designers and shoemakers; Polly Flinders, Fieldcrest/Cannon, Fitz & Floyd, Mikasa, and others are represented, and prices are up to 75% off retail. *4949 International Dr., Orlando, tel. 407/352–7110.*
Worth-It Rating ★★★★★

SHOPPERTOONITIES

QUALITY OUTLET CENTER Although this mall is not as complete as Belz, the Adidas, Great Western Boot, Florsheim, and Laura Ashley here are the only ones in the attractions area. *5437 International Dr. at Sand Lake Rd., Orlando, tel. 407/345–8676.*
Worth-It Rating ★★★★

FESTIVAL CENTERS

At these themed shopping centers, the entertainment value is high and the retail experience is offbeat and unique. Some have street entertainers or rides and activities for children. The shops are usually one-of-a-kind stores where you're greeted personally by the owners.

CHURCH STREET MARKET This is just across the courtyard from Church Street Station, and if you didn't know the politics of the place, you'd think it was part of the same complex. Actually, it was cleverly created by another developer to cash in on Church Street's popularity and its advertising. Still, it has a number of worthwhile shoppertoonities, including a **Sharper Image** and **Brookstone's**. For food, there's the politically incorrect **Hooter's**, a sports bar, featuring spicy chicken wings served by scantily clad young women, and **Jungle Jim's**, with a cute jungle theme the kids will love, and family-friendly prices. *55 W. Church St., Orlando, tel. 407/872–3500.*
Worth-It Rating ★★★★ Deduct 1 if you have to make a special trip.

CHURCH STREET EXCHANGE This is the shopping part of Church Street Station, with over 50 specialty stores, many of

them locally owned and operated. A flight-ready biplane hangs from the ceiling on the second floor, where there's also an excellent food court and **Commander Ragtime's Midway**, possibly Orlando's most extensive arcade, with about a zillion video games and claw machines. The fabulous **Buffalo Trading Company** has all kinds of western items including many, many fringed buckskin jackets. The **Bumby Emporium**, also huge, sells Church Street souvenirs and lots of old-timey stuff. *55 W. Church St., Orlando, tel. 407/872–3500.*
Worth-It Rating ★★★★★

MERCADO The Mediterranean-themed Mercado invites you to eat! shop! and party! The 60 festive shops include at least several that may well be unduplicated, including **Space 2000**, loaded with space souvenirs; **Conch Republic**, which caters to fans of Florida's own Jimmy Buffett; and my son's favorite, **U-Spy,** a whole store full of honest-to-gosh James Bond–type spy gear. Mercado is also home to **Blazing Pianos**, a nightclub featuring a pair of rock & rollers on dueling grand pianos. Talk about great balls of fire! *8445 International Dr., Orlando, tel. 407/345–9337.*
Worth-It Rating ★★★★★ Subtract 1 if you're not staying on I-Drive or if you're not eating.

SHOPPERTOONITIES

chapter 19
SLEEPING BEAUTIES

Florida state law requires each household to offer free accommodations to all friends, relatives, acquaintances, and acquaintances of acquaintances who pass through town. That's just a joke. But the truth is that despite the 100,000 hotel rooms around town (more than in almost any other city in the world) and despite the rock-bottom-budget prices of many of them, most locals maintain a guest room for both invited and uninvited visitors.

Since our family already has our quota of visiting out-of-towners, I'm going to give you the next best thing—the very best hotel values around town. First I'll give you my short list, my absolute favorites. Then I'll give you a range of other good bets for each of the several major lodging areas.

Why do you need my recommendations? When I started Visitor Information Television, I called on nearly every hotel and motel in the area to try to get them to carry our channel.

I have visited every one of the properties listed here again and again over the years. Hopefully, as a result, I know a few things that you don't. For instance:

- Florida swamps breed mosquitoes the size of butterflies and cockroaches the size of golf balls. If your motel was built over a swamp, as many properties were, the only way to keep the bugs under control is with chemicals. I have been in rooms that made my nose burn and my eyes turn blood red. I left those places off the list.
- Some tourist traps are seedy, sleazy, and just plain dirty. *They* won't tell you just how bad they are when you make reservations.
- Most resorts advertise in the local tourist publications. Many post rates daily on electric signs. Because I live and work here, I read the same publications and see the same signs that you will—but all the time. I have tried to include the places that regularly post the lowest rates and deliver the best value in each area, in each price category.

As I noted previously, access to transportation and ticket deals are important in determining the overall hotel value. Disney's on-property hotels have direct access to Disney transportation, an extra that's worth money. The resorts that have banded together with Universal Studios, Sea World, and Wet 'n Wild—all covered below—also provide complimentary transportation and special packages that include tickets. In choosing either a Disney or an Orlando resort, it is best to shop around for the best available package. If you choose one that participates in the Orlando FlexTicket package, be sure to refer to the special reader discount included in the coupon section in the back of the book.

I've called this chapter "Sleeping Beauties" because here in Orlando, your hotel will be an especially important part of the overall vacation experience and the number of theme properties is increasing. I've included them all, along with a good selection of those that stand out from the crowd and offer significant extra value, particularly when the prices are competitive. Not every place that didn't make my list is a flea bag or a toxic dump. Some were omitted just because I don't know them personally, others because I didn't think they delivered value equal to their rates. The ones I did include I can recommend without reservation. Information about the facilities follows my comments. Unless I tell you otherwise, all properties have an arcade with video games, at least one swimming pool, a no-pets-allowed policy, and transportation to and from some major area attractions (noted below when it's free).

If you're traveling with your kids, be on the lookout for "baby-sitting adventures"—that is, child-care with a theme, in a themed environment and often with costumed characters. They're usually available both day and night.

PRICE CATEGORIES Dollar-sign symbols indicate regular nightly rates for two people in a room (called rack rates in the hospitality industry):

Budget	$	under $49
Moderate	$$	$49–$99
Upscale	$$$	$99 and up

MAIN ATTRACTIONS AREAS Hotels in and around Orlando are clustered in three main areas:

International Drive: Universal Studios Florida is on the north end of this busy strip, Sea World on the south. It's also home to the Orlando Convention Center, Wet 'n Wild, and several smaller attractions. There are more rooms and places to eat here than in any other area.

Lake Buena Vista: This is the area around Route 535 at I–4 Exit 27, near Downtown Disney; it's convenient to Disney attractions.

The U.S. 192 corridor in Kissimmee: Also known as the Irlo Bronson Memorial Highway, the strip begins at the end of Disney property near the Magic Kingdom and Celebration, the new Disney planned community. It is close to Water Mania, Medieval Times, Old Town, Wild Bill's, and other sites. This is also where you'll find some of the area's lowest room rates. Parts of the area are also known as Maingate, because of their proximity to the main gate to the Magic Kingdom back when the Magic Kingdom was all there was to Walt Disney World. In downtown Kissimmee, U.S. 192 is known as Vine Street. Most of the time, it reminds me of a Hollywood movie set, all front with no back. Kissimmee/Osceola County is one of America's largest cattle-producing areas. Check it out: Just a few feet behind the strip, cows still graze.

Downtown Disney and Other Areas Inside WDW: On Walt Disney World property, some hotels are owned by Disney, some are not. The Disney-owned properties tend to be high-end; rooms tend to be small at those that are moderately priced or in the budget categories—not a problem if your group numbers four or fewer. Almost all hotels have terrific theme swimming pools and almost all are on lakes. They may have a beach and there's almost always a marina where you can rent zippy little speedboats called Water Sprites as well as other craft. Transportation around WDW is always free.

SLEEPING BEAUTIES

Hotels that are not Disney-owned are clustered in Downtown Disney in an area that used to be known as Hotel Plaza. These represent an exceptional value, and guests enjoy many of the perks available to those staying at WDW-owned hotels, including free transportation between hotels and Disney attractions, guaranteed admission to Disney theme parks during normal park operating hours (even on "sold-out" days), and preferential treatment when you want to book tee times on Walt Disney World championship golf courses. The Marketplace at Downtown Disney is within walking distance, and from there you can catch a bus to almost any other WDW destination.

If you are considering a hotel outside WDW that I haven't recommended, choose carefully: Base your decision only on recent personal visits by someone you trust, since there has been a lot of decline among some U.S. 192 properties in the last year or so, and a few sections of the strip are downright unwelcoming. Be sure to get the exact location of the property (or look it up on a map). And don't be misled by names. Some properties add the name of an area to its own (i.e. Maingate, Lake Buena Vista) in an effort to make you think they're closer than they are to the area in question. For instance, several hotels that have called themselves Orlando North (not on my list) are really in Maitland and Altamonte. That's 35 miles north of Disney property, or about an hour by car in morning rush hour traffic.

Note that I don't recommend downtown Orlando or, unless you're specifically looking for adult entertainment, the South Orange Blossom Trail (U.S. 441, known around town as the South Trail or SOBT).

SLEEPING BEAUTIES

My Short List

⭐⭐⭐⭐⭐

The following are my favorite hotels in Orlando, with the least expensive first.

RODEWAY INTERNATIONAL INN This simple, clean I-Drive motel with all the basics usually posts the area's lowest rates. The restaurant serves buffet-style, and there's a Japanese steak house. *6327 International Dr., Orlando 32819, tel. 407/351–4444 or 800/999–6327. 315 rooms. 2 restaurants, bar, babysitting, supervised children's program (summer only). Pets accepted.*
$

COMFORT INN LAKE BUENA VISTA This relatively new complex, with four five-story buildings, is very clean and well maintained. Convenient to Downtown Disney, it's visible from I–4; transportation to and from WDW attractions is complimentary. Kids eat free, and there are two swimming pools. *8442 Palm Pkwy., Orlando 32836, tel. 407/239–7300 or 800/999–7300. 640 rooms. Restaurant, bar. Pets accepted.*
$

HOLIDAY INN MAINGATE EAST I rate this property one of the best on U.S. 192 in its price range. Even among Orlando hotels, most of which are family-friendly, this one stands out. Free child care runs from 8 AM until midnight, and kids eat free with their parents in the restaurant. You can't get any better than that. There are two swimming pools. *5678 W. Irlo Bronson Memorial Hwy., Kissimmee 34746, tel. 407/396–4488 or*

800/FON–KIDS. 614 rooms, 89 suites. 2 restaurants, 2 bars, some kitchenettes, lighted tennis court, health club, 2 hot tubs, baby-sitting, supervised children's program, playground. Pets accepted.
$$

DISNEY'S ALL-STAR RESORTS These two resorts in the southwest corner of the property near Blizzard Beach and Downtown Disney are the best of the moderately priced properties at Walt Disney World, and others are planned. It's hard to beat the rates, anywhere. The **All-Star Sports Resort** can be recognized by its giant football helmet, immense basketball, and other sports-equipment sculptures. The **All-Star Music Resort** features a giant guitar, huge piano, and jumbo jukebox. The swimming pools (there are four in the complex) are like mini-water parks on the same themes. Staying at either gets you all Disney privileges, including unlimited free Disney transportation. It almost doesn't matter that the rooms are a little small. *WDW Central Reservations, Box 10100, Lake Buena Vista 32830, tel. 407/934–7639 or 407/824–3000. 3,840 rooms. 2 restaurants, 2 bars, baby-sitting.*
$$

RADISSON TWIN TOWERS HOTEL The largest Radisson hotel on earth, at the entrance to Universal Studios, is also one of the nicest, with its modern, spacious rooms. Proximity to the park makes it a frequent choice of visiting celebrities. In fact, you can't get much closer. *5780 Major Blvd., Orlando 32819, tel. 407/351–1000 or 800/843–8693. 760 rooms, 27 suites. Restaurant, 3 bars, health club, hot tub, baby-sitting, playground.*
$$–$$$

MY SHORT LIST

DOUBLETREE GUEST SUITES AT DOWNTOWN DISNEY This is the best pick on Disney property for families who need a lot of space at a reasonable price. Little touches abound, like the hot cookies on arrival and a children's registration area to entertain and occupy the little ones during check in and out. My editor stayed here with her extended family and said that the vacation worked because of the accommodations here: Each is a spacious suite that includes a living room with a TV, Sony PlayStation, and a double sleep sofa, plus either one bedroom (in units that sleep six) or two bedrooms (in those that accommodate ten); each bedroom has two double beds or a king bed and a TV. (Even the bathrooms have their own TVs.) For all this, the price is right—not too much more than at Disney's own bottom-of-the-line properties, which sleep just four to a room. *2305 Hotel Plaza Blvd., Lake Buena Vista 32830, tel. 407/934–1000. 229 suites. Restaurant, hot tub, 2 lighted tennis courts, playground.*
$$–$$$

THE CASTLE, DOUBLETREE RESORT Why stay in a hotel when you can stay in a castle? When hotelier Richard Kessler's young daughter asked her daddy why she couldn't stay in the Cinderella Castle, Kessler got the idea to build this magnificent medieval-style property, which dominates International Drive skyline. The attention to detail is awesome—there are intricate mosaics, fantasy medieval art, and special effects everywhere, even in-room sound effects (I like the ocean sounds). A medieval fountain with three giant bronze fish spouts at the center of the spacious round pool. The gift shop offers medieval collectibles, and the hotel is home to the eclectic Café Tu-Tu Tango and Austin's Steak House, which are both excellent. There's free transportation to both Disney and Orlando FlexTicket attractions. *8629 International Dr., Orlando 32819, tel. 800/95–CASTLE or 407/345–1511, fax 407/*

SLEEPING BEAUTIES

248–8181. 218 rooms, 12 suites. 2 restaurants, 4 bars, hot tub.
$$–$$$

DISNEY'S FORT WILDERNESS RESORT AND CAMPGROUND

At Tiffany's request, we spent her fourth birthday at this lakeside WDW campground and we had a great time. You'll find all the traditional camp activities: campfire sing-alongs (Chip and Dale show up), marshmallow roasts, and outdoor movies (some not screened anywhere else in the world). Don't let the campground idea keep you away if you're not a camper. Besides the tent and RV sites, you can rent suite-size digs with full kitchens in spiffy free-standing manufactured homes (like deluxe RVs on foundations)—and you'll pay about the same as a regular room elsewhere in WDW. Plus, there are three swimming pools and loads of other facilities: horseback riding, fishing, and nature trails. The campground is right next to River Country, and Disney transportation is free. *WDW Central Reservations, Box 10100, Lake Buena Vista 32830, tel. 407/934–7639 or 407/824–3000. 408 rooms, 387 RV sites, 390 tent sites. 2 restaurants, bar, lighted tennis court, babysitting, playground.*
$$–$$$

CARIBE ROYALE RESORT SUITES Lush landscaping, waterfalls, and a moat mark one of the most impressive layouts in town. A 75-foot water slide passes over the waterfalls into the enormous free-form pool. Nearby is a children's wading pool with aim-and-squirt water cannons. The playground is modern and full of climbing things, tunnels, and slides. All accommodations are in one- or two-bedroom suites, which sleep between six and ten; the living rooms have sofa beds, wet bars, microwaves, and refrigerators. Breakfast is free, and so is transportation to and from Disney. When you figure in

MY SHORT LIST

the money you can save by occasionally eating in your room, you could save money at this deluxe resort. *14300 International Dr. Orlando 32821, tel. 407/238–8000 or 800/823–8300. 1,200 suites. Restaurant, bar, deli, pool, 2 jacuzzis, 2 exercise rooms.*
$$$

CLARION PLAZA HOTEL This really nice 12-story hotel right in the middle of things on I-Drive, near the convention center, is very pretty, with a wonderful big pool and a spacious patio that never seems overcrowded; you can usually find a chair. The grounds are attractively landscaped and the lobby is huge. The food in the restaurant is excellent. And with VCRs in every unit and lots of facilities for the money, it's a wallet-pleaser as well. When reserving, check to see whether there will be a major convention there during your stay; if so, you should probably go elsewhere. *9700 International Dr., Orlando 32819-8114, tel. 407/352–9700 or 800/627–8258. 810 rooms, 32 suites. 2 restaurants, 3 bars, golf, baby-sitting, playground.*
$$$

THE GRAND FLORIDIAN At Disney, you can't do better than this stately white re-creation of a turn-of-the-century resort with a vintage white Rolls-Royce out front. Overlooking the Seven Seas Lagoon, directly opposite the Magic Kingdom, it's incredibly convenient. And the view of the Magic Kingdom fireworks across the lake is breathtaking—as is the view of the splendid nightly Electrical Water Pageant. *WDW Central Reservations, Box 10100, Lake Buena Vista 32830, tel. 407/934–7639 or 407/824–3000. 961 rooms, 71 suites. 6 restaurants, 3 bars, health club, hot tub, golf, lighted tennis court, baby-sitting.*
$$$

SLEEPING BEAUTIES

MARRIOTT'S ORLANDO WORLD CENTER This gorgeous high-rise is the best hotel not only in the Lake Buena Vista area but in all Orlando. General Manager Jim McDonnell runs the tightest ship in town. You can't miss it—it's the area's tallest structure, and it's near Epcot's main entrance. From higher floors, you can get the clearest aerial view anywhere of all three parks. Of the five pools, the free-form pool is the best, with waterfalls and a water slide. There's also miniature golf. *8701 World Center Dr., Orlando 32821, tel. 407/239–4200 or 800/228–9290. 1,503 rooms. 6 restaurants, 2 bars, health club, 3 hot tubs, golf, 8 lighted tennis courts, baby-sitting, supervised children's program, playground.*
$$$

THE BUENA VISTA PALACE This towering structure is almost as tall as Marriott's Orlando World Center, and the lounge on top and the west-facing rooms above the ninth floor have a clear and close-up view of the nightly pyrotechnics in the Magic Kingdom, Epcot, Disney–MGM, and Pleasure Island. Of all the Downtown Disney properties, the Buena Vista is the closest to the theme parks, so if you use the hotel transportation you'll be the last on and the first off. It's also the most luxurious property. It has three heated swimming pools, volleyball, a marina with boat rentals, jogging trails, and a large, serious spa, with complete facilities. The complex includes a concierge floor, several non-smoking "Evergreen Rooms" designed to remain odor-free, and an adjacent complex of one- and two-bedroom suites. And all rooms and suites have a balcony or patio. Arthur's 27 is known as one of the area's finest restaurants—it also has the fireworks view—and the Laughing Kookaburra is a top hangout for the local party kids. *1900 Buena Vista Dr., Lake Buena Vista 32830, tel. 407/827–2727, 800/327–2990. 984 rooms, 30 suites. 5 restaurants,*

MY SHORT LIST

4 bars, hot tub, 3 lighted tennis courts, supervised children's program, playground.
$$$

STAR ISLAND/RESORT WORLD Established to accommodate visiting celebs in style while remaining affordable to family vacationers, this resort is my pick as Central Florida's very best time-share—and you don't have to be an owner to stay here. Every year it hosts the annual NBA Fantasy Basketball Camp. This is also where I send my friends and business contacts. Every unit is a 1,400-square-foot suite with a kitchen; a wet bar, large-screen color TV, VCR, stereo system, and balcony in the living room; plus large TVs in every bedroom, giant sunken whirlpool tubs in the master baths, and smaller whirlpools in the guest baths. Swimming, fishing, boating, lake cruises, water skiing, and jet skiing are all available on adjacent Lake Cecile. The playground is large and elaborate. There are four swimming pools, an elaborate health club, and a T.G.I. Friday's restaurant. The location is excellent, too; it's on U.S. 192 just down the street from Disney's Celebration. *2800 N. Poinciana Blvd., Kissimmee 34746-5258, tel. 407/397–7827 or 800/423–8604. 523 suites. 3 restaurants, 2 bars, 3 hot tubs, golf, 6 lighted tennis courts, health club, baby-sitting, supervised children's program, playground.*
$$$

OMNI ROSEN The signature property of local hotelier Harris Rosen is the most luxurious hotel on I-Drive. The rooms are large, and the beds, pillows, and towels are oversized and fluffy; everything is flawlessly maintained. The heated pool is jumbo, and access to a nearby golf course is included in the room rate. *9840 International Dr., Orlando 32819, tel. 407/*

354–9840 or 800/627–8258. 1,334 rooms, 89 suites. 3 restaurants, 3 bars, lighted tennis court, baby-sitting, hot tubs, fitness center, playground.
$$$

Other Good Bets

These hotels and motels yield good value-for-dollar, and I recommend them wholeheartedly. Many are perfectly wonderful, and I've given them my highest rating, but for whatever reason, they just aren't extra-special *to me* personally and I haven't put them on my short list. You may well feel otherwise.

INTERNATIONAL DRIVE AREA: UNIVERSAL CITY RESORTS

Until Universal opens its own four hotels on-property in 1999, the following properties give you Universal's answer to the special deals and amenities available at Disney properties: free transportation to Universal, Sea World, and Wet 'n Wild, as well as discount vacation packages that include the Orlando FlexTicket. For more information and the latest rates, call Universal City Travel at 800/711–0080.

ECONOLODGE INTERNATIONAL DRIVE This clean, basic motel provides economy lodging at rates tailored to the lowest budgets. It's only 2 miles from Universal Studios, just off

of International Drive. *5859 American Way, Orlando 32819, tel. 407/351–2000. 192 rooms. Bar.*
Worth-It Rating ★★★
$$

LAS PALMAS HOTEL This is a good basic choice that's an especially good deal on Universal City Travel packages. It's secure, with inside-entrance rooms, and it's got a great location on International Drive, directly across from Wet 'n Wild and just a couple of minutes from Universal Studios. *6233 International Dr., Orlando 32819, tel. 407/351–3900. 262 rooms. Bar.*
Worth-It Rating ★★★★
$–$$

HOLIDAY INN UNIVERSAL STUDIOS In this Holiday Inn at Universal's main entrance, every spacious room has its own balcony or patio. There's also a special pool for kids. *5905 Kirkman Rd., Orlando 32819, tel. 407/351–3333. 256 rooms. Restaurant.*
Worth-It Rating ★★★★
$–$$

DELTA ORLANDO RESORT This 25-acre resort has large grounds, with well-planned and well-maintained recreational areas, including three swimming pools, two wading pools, and miniature golf. It provides free transportation to Sea World, Wet 'n Wild, and nearby Universal. *5715 Major Blvd., Orlando 32819-7988, tel. 407/351–3340. 800 rooms. 3 restaurants, bar, 3 hot tubs, 2 lighted tennis courts, supervised children's program, playground. Pets accepted.*
Worth-It Rating ★★★★
$$

SLEEPING BEAUTIES

COMFORT SUITES UNIVERSAL You can get a suite with a microwave and fridge for the price of a budget room here; the one-bedroom suites sleep up to five. The pool complex includes a wading pool, and the location is just 2 miles from Universal Studios. *9350 Turkey Lake Rd., Orlando 32819, tel. 407/351–5050. Restaurant, bar, playground.*
Worth-It Rating ★★★★
$–$$

EMBASSY SUITES Less than five minutes' drive from Universal is this excellent example of Embassy's consistently high quality. Every unit is a suite that sleeps up to six in its bedroom and sofa-bedded living room; there's always a wet bar, refrigerator, microwave oven, and two TVs. Breakfast is cooked to order—and it's free. This is a bit nicer than the Comfort Suites, but more expensive. *8250 Jamaican Ct., Orlando 32819, tel. 407/345–8250. 26 suites. Bar, exercise room, hot tub.*
Worth-It Rating ★★★★
$$

HILTON GRAND VACATIONS CLUB Grand Vacations is Hilton's time-share division, but you don't have to own to stay in this one right next to Sea World, minutes away from Universal Studios. Rooms are very big and nicely appointed—they even have chandeliers. *6878 Sea Harbor Dr., Orlando 32821, tel. 407/239–0100, 800/448–2736. Restaurant, bar, 2 pools, exercise room, 4 hot tubs, playground.*
Worth-It Rating ★★★★
$$$

OTHER GOOD BETS

OTHER I-DRIVE RESORTS

QUALITY INN INTERNATIONAL Proof that not all motels are created equal, this Quality Inn has clean, spacious rooms and two swimming pools, as well as rates that are consistently some of the strip's lowest. Kids eat free at the restaurant's all-you-can-eat breakfast and dinner buffets; Mickey D's, the world's largest McDonald's, is next door. *7600 International Dr., Orlando 32819, tel. 407/351–1600 or 800/875–7600. 728 rooms. Restaurant, bar. Pets accepted.*
Worth-It Rating ★★★★★
$

HOLIDAY INN INTERNATIONAL DRIVE RESORT This well-laid-out 13-acre resort is on the older side, with some of the problems that go with the territory. But its age also means that the landscaping is lush and mature, and it's cool and pleasant even on the hottest days. *6515 International Dr., Orlando 32819, tel. 407/351–3500 or 800/465–4329. 652 rooms. 2 restaurants, bar, pool, jacuzzi, health club, baby-sitting.*
Worth-It Rating ★★★★
$$–$$$

PEABODY HOTEL ORLANDO This 27-story luxury hotel is famous as home of the Peabody ducks. Every day, in an amazing spectacle, they take the elevator to the ground floor, and then, to the strains of John Phillip Sousa, march single file through the lobby to the fountain in the middle. Every afternoon the ceremony is reversed. The restaurants are among Orlando's best, and rooms are large, with big TV-equipped bathrooms. In west-facing rooms above the 20th floor, you can see Disney fireworks off in the distance. *9801 Interna-*

tional Dr., Orlando 32819, tel. 407/352–4000 or 800/PEABODY. 891 rooms, 57 suites. 3 restaurants, 2 bars, health club, hot tub, 4 lighted tennis courts, baby-sitting.
Worth-It Rating ★★★★
$$$

AT WDW: DISNEY HOTELS

DISNEY'S DIXIE LANDINGS RESORT The world of Mark Twain's Tom Sawyer and Huck Finn was one of Walt Disney's favorite themes. With its riverboat-landing motif, this moderately priced Disney resort near Downtown Disney harks back to those days. There are six swimming pools; the fanciest one has slides, swings, playgrounds, and a quiet area for anyone who insists on acting like a grown-up. *WDW Central Reservations, Box 10100, Lake Buena Vista 32830, tel. 407/934–7639 or 407/824–3000. 2,048 rooms. Restaurant, bar, golf, playground.*
Worth-It Rating ★★★★
$$

DISNEY'S PORT ORLEANS RESORT The ubiquitous sound system plays New Orleans jazz in this Disney version of a Bourbon Street bivouac, near Downtown Disney. The pool, a mini-water park, has a Little Mermaid theme, and the slide is supposed to be King Neptune's; there's also a wading pool. *WDW Central Reservations, Box 10100, Lake Buena Vista 32830, tel. 407/934–7639 or 407/824–3000. 1,008 rooms. Restaurant, bar, health club, hot tub, baby-sitting.*
Worth-It Rating ★★★★
$$

OTHER GOOD BETS

DISNEY'S BOARDWALK INN Since Terrie and I spent our 18th anniversary at this faithful Disney's BoardWalk re-creation of the Atlantic City I remember from the 1950s, it's our new favorite among WDW hotels. The architecture is perfectly detailed, right down to the giant Art Deco signs. The hotel's Luna Park water play area features a flumelike 200-foot slide. And the fun never stops in the BoardWalk shopping, dining, and entertainment attraction at your doorstep. *WDW Central Reservations, Box 10100, Lake Buena Vista 32830, tel. 407/934–7639 or 407/824–3000. 378 rooms, 14 suites. 4 restaurants, 4 bars, health club, hot tub, golf, 2 lighted tennis courts, baby-sitting, supervised children's program, playground.*
Worth-It Rating ★★★★
$$$

DISNEY'S CONTEMPORARY RESORT There's only one resort that's truly a walk away from the Magic Kingdom, and that's this five-story lakeside A-frame tower. And the monorail runs right through the middle of its giant atrium. I once stayed in the corner suite up top and had my best view ever of the Magic Kingdom's fireworks: I thought I should duck. Right on the white sand beach, there's a notable water playground-cum-pool area (one of three swimming pools) with a wading pool. *WDW Central Reservations, Box 10100, Lake Buena Vista 32830, tel. 407/934–7639 or 407/824–3000. 1,053 rooms. 3 restaurants, 3 bars, golf, 6 lighted tennis courts, health club, baby-sitting.*
Worth-It Rating ★★★★
$$$

DISNEY'S OLD KEY WEST RESORT This all-suite resort near Downtown Disney is part of the Disney Vacation Club time-share program. However, you don't have to buy in to stay here, and the accommodations, all suites, are all extremely

SLEEPING BEAUTIES

spacious and perfectly appointed, right down to the kitchens. Like many romantics, Terrie loves lighthouses. This place has several, including an impressive example that's the centerpiece of the dolphin-theme pool area, a mini-water park that's actually one of four (count 'em) swimming pools. *WDW Central Reservations, Box 10100, Lake Buena Vista 32830, tel. 407/934–7639 or 407/824–3000. 497 suites. 2 restaurants, 2 bars, 2 hot tubs, golf, 2 lighted tennis courts, health club, baby-sitting, supervised children's program, playground.*
Worth-It Rating ★★★★
$$$

DISNEY'S POLYNESIAN VILLAGE RESORT Imagine the huts of a Polynesian village, blown up to giant size. That's the Poly, as it's known informally around here. On monorail and on the shores of the Seven Seas Lagoon, it's also directly across the water from the Magic Kingdom, so you get a clear view of the Magic Kingdom fireworks and of the floating Electrical Water Pageant, which makes its first nightly stop here at 9 PM. The Poly is also the site of the Ohana Grill (and its fabulous island-theme show-and-feast), the wonderful Neverland Club (a kids' program), and WDW's beloved Luau—all three open to all but most convenient for hotel guests. *WDW Central Reservations, Box 10100, Lake Buena Vista 32830, tel. 407/934–7639 or 407/824–3000. 853 rooms, 12 suites. 3 restaurants, bar, golf, health club, baby-sitting, supervised children's program, playground.*
Worth-It Rating ★★★★
$$$

DISNEY'S WILDERNESS LODGE Not many Florida hotels have fireplaces. But at this upscale re-creation of a Rocky Mountain resort, tucked away near Fort Wilderness there are

OTHER GOOD BETS

huge stone ones in the lobby, along with some totem poles—pretty striking in this subtropical setting. Along with one basic pool, there's another replete with waterfalls and a slide down huge rocks. *WDW Central Reservations, Box 10100, Lake Buena Vista 32830, tel. 407/934–7639 or 407/824–3000. 699 rooms, 29 suites. 2 restaurants, bar, golf, baby-sitting, supervised children's program. Pets accepted.*
Worth-It Rating ★★★★★
$$$$

DISNEY'S YACHT AND BEACH CLUB RESORT These lakeside siblings near Epcot are almost like a single hotel, sharing amenities such as a mini-water park complete with a shipwreck where your pint-sized swabs can climb up to a crow's nest, then slide down the "plank" and plunk into the not-at-all-briny deep. Both hotels look as if they were moved straight from some vintage northeastern seaside resort. *WDW Central Reservations, Box 10100, Lake Buena Vista 32830, tel. 407/934–7639 or 407/824–3000. 1,219 rooms, 71 concierge rooms, 40 suites. 2 restaurants, 4 bars, golf, 2 lighted tennis courts, health club, baby-sitting, supervised children's program, playground.*
Worth-It Rating ★★★★
$$$

THE VILLAS AT THE DISNEY INSTITUTE You don't have to be attending the Disney Institute (*see* Chapter 15) to stay in these Downtown Disney-area villas, which come in several styles (all with kitchenettes). The Treehouse Villas, surrounded by woods, are a personal favorite—two-story houses with a spiral staircase between floors and one bedroom downstairs and two, with balconies, upstairs. The two-story town houses are similar in size, though more traditional. And

there are five swimming pools! *WDW Central Reservations, Box 10100, Lake Buena Vista 32830, tel. 407/934–7639 or 407/824–3000. 585 suites. Restaurant, bar, hot tub, golf, 4 lighted tennis courts, health club, baby-sitting, playground.*
Worth-It Rating ★★★★
$$$

AT WDW IN DOWNTOWN DISNEY: NON-DISNEY HOTELS

THE HILTON AT DOWNTOWN DISNEY Rooms at this former convention hotel are clean and fresh from a 1997 renovation, and each has a spacious sitting area and Sony PlayStations. There are two heated swimming pools, one with a spray-equipped wading pool. The Vacation Station kids' hotel, a hotel-within-a-hotel, was a baby-sitting adventure pioneer at WDW. *1751 Hotel Plaza Blvd., Lake Buena Vista 32830, tel. 407/827–4000. 786 rooms, 27 suites. 7 restaurants, 2 bars, hot tub, health club, supervised children's program.*
Worth-It Rating ★★★★
$$–$$$

GROSVENOR RESORT At the time of my inspection, the home of the excellent MurderWatch Mystery Theatre dinner show, was getting a much-needed refurb. The tower section has a nice view of Downtown Disney and the fireworks, and rooms have VCRs. Kids can help themselves at the kids-only buffet alongside the adult spread. And character breakfasts and dinners are held frequently on site. *1850 Hotel Plaza Blvd., Lake Buena Vista 32830, tel. 407/828–4444. 626 rooms, 6*

OTHER GOOD BETS

suites. 2 restaurants, 3 bars, hot tub, 2 lighted tennis courts, health club, playground.
Worth-It Rating ★★★
$$–$$$

TRAVELODGE HOTEL For the price of a room in a Disney-owned hotel, you can rent one of the four gorgeous tropical-theme penthouse suites here. Even regular rooms are fine, and all units have a balcony, with views of Disney pyrotechnics from upper floors facing every direction but east. The buffet breakfast is lavish and yummy. *1805 Hotel Plaza Blvd., Lake Buena Vista 32830, tel. 407/828–2424 or 800/348–3765. 325 rooms, 4 suites. Restaurant, bar, baby-sitting, playground.*
Worth-It Rating ★★★ Penthouse suites **★★★★★**
$$–$$$

COURTYARD BY MARRIOTT Standard rooms here are larger than any other comparable accommodations in Downtown Disney. There's a convenient deli in the lobby, and there are two swimming pools, one with a wading pool. In the restaurant, children under six eat free when accompanied by a paying adult. *1805 Hotel Plaza Blvd., Lake Buena Vista 32830. 323 rooms. Restaurant, exercise room, hot tub, playground.*
Worth-It Rating ★★★★
$$–$$$

HOTEL ROYAL PLAZA Rooms here have emerged from a recent renovation minus their balconies but, instead, now equipped with large whirlpool bathtubs (a good trade-off, in my opinion). They also have VCRs. *1905 Hotel Plaza Blvd., Lake Buena Vista 32830, tel. 407/828–2828 or 800/248–7890. 372*

rooms, 22 suites. Restaurant, hot tub, 4 lighted tennis courts, health club, baby-sitting, supervised children's program.
Worth-It Rating ★★★
$$–$$$

U.S. 192/KISSIMMEE

DAYS INN/DAYS SUITES EAST OF THE MAGIC KINGDOM
Kids eat free and you can buy up to 10 gallons of gas half-price at this motel next to the Disney's Celebration and the Old Town shopping-dining-rides attraction. Every suite has a kitchenette, and breakfast is free. *5820 W. Irlo Bronson Memorial Hwy., Kissimmee 34746, tel. 407/396–7900 or 800/327–9126. 404 rooms, 604 suites. 4 restaurants, hot tub, health club, baby-sitting, playground. Pets accepted.*
Worth-It Rating ★★★
$–$$

HOLIDAY INN NIKKI BIRD RESORT
Rooms here are colorful and tropical. There are three swimming pools and two wading pools. Kids eat free. *7300 W. Bronson Hwy., Kissimmee 34746, tel. 407/396–7300 or 800/206–2747. 529 rooms. Restaurant, bar, 3 hot tubs, lighted tennis court, playground.*
Worth-It Rating ★★★★
$$

HYATT ORLANDO
Dominating the corner of I–4 and U.S. 192, this rambling, well-appointed 56-acre resort is one of the most convenient in the area. There are four swimming pools, each with its own wading pool. It's not your usual Hyatt—it's simpler, though still comfortable, more like a Hyatt motel.

OTHER GOOD BETS

And without the higher Hyatt rates. *6375 W. Irlo Bronson Memorial Hwy., Kissimmee 34746, tel. 407/396–1234 or 800/233–1234. 922 rooms, 29 suites. 4 restaurants, bar, health club, 4 hot tubs, 3 lighted tennis courts, baby-sitting, playground.*
Worth-It Rating ★★★★
$$

chapter 20
CRUISING LIKE A PRO

Back in the 1980s, the gang at Premier Cruise Lines had a neat idea: Put some of the theme-park characters on a cruise ship sailing from Port Canaveral, less than an hour from Orlando, and package a short cruise with a theme-park visit and hotel accommodations. The *Big Red Boat* was such a success that it refocused cruise lines on the family market. For 1998, Disney inaugurates its own cruise line with the *Disney Magic,* the first of two megaships that will function as yet another Walt Disney World destination attraction. The Premiere Cruise Line's *Big Red Boat* and ships from other lines continue to offer year-round land-sea packages from Port Canaveral with hotel accommodations and tickets for WDW and Universal Studios; you can also buy the three- or four-day cruise alone, without the land arrangements. Note: All rates given below are per person based on double occupancy.

THE DISNEY MAGIC

This Disneyesque fantasy re-creates the grandeur of the great sailing ships of the last century and the earlier part of this one. But you could also call it the water launch to the fifth theme park. I think back on the original concept for the Magic Kingdom—a theme park that's more or less surrounded by water, that's on an island reachable only by Disney transportation; the *Disney Magic* is the only transportation to Castaway Cay, Disney's own private island destination in the Bahamas. With a land-and-sea package, you'll have a vacation that is all Disney, from the time you arrive in Orlando until you're dropped off at the airport, homeward bound. Disney Cruise Line buses transport you to a Walt Disney World resort, where you check in for your entire holiday; when it's time to head for the Disney Cruise Line's own Port Canaveral terminal, you're picked up at your hotel by another Disney bus, complete with smiling Disney staffers. At the end of the trip, another Disney bus transports you back to your original hotel.

Meals and Entertainment: You'll find Broadway-style shows, first-run movies, and more dining experiences than there are meals to try them. At **Animators' Palate,** the room is transformed as you work your way through a meal of California cuisine from the first black-and-white sketch of the animator's pen into a completely animated spectacle of light and sound. **Lumière's,** named for Jerry Orbach's memorable singing candle in *Beauty and the Beast,* offers elegant five-course meals by candlelight (of course). **Parrot Cay** has a casual Caribbean theme and serves spicy Jamaican jerk meat and other island specialties. **Palo,** a grown-up restaurant, serves northern Italian fare with an ocean panorama. At night, the ship becomes the equivalent of a floating Pleasure Island, complete with a nighttime entertainment district, **Beat Street,** with a country-rock bar, a

CRUISING LIKE A PRO

comedy club, a piano bar, and a sports bar. A family entertainment area, in the form of a replica TV studio, has live bands and does game shows with plenty of audience participation.

Sports: There are three pools—a wading pool, a pool for families, and another for adults only—all on Deck 9, where you'll also find a spa and fitness areas. One deck above is volleyball, Ping-Pong, and a workout room.

For Children: Kids and teens have their own activities. Grade-schoolers can join their favorite Disney characters in audience-participation skits, and Disney's **Ocean-ear Club** supervises the kids and sends their parents off, equipped with pagers, to play on their own. The nine-to-twelve set has its own gadget-laden adventure area, and teens have a coffee house with music, big-screen TV, computers, participatory activities, and a lounge for get-togethers.

Ashore Just when you get your sea legs, you dock in Nassau for a day, and, the next day, sail to Disney's own Castaway Cay, where turquoise Caribbean waters lap at both a secluded adults-only beach and a family beach. You can play beach volleyball or go bicycling, snorkeling, and lots more. Don't be surprised to see a dolphin.

Itineraries, Prices, Info *Cruises Fri. to Fri., with 3 days in WDW and a 4-day cruise; Mon. to Mon., with 4 days in WDW and a 3-day cruise. Rates: $1,309–$3,619, including airfare from major gateways cities (lowest late Aug.–early Dec., highest Mar.–Apr. and the year-end holidays). Disney Cruises, tel. 800/951–3532, 407/566–7000; www.disney.com/DisneyCruise.*

THE BIG RED BOAT

The original is still around, part of the Premier Cruise Lines fleet, and it certainly will be for a long time. It sails the same azure ocean as Disney, but at a lower price and with a casino and duty-free shopping. And the packages include not only WDW but also my favorite theme park, Universal Studios Florida.

You can have breakfast and photos with Looney Toons' Sylvester, Tweetie, Wile E. Coyote, Daffy Duck, Yosemite Sam, Foghorn Leghorn, Bugs Bunny, and the Tasmanian Devil. A nifty touch for the little ones is at bedtime, when you can have one of the toons tuck your kids into bed, an amazing once-in-a-lifetime tuck-in photograph!

Meals and Entertainment: As on any cruise worth its saltwater, a major objective is to feed you to death, beginning with a lavish welcome-aboard buffet. Every night brings a different theme dinner—Italian, French, American, Caribbean—with appropriate fare (or, if you must, low-fat, low-cholesterol meals that meet American Heart Association guidelines). There's even a private kids-only meal. For diversion, there are planned activities ranging from a family karaoke contest to a game show based on TV's old Family Feud.

Sports: A transparent cover turns the entire Riviera deck into an indoor recreation area in inclement weather; it's the site of two large interconnecting pools and three hot tubs. There's also a fitness center with exercise equipment, and a jogging track.

For Children: There's around-the-clock child care for youngsters two and up. There are no organized kids' programs.

Ashore: Shore excursions take you to Nassau, where you can ride in a horse-drawn carriage past pink colonnaded British Colonial buildings and more. While Port Lucaya is not a private island like Disney's Castaway Cay, it is the next best thing, because the *Big Red Boat* is the only ship that calls here. There, as part of the Underwater Explorers Society's Dolphin Experience, you can swim with a live dolphin. Sailing, windsurfing, parasailing, jet-skiing, snorkeling, scuba diving, and sport fishing are also available.

Itineraries, Prices, Info: Options include a 4-night cruise plus 3-night land package that includes two days at Universal Studios Florida and one day's admission to downtown Orlando's nightlife focal point, Church Street Station; or a 3-night cruise plus 4 nights' accommodations and a 4-day, 3-park Orlando FlexTicket. Both packages also include early admission to Universal Studios Florida on selected days, a Nickelodeon Kids' Park Pack, and unlimited transportation between your hotel, Universal Studios Florida, Sea World, and Wet 'n Wild. Rates: $621–$2,159 (lowest late Aug.–early Dec., highest Mar.–mid-July and during the year-end holidays). *Universal City Travel, tel. 800/711–0080, 407/224–7096, fax 407/224–7001; www.destinationuniversal.com.*

CARNIVAL CRUISE LINES

You've seen the TV ads for the world's most popular cruise line. Well, Terrie and I went on our honeymoon on the original "fun ship" (that's what Carnival calls each of its craft), the *Mardi Gras,* from Port Everglades, Miami. That was back in nineteen-eighty-something and we had the time of our lives. The *Fantasy,* the first of Carnival's new megaships, sails year-round from Port Canaveral on three- and four-day Caribbean cruises that call at Nassau and Freeport, both in the Bahamas.

The ship's striking seven-deck-high atrium, with panoramic windows on the sea, computerized white mini-lights, and two glass elevators, is the ship's spectacular focal point.

Meals and Entertainment: The *Fantasy* casino is one of the largest afloat, with more than 200 slot machines and 15 blackjack tables, along with roulette, a wheel of fortune, and Caribbean stud poker. Entertainment is Vegas-style—big musical productions with elaborate sets, costumes, and special effects in one lounge, comedians, singers, and bands elsewhere.

Terrie and I first began the trek from svelte youth to paunchy middle age on a Carnival ship, and if you take advantage of all the food put before you, you will definitely put on some pounds, although you can request vegetarian dishes or spa fare, which is low in fat, sodium, cholesterol, and calories. In the two main dining rooms, there are several theme meals and one gala, usually the first night out. You can also eat on the Lido Deck at the casual, indoor–outdoor Windows on the Sea. There's also Cleopatra's, a piano bar with an ancient Egyptian theme, the Cats' Lounge, decorated with giant objects as seen from a cat's-eye view, and a disco.

Sports: The 12,000-square-foot Nautica Spa offers a fine sea view as well as high-tech exercise equipment, workout areas, body and facial treatments, whirlpools, saunas, and steam rooms. There are three swimming pools, including a children's pool; the main pool has a 14-foot-high water slide.

For Children: Carnival's supervised children's program, **Camp Carnival**, offers a variety of activities, and like Disney's, has something for each age group: 2–4, 5–8, 9–12, and 13–17.

Itineraries, Prices, Info: 7-day Fantasy cruise packages include 3-night Bahamas cruise with 4 nights' Orlando hotel accommodations, and a 3-park Orlando FlexTicket; or a 4-night cruise with 3 nights in Orlando and a 3-park Orlando FlexTicket. Both packages include a tour of Kennedy Space Center and an Alamo rental car with unlimited mileage for four days. Rates: $979–$2,389 (lowest late Aug.–early Dec., highest Mar.–mid-July and during the year-end holidays). Universal City Travel, tel. 800/711–0080, or 407/224–7096, fax 407/224–7001; www.destinationuniversal.com.

index

A

Admission prices, *33–35*
Adventureland, *104–106*
Africa, *147–148*
Air Orlando, *207*
Alfred Hitchcock—the Art of Making Movies, *43*
AMC 24 Theater Complex, *154*
American Adventure, The, *124–125*
American Film Institute Showcase, The, *142*
Anheuser-Busch Hospitality Center (Busch Gardens), *73*
Anheuser-Busch Hospitality Center (Sea World), *66*
Animal Actors Stage, *49*
Animal Nursery Tour, *77*
Arrival and departure times, *25*
Astro Orbiter, *91*
AT&T at the Movies, *50*

B

Back Lot Studio Tour, *52–53*
Backstage Studio Tour, *141–142*
Back to the Future: The Ride, *48–49*
Bargain World, *227*
Barney, *49*
Barnstormer at Goofy's Wiseacres Farm, *95*
Bayside Water Ski Stadium, *66*
Beaches, *218–225*
Beauty and the Beast Stage Show, *143*
Beetlejuice's Rock and Roll Graveyard Revue, *46*
Belz Factory Outlet World, *228*
Big Thunder Mountain Railroad, *103*
Bird Show Theater, *73*
Blizzard Beach, *190*
Blues Brothers in Chicago Bound, *46*
Body Wars, *115*
Bok Tower Gardens, *201–202*
Bone Yard, *44*
Bongos Cuban Cafe, *154*
Busch Gardens, *68–80*
BYO drinks and food, *20–21*

C

Cameras, *31*
Canada pavilion, *120–121*
Caribbean Tide Pool, *62–63*
Carousel of Progress, *91–92*
Center Court, *116*
Child-oriented approach to vacationing, *32*
China pavilion, *129*
Church Street Exchange, *229–230*
Church Street Market, *229*
Church Street Station, *175–179*
Cinderella's Golden Carrousel, *96*
Cirque du Soleil, *152*
Clothing, *28–29*
Clydesdale Hamlet (Busch Gardens), *79–80*
Clydesdale Hamlet (Sea World), *65*
Cocoa Beach, *224–225*
Congo River Golf & Exploration Co., *207, 209–210*
Congo River Rapids, *75–76*
Cost of vacation, calculation of, *2–3, 7–8*
Country Bear Jamboree, *102*
Cranium Command, *115*
Curiosity Caverns, *78*
Cypress Gardens, *202*

D

David Copperfield's Magic Underground, *155–156*
Daytona Beach, *218–220*
Diamond Horseshoe Revue, *102*
Dinoland U.S.A., *147*
Directions for getting around, *22*
Discovery Island, *204–205*
Disney BoardWalk, *179–180*
Disney Character Breakfasts, *173–174*
Disney Institute, *203–204*
Disney-MGM Studios Theme Park, *24, 131–144*
Disneyquest, *152–153*
Disney's All-Star Resorts, *237*
Disney's Animal Kingdom, *145–148*
Disney's Fantasia Miniature Golf, *204*
Disney's Wide World of Sports, *192–194*

INDEX

261

Dolphin Interactive Program, *63*
Dolphin Nursery, *62*
Dolphin Theater, *76*
Donald's Boat, *94*
Downtown Disney, *149–164*
Dragon Flume Ride, *74*
Dumbo the Flying Elephant, *96*
Dynamite Nights Stuntacular, *54*

E

Earthquake: The Big One, *47*
Electrical Water Pageant, *205*
Epcot Center, *24, 107–130*
E.T. Adventure, *50*
Extraterrestrial Alien Encounter, *90–91*

F

Fantasyland, *95–99*
Festhaus, The, *77*
Fievel's Playland, *50*
Food Rocks, *113*
Fort Christmas County Park, *216*
France pavilion, *121–122*
Front-car opportunities at rides, *30*
Frontierland, *101–104*
Frontierland Shootin' Arcade, *102*
Funtastic World of Hanna-Barbera, *42*
Future World, *110–117*

G

Gatorland, *199–200, 227*
Germany pavilion, *128*
GM World of Motion, *114*
Gory, Gruesome & Grotesque Horror Make-up Show, *51*
Grand Prix Raceway, *92*
Great Movie Ride, *135–136*
Greenhouse Tour, *113*
Green Meadows Farm, *209*
Guitar Gallery by George's Music, *153–154*

H

Hall of Presidents, The, *100*
Hard Rock Café, *169*
Harvest Theater, *113*
Haunted Mansion, *99*
Heat-beating tips, *31–32*
Hercules and Xena: Wizards of the Screen, *43*
Homosassa Springs State Wildlife Park, *201*
Honey, I Shrunk the Kids Movie Set Adventure, *140*
Hotel Clyde and Seamore, *64*
Hotels, *231–235*
  best bets, *236–254*
  freebies from, *13*
  International Drive, *243–247*
  Kissimmee, *253–254*
  Lake Buena Vista, *236*
  money-saving tips, *10–12*
House of Blues, *152*

I

Illuminations, *130*
Image Works, *114*
Indiana Jones Stunt Spectacular, *136*
Information, *33–35*
Innoventions East and West, *111*
Inside the Magic, *141*
Islands of Adventure, *45, 55–58*
Italy pavilion, *127–128*
It's a Small World, *97*

J

Japan pavilion, *123–124*
Jaws, *47*
Jim Henson's Muppet Vision 4D, *140*
John F. Kennedy Space Center Visitor Center, *212–215*
Journey into Imagination, *113–114*
Journey to Atlantis, *64–65*
Jungle Adventure, *216–217*
Jungle Cruise, *105–106*
Jungleland, *210*
Jurassic Park, *56*

K

Key West at Sea World, *64*
King Tut's Tomb, *80*
Kissimmee
  attractions, *208–210*
  hotels, *253–254*
  water parks, *188–189*
Kongfrontation, *45*
Kumba, *76*

L

Land, The, *112*
Left lanes at rides, *26*
Legend of the Lion King, *97*
Liberty Belle Riverboat, *100*
Liberty Square, *99–101*

INDEX

Line waits, tips for minimizing, 22–28
Living Seas, The, 112
Living with the Land, 112
Lockers, 29–30
Lost Continent, 56–57
Lucy: A Tribute, 52

M

Mad Tea Party, 95
Magic Eye Theater, 113–114
Magic Kingdom, 23, 81–106
Magic of Disney Animation, The, 142
Main Street Cinema, 87
Main Street USA, 86–90
Making of . . . , The, 142
Making of Me, The, 116
Manatees, the Last Generation?, 63
Marineland of Florida, 202–203
Marketplace at Downtown Disney, The, 159–164
Medieval Life, 208
Mercado, 230
Mexico pavilion, 125–127
Mickey's Country House, 94
Mickey's Toontown Fair, 93–95
Midway Airboat Rides, 217
Midway and Arcade, 77
Mike Fink Keelboats, 100
Miniature golf, 207–208, 209–210
Minnie's Country House, 94
Mr. Toad's Wild Ride, 96
Montu, 80
Moroccan Palace Theater, 72
Morocco pavilion, 122–123
Movie Rider, 206–207
Myombe Reserve, 78

N

New Smyrna Beach, 223–224
Nickelodeon Studios Tour, 42
Nightlife, 157–159
Norway pavilion, 119–120

O

Oasis, The, 146
Off-Premises Contractors (OPCs), 12, 16–17
Off-season travel, 10
Old Town, 209
Orlando Science Center and Loch Haven Park, 205–208
Ormond Beach, 220

P

Pacific Point Preserve, 64
Paintball World, 208–209
Park-hopping, 18–19
Parking, 23–24
Penguin Encounter, 64
Peter Pan's Flight, 97
Pirate's Cove Adventure Golf, 207–208
Pirate's Island Adventure Golf, 210
Pirates of the Caribbean, 105
Planet Hollywood, 154–155
Pleasure Island, 157–159
Pointe Orlando, 228
Production Center, Soundstage Walk-Throughs, 44, 55–53
Python, The, 75

Q

Quality Outlet Center, 229
Questor, 79

R

Rainforest Café, 160
Restaurants, 171–185. *See also under specific theme parks*
breakfasts and brunches, 173
celebrity theme restaurants, 152, 154, 174–175
dinner theaters, 173, 180–183
family buffets, 172–173
lobster feasts, 171–172
sushi and seafood, 184
Ripley's Believe It or Not!, 206
River Country, 190–191
Ron Jon Surf Shop, 228

S

Safari Village, 146–147
St. Augustine, 221–223
Sand Dig, 80
Sand Storm, 75
Scheduling for vacation activities, 8–10
Scorpion, 77
Sea Lion and Otter Stadium, 64
Sea World, 59–67
Sea World Theatre, 62
Shamu Adventure, 65
Shamu Close-Up, 65
Shamu's Happy Harbor, 65–66
Shamu World Focus, 65
Shipping of purchases, 29

INDEX

Shopping, 226. *See also under specific theme parks*
discount souvenirs, 227
festival centers, 229–230
one of a kind shops, 153–154, 156
shopping centers, discount malls, 228–229
Shopping passes, 21
Shuttle services, 21
Silver Springs, 199
Skyway to Fantasyland, 92
Skyway to Tomorrowland, 98
Snow White's Adventure, 96
Space Coast, 211–217
Space Mountain, 92
Spaceship Earth, 110–111
Splash Mountain, 103
Sports Dominator, 227
Stage 54, 43–44
Stanley Falls, 75
Star Island/Resort World, 242
Star Tours, 137
Seuss Landing, 57–58
Sultan's Tent, 72
Sunscreen, 31
Superstar Television, 136
Swiss Family Treehouse, 106

T

Take Flight, 91
Tanganyika Tidal Wave, 74
Terminator 2: 3D, 51–52
Terror on Church Street, 208
Terrors of the Deep, 65
Test Track, 114
Tickets
 freebies from hotels, 13–16
 freebies from time-share operators, 16–17
 money-saving tips, 12
 multi-day passes, 18–20
 one-day, one-park tickets, 18–20
 prices, 33–35
Timekeeper, 90
Time-share resorts, 16–18
Tomorrowland, 90–93
Tomorrowland Transit Authority, 91
Tom Sawyer Island, 102
Toon Lagoon, 56
Toon Park, 94
Toontown Fair Hall of Fame, 95
Toontown Fair Train Station, 95
Trainland Toy Train Museum, 207
Trans-Veldt Railroad, 74

Tropical Reef, 62
Tropical Serenade, 104–105
TV show tapings
 Disney-MGM Studios Theme Park, 133
 Universal Studios Florida, 39
Twilight Zone Tower of Terror, 143
Twister, 45
Typhoon Lagoon, 189–190

U

Ubanga-Banga, 75
United Kingdom pavilion, 118–119
Universal's Citywalk, 165–170
Universal Studios Florida, 36–58
Universe of Energy, 116–117
U.S. Astronaut Hall of Fame, 215–216, 227

V

Virgin Megastore, 153
Visitor information, 227–229
Voyage of the Little Mermaid, 141

W

Walt Disney Theater, 141
Walt Disney World. *See also* Disney-MGM Studios Theme Park; Epcot Center; Magic Kingdom
 Discovery Island, 204–205
 Disney Character Breakfasts, 173–174
 Disney Institute, 203–204
 Disney's Fantasia Miniature Golf, 204
 Electrical Water Pageant, 205
 hotels, 236, 237–239, 247–251
 water parks, 189–191
Walt Disney World Railroad, 87
Watermania, 188–189
Water parks, 186–191
Waterproof clothes and cameras, 31
Weather conditions, 27–28
Weeki Wachee Springs City of Mermaids, 201
Wet 'N' Wild, 188
Whale and Dolphin Show, 63
Wider World of Sports, The, 192–196
Wild, Wild, Wild West Stunt Show, 47
Wild Arctic, 66
Wild Horse Saloon, 159
Wolfgang Puck Café, 153
Wonders of Life, 115–116
World of Denim, 228
World Showcase, 117–130

INDEX

264

coupons

INTERNATIONAL DRIVE, ORLANDO

Save $2
on admission

Experience Wet 'n Wild's thrills for $2 off the regular all day admission. Coupon good for up to six people. Not to be used in conjunction with any other discounted offer or afternoon pricing.

Fodor's
PLU 1688A
PLU 1689C

Why stay in a hotel,
When you can have
The Castle
for 10% off?

The Castle DoubleTree Resort
8629 International Drive
Orlando, FL 32819 (407) 345-1511
fax: (407) 248-8181 - 1(800)-952-2785

* On I-Drive near attractions and convention center
* In-room refrigerator and safe
* Remote control TV & coffeemaker
* Grand swimming pool, hot tub and pooside bar
* Fitness center and game room * Kids stay free
Not valid with other offers - subject to availability

A PRO DISNEY LIKE A PRO DISNEY LIKE A PRO DISNEY LIKE
DISNEY LIKE A PRO DISNEY LIKE A PRO DISNEY LIKE A PR
EY LIKE A PRO DISNEY LIKE A PRO DISNEY LIKE A PRO DISNE
A PRO DISNEY LIKE A PRO DISNEY LIKE A PRO DISNEY LIKE
DISNEY LIKE A PRO DISNEY LIKE A PRO DISNEY LIKE A PR
EY LIKE A PRO DISNEY LIKE A PRO DISNEY LIKE A PRO DISNE
A PRO DISNEY LIKE A PRO DISNEY LIKE A PRO DISNEY LIKE
DISNEY LIKE A PRO DISNEY LIKE A PRO DISNEY LIKE A PR
EY LIKE A PRO DISNEY LIKE A PRO DISNEY LIKE A PRO DISNE
A PRO DISNEY LIKE A PRO DISNEY LIKE A PRO DISNEY LIKE
DISNEY LIKE A PRO DISNEY LIKE A PRO DISNEY LIKE A PR
EY LIKE A PRO DISNEY LIKE A PRO DISNEY LIKE A PRO DISNE
A PRO DISNEY LIKE A PRO DISNEY LIKE A PRO DISNEY LIKE
DISNEY LIKE A PRO DISNEY LIKE A PRO DISNEY LIKE A PR
EY LIKE A PRO DISNEY LIKE A PRO DISNEY LIKE A PRO DISNE
A PRO DISNEY LIKE A PRO DISNEY LIKE A PRO DISNEY LIKE
DISNEY LIKE A PRO DISNEY LIKE A PRO DISNEY LIKE A PR
EY LIKE A PRO DISNEY LIKE A PRO DISNEY LIKE A PRO DISNE
A PRO DISNEY LIKE A PRO DISNEY LIKE A PRO DISNEY LIKE
DISNEY LIKE A PRO DISNEY LIKE A PRO DISNEY LIKE A PR
EY LIKE A PRO DISNEY LIKE A PRO DISNEY LIKE A PRO DISNE
A PRO DISNEY LIKE A PRO DISNEY LIKE A PRO DISNEY LIKE
DISNEY LIKE A PRO DISNEY LIKE A PRO DISNEY LIKE A PR
EY LIKE A PRO DISNEY LIKE A PRO DISNEY LIKE A PRO DISNE
A PRO DISNEY LIKE A PRO DISNEY LIKE A PRO DISNEY LIKE
DISNEY LIKE A PRO DISNEY LIKE A PRO DISNEY LIKE A PR
EY LIKE A PRO DISNEY LIKE A PRO DISNEY LIKE A PRO DISNE
A PRO DISNEY LIKE A PRO DISNEY LIKE A PRO DISNEY LIKE
DISNEY LIKE A PRO DISNEY LIKE A PRO DISNEY LIKE A PR
EY LIKE A PRO DISNEY LIKE A PRO DISNEY LIKE A PRO DISNE
A PRO DISNEY LIKE A PRO DISNEY LIKE A PRO DISNEY LIKE
DISNEY LIKE A PRO DISNEY LIKE A PRO DISNEY LIKE A PR
EY LIKE A PRO DISNEY LIKE A PRO DISNEY LIKE A PRO DISNE
A PRO DISNEY LIKE A PRO DISNEY LIKE A PRO DISNEY LIKE
DISNEY LIKE A PRO DISNEY LIKE A PRO DISNEY LIKE A PR
EY LIKE A PRO DISNEY LIKE A PRO DISNEY LIKE A PRO DISNE
A PRO DISNEY LIKE A PRO DISNEY LIKE A PRO DISNEY LIKE
DISNEY LIKE A PRO DISNEY LIKE A PRO DISNEY LIKE A PR
EY LIKE A PRO DISNEY LIKE A PRO DISNEY LIKE A PRO DISNE
A PRO DISNEY LIKE A PRO DISNEY LIKE A PRO DISNEY LIKE

coupons

ORLANDO

"Kingdom of Rock 'N Roll" at Universal Studios Florida (407) 351-ROCK

Bring this coupon to the Hard Rock Cafe
and receive a free collector's souvenir
with a purchase of $15.00 or more in our
restaurant or merchandise store.

Limit one per person per visit

$4.00 Off

Experience the Exciting World of Mystery and Intrigue!

* An intriguing mystery that you try to solve
* Delicious dinner and desert
* Unlimited beer and wine
* Audience participation and family fun
* Open 7 mysterious nights a week

Nightly at 6 and/or 9pm
Reservations 407-363-1985
800-393-1985
7508 Republic Dr. behind Wet 'n Wild
Not valid with any other offers

Comedy mysteries where you solve the crime!

Limit 6 guests, tickets must be purchased at the door

coupons

ASTRONAUT HALL OF FAME
HOME OF U.S. SPACE CAMP
$1 OFF Any admission with this coupon.

Tumble through space and hang on for all you're worth as you are hurled into G-Force territory at the Astronaut Hall of Fame

Where history is a wild ride!

JUST WEST OF THE KENNEDY SPACE CENTER. OPEN SEVEN DAYS A WEEK. 407-269-6100 TITUSVILLE, FLORIDA

THIS OFFER NOT GOOD IN COMBINATION WITH ANY OTHER DISCOUNTS
Fodor's OLAP '98

SINK INTO SOME FUN IN ORLANDO

STRAP IN & HANG ON!

Orlando Museum

8201 International Drive
Ripley's and Believe It or Not are registered trademarks of Ripley Entertainment Inc.

ALAP   Present this coupon for   CLAP
$1.50 OFF EACH ADULT
$1.00 OFF EACH CHILD
Not valid with any other offer - Good for up to 6 people.

OLAP   Present this coupon for   OLAP
$2.00 OFF
EACH PERSON - IT'S FUN!
Not valid with any other offer - Good for up to 6 people.

A PRO DISNEY LIKE A PRO DISNEY LIKE A PRO DISNEY LIKE
DISNEY LIKE A PRO DISNEY LIKE A PRO DISNEY LIKE A PR
EY LIKE A PRO DISNEY LIKE A PRO DISNEY LIKE A PRO DISN
A PRO DISNEY LIKE A PRO DISNEY LIKE A PRO DISNEY LIKE
DISNEY LIKE A PRO DISNEY LIKE A PRO DISNEY LIKE A PR
EY LIKE A PRO DISNEY LIKE A PRO DISNEY LIKE A PRO DISN
A PRO DISNEY LIKE A PRO DISNEY LIKE A PRO DISNEY LIKE
DISNEY LIKE A PRO DISNEY LIKE A PRO DISNEY LIKE A PR
EY LIKE A PRO DISNEY LIKE A PRO DISNEY LIKE A PRO DISN
A PRO DISNEY LIKE A PRO DISNEY LIKE A PRO DISNEY LIKE
DISNEY LIKE A PRO DISNEY LIKE A PRO DISNEY LIKE A PR
EY LIKE A PRO DISNEY LIKE A PRO DISNEY LIKE A PRO DISN
A PRO DISNEY LIKE A PRO DISNEY LIKE A PRO DISNEY LIKE
DISNEY LIKE A PRO DISNEY LIKE A PRO DISNEY LIKE A PR
EY LIKE A PRO DISNEY LIKE A PRO DISNEY LIKE A PRO DISN
A PRO DISNEY LIKE A PRO DISNEY LIKE A PRO DISNEY LIKE
DISNEY LIKE A PRO DISNEY LIKE A PRO DISNEY LIKE A PR
EY LIKE A PRO DISNEY LIKE A PRO DISNEY LIKE A PRO DISN
A PRO DISNEY LIKE A PRO DISNEY LIKE A PRO DISNEY LIKE
DISNEY LIKE A PRO DISNEY LIKE A PRO DISNEY LIKE A PR
EY LIKE A PRO DISNEY LIKE A PRO DISNEY LIKE A PRO DISN
A PRO DISNEY LIKE A PRO DISNEY LIKE A PRO DISNEY LIKE
DISNEY LIKE A PRO DISNEY LIKE A PRO DISNEY LIKE A PR
EY LIKE A PRO DISNEY LIKE A PRO DISNEY LIKE A PRO DISN
A PRO DISNEY LIKE A PRO DISNEY LIKE A PRO DISNEY LIKE
DISNEY LIKE A PRO DISNEY LIKE A PRO DISNEY LIKE A PR
EY LIKE A PRO DISNEY LIKE A PRO DISNEY LIKE A PRO DISN
A PRO DISNEY LIKE A PRO DISNEY LIKE A PRO DISNEY LIKE
DISNEY LIKE A PRO DISNEY LIKE A PRO DISNEY LIKE A PR
EY LIKE A PRO DISNEY LIKE A PRO DISNEY LIKE A PRO DISN
A PRO DISNEY LIKE A PRO DISNEY LIKE A PRO DISNEY LIKE
DISNEY LIKE A PRO DISNEY LIKE A PRO DISNEY LIKE A PR
EY LIKE A PRO DISNEY LIKE A PRO DISNEY LIKE A PRO DISN
A PRO DISNEY LIKE A PRO DISNEY LIKE A PRO DISNEY LIKE
DISNEY LIKE A PRO DISNEY LIKE A PRO DISNEY LIKE A PR
EY LIKE A PRO DISNEY LIKE A PRO DISNEY LIKE A PRO DISN
A PRO DISNEY LIKE A PRO DISNEY LIKE A PRO DISNEY LIKE
DISNEY LIKE A PRO DISNEY LIKE A PRO DISNEY LIKE A PR
EY LIKE A PRO DISNEY LIKE A PRO DISNEY LIKE A PRO DISNE
A PRO DISNEY LIKE A PRO DISNEY LIKE A PRO DISNEY LIKE

coupons

---

3 DAYS • 2 NIGHT STAY

ONLY **VALUE**

$200 **$550**

Tax Not Included

STAR ISLAND RESORT & COUNTRY CLUB

AWARD WINNING!
3-BEDROOM 2-BATH CONDOS
Subject to availability • Expires 12/31/99

CALL (800) 423-8604   ORLANDO RESORT AREA

Save $300 Off Published Rates!

This offer not good in combination with any other discounts or offers.
FODOR'S OLAP '98

Celebrity Pass
See Where the Stars Vacation!

STAR ISLAND RESORT & COUNTRY CLUB

CALL (800) 696-2782
*For a **FREE** Courtesy Tour of Star Island Resort & Country Club*

Orlando • Disney Area

FODOR'S OLAP '98

A PRO DISNEY LIKE A PRO DISNEY LIKE A PRO DISNEY LIKE
DISNEY LIKE A PRO DISNEY LIKE A PRO DISNEY LIKE A PR
EY LIKE A PRO DISNEY LIKE A PRO DISNEY LIKE A PRO DISN
A PRO DISNEY LIKE A PRO DISNEY LIKE A PRO DISNEY LIKE
DISNEY LIKE A PRO DISNEY LIKE A PRO DISNEY LIKE A PR
EY LIKE A PRO DISNEY LIKE A PRO DISNEY LIKE A PRO DISN
A PRO DISNEY LIKE A PRO DISNEY LIKE A PRO DISNEY LIKE
DISNEY LIKE A PRO DISNEY LIKE A PRO DISNEY LIKE A PR
EY LIKE A PRO DISNEY LIKE A PRO DISNEY LIKE A PRO DISN
A PRO DISNEY LIKE A PRO DISNEY LIKE A PRO DISNEY LIKE
DISNEY LIKE A PRO DISNEY LIKE A PRO DISNEY LIKE A PR
EY LIKE A PRO DISNEY LIKE A PRO DISNEY LIKE A PRO DISN
A PRO DISNEY LIKE A PRO DISNEY LIKE A PRO DISNEY LIKE
DISNEY LIKE A PRO DISNEY LIKE A PRO DISNEY LIKE A PR
EY LIKE A PRO DISNEY LIKE A PRO DISNEY LIKE A PRO DISN
A PRO DISNEY LIKE A PRO DISNEY LIKE A PRO DISNEY LIKE
DISNEY LIKE A PRO DISNEY LIKE A PRO DISNEY LIKE A PR
EY LIKE A PRO DISNEY LIKE A PRO DISNEY LIKE A PRO DISN
A PRO DISNEY LIKE A PRO DISNEY LIKE A PRO DISNEY LIKE
DISNEY LIKE A PRO DISNEY LIKE A PRO DISNEY LIKE A PR
EY LIKE A PRO DISNEY LIKE A PRO DISNEY LIKE A PRO DISN
A PRO DISNEY LIKE A PRO DISNEY LIKE A PRO DISNEY LIKE
DISNEY LIKE A PRO DISNEY LIKE A PRO DISNEY LIKE A PR
EY LIKE A PRO DISNEY LIKE A PRO DISNEY LIKE A PRO DISN
A PRO DISNEY LIKE A PRO DISNEY LIKE A PRO DISNEY LIKE
DISNEY LIKE A PRO DISNEY LIKE A PRO DISNEY LIKE A PR
EY LIKE A PRO DISNEY LIKE A PRO DISNEY LIKE A PRO DISN
A PRO DISNEY LIKE A PRO DISNEY LIKE A PRO DISNEY LIKE
DISNEY LIKE A PRO DISNEY LIKE A PRO DISNEY LIKE A PR
EY LIKE A PRO DISNEY LIKE A PRO DISNEY LIKE A PRO DISN
A PRO DISNEY LIKE A PRO DISNEY LIKE A PRO DISNEY LIKE
DISNEY LIKE A PRO DISNEY LIKE A PRO DISNEY LIKE A PR
EY LIKE A PRO DISNEY LIKE A PRO DISNEY LIKE A PRO DISN
A PRO DISNEY LIKE A PRO DISNEY LIKE A PRO DISNEY LIKE
DISNEY LIKE A PRO DISNEY LIKE A PRO DISNEY LIKE A PR
EY LIKE A PRO DISNEY LIKE A PRO DISNEY LIKE A PRO DISN
A PRO DISNEY LIKE A PRO DISNEY LIKE A PRO DISNEY LIKE
DISNEY LIKE A PRO DISNEY LIKE A PRO DISNEY LIKE A PR
EY LIKE A PRO DISNEY LIKE A PRO DISNEY LIKE A PRO DISN
A PRO DISNEY LIKE A PRO DISNEY LIKE A PRO DISNEY LIKE

coupons

World Famous Boston Lobster Feast!

Save up to $20!
World famous all-you-can-eat Boston Lobster Feast only $19.95

GIANT LOBSTERS LIVE IN THE TANK
EXCELLENT LANDLUBBER MENU
KIDS MENU, FULL BAR, WINE LIST
ACCOMMODATIONS FOR GROUPS

On the corner of Sand Lake Road and South Orange Blossom Trail in front of the Florida Mall.
407 438-0607

$5.00 off regular price of $24.95 after 6pm.
Good for up to 4 diners per coupon.
Not valid with any other offers or discounts.
Tax and tip not included.
Fodor's OLAP 98

A PRO DISNEY LIKE A PRO DISNEY LIKE A PRO DISNEY LIKE
DISNEY LIKE A PRO DISNEY LIKE A PRO DISNEY LIKE A PR
EY LIKE A PRO DISNEY LIKE A PRO DISNEY LIKE A PRO DISNE
A PRO DISNEY LIKE A PRO DISNEY LIKE A PRO DISNEY LIKE
DISNEY LIKE A PRO DISNEY LIKE A PRO DISNEY LIKE A PR
EY LIKE A PRO DISNEY LIKE A PRO DISNEY LIKE A PRO DISNE
A PRO DISNEY LIKE A PRO DISNEY LIKE A PRO DISNEY LIKE
DISNEY LIKE A PRO DISNEY LIKE A PRO DISNEY LIKE A PR
EY LIKE A PRO DISNEY LIKE A PRO DISNEY LIKE A PRO DISNE
A PRO DISNEY LIKE A PRO DISNEY LIKE A PRO DISNEY LIKE
DISNEY LIKE A PRO DISNEY LIKE A PRO DISNEY LIKE A PR
EY LIKE A PRO DISNEY LIKE A PRO DISNEY LIKE A PRO DISNE
A PRO DISNEY LIKE A PRO DISNEY LIKE A PRO DISNEY LIKE
DISNEY LIKE A PRO DISNEY LIKE A PRO DISNEY LIKE A PR
EY LIKE A PRO DISNEY LIKE A PRO DISNEY LIKE A PRO DISNE
A PRO DISNEY LIKE A PRO DISNEY LIKE A PRO DISNEY LIKE
DISNEY LIKE A PRO DISNEY LIKE A PRO DISNEY LIKE A PR
EY LIKE A PRO DISNEY LIKE A PRO DISNEY LIKE A PRO DISNE
A PRO DISNEY LIKE A PRO DISNEY LIKE A PRO DISNEY LIKE
DISNEY LIKE A PRO DISNEY LIKE A PRO DISNEY LIKE A PR
EY LIKE A PRO DISNEY LIKE A PRO DISNEY LIKE A PRO DISNE
A PRO DISNEY LIKE A PRO DISNEY LIKE A PRO DISNEY LIKE
DISNEY LIKE A PRO DISNEY LIKE A PRO DISNEY LIKE A PR
EY LIKE A PRO DISNEY LIKE A PRO DISNEY LIKE A PRO DISNE
A PRO DISNEY LIKE A PRO DISNEY LIKE A PRO DISNEY LIKE
DISNEY LIKE A PRO DISNEY LIKE A PRO DISNEY LIKE A PR
EY LIKE A PRO DISNEY LIKE A PRO DISNEY LIKE A PRO DISNE
A PRO DISNEY LIKE A PRO DISNEY LIKE A PRO DISNEY LIKE
DISNEY LIKE A PRO DISNEY LIKE A PRO DISNEY LIKE A PR
EY LIKE A PRO DISNEY LIKE A PRO DISNEY LIKE A PRO DISNE
A PRO DISNEY LIKE A PRO DISNEY LIKE A PRO DISNEY LIKE
DISNEY LIKE A PRO DISNEY LIKE A PRO DISNEY LIKE A PR
EY LIKE A PRO DISNEY LIKE A PRO DISNEY LIKE A PRO DISNE
A PRO DISNEY LIKE A PRO DISNEY LIKE A PRO DISNEY LIKE
DISNEY LIKE A PRO DISNEY LIKE A PRO DISNEY LIKE A PR
EY LIKE A PRO DISNEY LIKE A PRO DISNEY LIKE A PRO DISNE
A PRO DISNEY LIKE A PRO DISNEY LIKE A PRO DISNEY LIKE
DISNEY LIKE A PRO DISNEY LIKE A PRO DISNEY LIKE A PR
EY LIKE A PRO DISNEY LIKE A PRO DISNEY LIKE A PRO DISNE
A PRO DISNEY LIKE A PRO DISNEY LIKE A PRO DISNEY LIKE

coupons

Save over $2,000 with this coupon alone!

SAVE ON EVERYTHING!

One Call Does It All! **1-800-396-1883**

Exchange this coupon for your free card at CFTIC!

ORLANDO ACCESS

Tickets • Dining • Transportation • Shopping • Accommodations

Your Ticket to Savings in the ORLANDO Resort Area

Save on these particpating attractions, restaurants, dining and more!

Shopping: Florida Mall, Lake Buena Vista Factory Stores, Gold Hut, Teams of Old Town, Jeans Warehouse, Magic Gifts, Sneaker Tree II, $1.99 Outlet, Gold Factory, Electric Town, Royal Market, Tokio Electronics, T-Shirt King, Royal Electronics, Off Broadway Shoes, Edwin Watts Golf and more!

Dining: Kobe Japanese Steak House, Pacino's, Key W. Kools, New China, Boston Creamery, Golden Corral, Ruby Tuesday, Ocean Grill, Key Largo, Magic Bull Steak House, Magic Mining Company, Captain Nemo's and more!

Hotels: Omni Rosen, Clarion Plaza, Parc Corniche, Inn at Maingate, Best Western Plaza International, Ramada Fountain Park, Delta Orlando, Ramada Vacation Suites, Enclave Suites, Howard Johnsn's S. International and more!

Dinner Theaters: Medieval Times, Arabian Nights, Wild Bill's, Sleuth's, King Henry's, Pirates Adventure and more!

Plus savings on Golf, Cruises, Attraction Tickets, Car Rentals and much, much more!

Participating Offers May Vary

Visit our site on the world wide web @www.orlando-visitor.com

USE YOUR ORLANDO ACCESS DISCOUNT CARD TO GET BIG DISCOUNTS ON ALL OF YOUR DINING, ATTRACTIONS & ENTERTAINMENT!

FODORS 98

coupons

Getaway Today! | Sneak a Week!

It's Playtime for 4 Days & 3 Nights! | **One Week Wonder Package: 7 Days & 6 Nights!**

YOU PAY **$139*** — Retail Value at least $199 — FVG14

YOU PAY **$249*** — Retail Value at least $382 — FVG17

CENTRAL FLORIDA TOURIST INFORMATION CENTERS — YOUR TICKET TO SAVINGS

*per person, plus tax, double occupancy, value-season rate based on availability

*per person, plus tax, double occupancy, value-season rate based on availability

INCLUDES

Accommodations for up to 4 persons plus tickets to your favorite attractions! Additional nights available for $19.50 per person, based on double occupancy.

INCLUDES

Accommodations for up to 4 persons plus tickets to your favorite attractions! Bonus: 2 adult tickets to Arabian Nights Dinner Show and 2 more tickets to another exciting attraction!

2 adult tickets to Universal Studios of Florida

7 days unlimited admission for 2 to Universal Studios

2 adult tickets to Arabian Nights Dinner Show

Family Pass (up to 10 persons) to Water Mania

7 days unlimited admission for 2 to Sea World

7 days unlimited admission for 2 to Wet N' Wild

ORLANDO PACKAGES 1-800-396-1883

Convenient Locations Throughout Orlando. Your Exclusive Resource for the Orlando Access Discount Card.

This value-season pricing is valid through 3/31/99 except during peak and holiday seasons. Similar savings available in peak times. Visit us at www.orlando-visitor.com

FODORS OLAP 98